RIDERS OF THE STORM

Ian Cameron was born in 1924 and educated at Charterhouse and Corpus Christi College, Oxford. In the Second World War he was a pilot in the Fleet Air Arm, and saw service on Atlantic and Russian convoys. He has been a full-time writer since 1956 and his books have been translated into fourteen languages.

RIDERS

OF THE STORM

The Story of the Royal National Lifeboat Institution

IAN CAMERON

An Orion paperback

First published in Great Britain in 2002
by Weidenfeld & Nicolson
This paperback edition published in 2009
by Orion Books Ltd,
Orion House, 5 Upper St Martin's Lane,
London WC2H 9EA

An Hachette UK company

10 9 8 7 6 5 4 3 2 1

Copyright © Donald Payne 2002

The right of Donald Payne to be identified
as the author of this work has been asserted
by him in accordance with the Copyright,
Designs and Patents Act 1988.

A CIP catalogue record for this book is
available from the British Library.

ISBN 978-0-7528-8344-1

Printed in Italy by Printer Trento S.r.l.

The Orion Publishing Group's policy is to
use papers that are natural, renewable and
recyclable products and made from wood
grown in sustainable forests. The logging
and manufacturing processes are expected
to conform to the environmental
regulations of the country of origin.

www.orionbooks.co.uk

PICTURE ACKNOWLEDGEMENTS

Unless otherwise indicated, all photographs are from the RNLI *Archive.*
8 RNLI/ Grahame Farr Archive; 10 Mary Evans Picture Library; 12 RNLI/ *Journal
of the Life Boat Institution;* 16 (right) RNLI/ Eric C. Fry, *The Shell Book of Lifeboat
Design and Development;* 17 (right) Eric C. Fry, *The Shell Book of Lifeboat Design and
Development:* 20 The National Maritime Museum; 24 RNLI/ photograph courtesy
the *Irish Times;* 29 RNLI/ *Journal of the Lift Boat Institution;* 30 Mary Evans Picture
Library; 34 (top and bottom) RNLI/ paintings by Henry Perlee Parker; 35 (top)
Mary Evans Picture Library; 3 6-3 7 painting by Tim Thompson; 39 Science &
Society Picture Library; 40 painting by Tim Thompson; 41 RNLI/ painting by
Thomas Cantrell Dugdale ARA; 45 RNLI/ Fox Photos, presented to the RNLI by Mr
W. Brown; 48 Mary Evans Picture Library; 55 RNLI/ Grahame Farr Archive; 56
(top National Portrait Gallery; 57 painting by Tim Thompson; 59 RNLI/ Eric C. Fry,
The Shell Book of Lifeboat Design and Development; 61 Mary Evans Picture Library;
62-66 RNLI/ Eric C. Fry, *The Shell Book of Lifeboat Design and Development;* 70
painting by Tim Thompson; 72 RNLI/ Grahame Farr Archive; 88 (top) RNLI/
photograph courtesy Lytham Lifeboat Museum; 90-91 RNLI/ Graham Farr
Archive; 92 RNLI/ photograph courtesy *Weekend* magazine; 93 RNLI/ photograph
by Peter Daniels; 96 Apex Photo Agency Ltd; 97 RNLI/ Keystone View Co.; 98-99
painting by Tim Thompson; 100 RNLI/ Graham Farr Archive; 106 RNLI/
Grahame Farr Archive; 111 *Illustrated London News;* 113 RNLI/ photograph by
Oscar Way; 115 (left) National Portrait Gallery; 116 painting by Tim Thompson;
118-119 painting by Tim Thompson; 122 painting by Tim Thompson; 129 RNLI/
photograph by Jeff Morris; 132 RNLI/ photograph courtesy *Yorkshire Post;* 142
RNLI/ photographs by Derek King; 146 (left) RNLI/ photograph courtesy National
Army Museum; 147 (bottom left) RNLI/ photograph by Derek King, (bottom right)
RNLI/ photograph courtesy *Plymouth Evening Herald/West* Country Publications;
151 (top) RNLI/ photograph by Derek King, (bottom left) RNLI/ Grahame Farr
Archive, (bottom right) RNLI/ photograph by Edward Mallinson; 160 (top left,
bottom left and bottom right) RNLI/ photographs by Steve Edwards, (top right)
RNLI/ photograph courtesy *Glasgow Herald;* 163 RNLI/ Hayling Island Crew; 165
(top) RNLI/ photograph by Edward Mallinson, (bottom) photograph by Michael
Walsh, RNLI CoM; 166 RNLI/ Hayling Island Crew; 169 RNLI/ photograph by
Dennis Coutts; 173 painting by Tim Thompson; 176 The National Maritime
Museum; 181 RNLI/ photograph by Sue Denny; 183 *The Argus/* Newsquest
(Sussex) Ltd.; 185 RNLI/ photographs by John Dodds Studio; 188 (top) RNLI/
photograph by J.H.Bottrell, (bottom) RNLI/ photograph by H.H.Tansley; 190
RNLI/ photograph by Peter Thompson, 194-195 (inset) *Illustrated London News,*
(main) RNLI/ Royal Bank of Scotland/ photograph by Rick Tomlinson; 205 RNLI/
photograph by Gilbert Hampton; 207 (inset) RNLI/ photograph by Robert
Townsend, (main) RNLI/ Royal Bank of Scotland/ photograph by Rick Tomlinson;
209-215 RNLI/ Royal Bank of Scotland/ photographs by Rick Tomlinson; 220
RNLI/ photograph by Campbell MacCallum; 223 RNLI/ photograph by
H.H.Tansley; 228 RNLI/ photograph by Derek King; 241 (left) RNLI/ photograph
courtesy Marine Coastguard Agency, (right) RNLI/ photograph by Graeme Storey;
242 RNLI/ photograph by Graeme Storey; 243 RNLI/ photograph by Kieran
Murray; 244 RNLI/ photograph courtesy Marine Coastguard Agency: 250 RNLI/
photograph by Paul Taylor; 251 National Portrait Gallery

Contents

Acknowledgements 7

Introduction 8

1 'Beyond all human aid' 10

2 The founding of the Shipwreck Institution 20

3 The age of oars 30
   FACT BOX Willian Darling – Lighthouse Keeper 34
   FACT BOX Animals to the Rescue 44

4 The age of sail 48
   FACT BOX Medals and Awards 68

5 Steam boats and motor sailers 70
   FACT BOX Women's Work 94

6 The World Wars 98

7 From petrol to diesel 122

8 'Bring 'em back alive!' 142
   FACT BOX The Lifesaving Jacket 146
   FACT BOX Overseas Rescue Operations 154
   FACT BOX Helicopters 164

9 'It is not walls that make a city, but those who man them' 168

10 The RNLI in the 21st Century 190
    FACT BOX Tractors 198

11 The RNLI moving forward 228

APPENDICES

I Endnotes 246

II Key events in the history of the RNLI 248

III The Beaufort Scale 251

IV Annual receipts 252

V Members of the International Lifeboat Federation 253

VI Lives saved by RNLI lifeboats: cumulative annual total 254

VII The Lifeboat Enthusiasts' Society 256

Select bibliography 257

Index 258

'A lifeboatman must be strong
and muscular, possess great
courage, a spirit of self-sacrifice
and a waterproof hat.'

Extract from an entry for the schools' competition:
'Describe the kind of man a good lifeboatman should be.'

Acknowledgements

Without the goodwill of the RNLI *Riders of the Storm* could not have been written, and I acknowledge gratefully all the help and encouragement the Institution have given me.

My special thanks are due to Edward Wake-Walker (Public Relations Director), Derek King (Photographic and Presentations Assistant) and Barry Cox (Honorary Librarian). Barry Cox in particular was a great help, painstakingly and cheerfully checking a large number of often obscure facts and figures, and making sure I never strayed from accuracy. I would also like to thank Liz Cook (Editorial Manager of the RNLI's Publication Team) for her help in bringing this paperback edition up to date.

Riders of the Storm has been very much a team effort.

Ian Cameron

Introduction

bout 185 years ago an idiosyncratic Quaker, Sir William Hillary, founded a charity dedicated to 'the Preservation of Lives and Property from Shipwreck'. Its boats were few in number, were powered and often steered by oars, and could operate only close to the beaches from which they had been launched. Its affairs were managed – none too efficiently – by a conglomeration of part-time aristocratic patrons.

The Royal National Lifeboat Institution (RNLI) today might seem a totally different animal. It operates over 300 high-powered craft from over 230 stations. It provides a swift and efficient rescue service up to fifty miles offshore anywhere round the coast of the United Kingdom and Republic of Ireland. Each year its lifeboats answer about 8000 calls and assist over 8000 people, of whom several hundred would otherwise have lost their lives. Its affairs are in the hands of a full-time management team, who ensure its finances are sound and its boats and equipment state of the art.

The *Jeune Hortense* of Nantes aground off the coast of Cornwall, 17 May, 1888. Her Crew of three men and a boy were rescued by the Penzance lifeboat *Dora*.

Yet in spite of these obvious differences, the RNLI of today is still very much the child of the Shipwreck Institution of yesterday. It is still a charity, deriving no financial support from the government. And it still depends on the expertise and courage of the largely unpaid crews who man its lifeboats.

The work of these dedicated lifeboatmen and women is the thread that runs through the history of the RNLI. In an age when human frailty and wickedness are seldom out of the news, *Riders of the Storm* is a pleasant reminder that we are capable of better things: that ordinary people from every walk of life are prepared to give their time and even, if need be, their lives to help others.

1

'Beyond

all human aid'

quiet morning. No clouds, no wind, and the sea calm and dappled with that luminous phosphorescence that indicates shoals of fish. As the 400 or so ships of the Manx herring fleet put to sea on 21 September 1789 their crews have no premonition of disaster.

But there is an old Gaelic saying on the Isle of Man: '*Yn chiuney smoo erbee geay jiass smessey jee*' (The greater the calm, the nearer the south wind). And a south wind in the Irish Sea is a harbinger of storm.

All morning the Manx fishermen cast their nets into waters alive with herring. But a little after midday a breeze springs up from the south, and the more experienced crews look at the sky and begin to haul in their nets. The herring fleet disperses and the individual ships make for the safety of harbour. Some head for Ramsey, more than twenty miles away but offering a safe haven for those that can reach it in time. Others head for Douglas, closer but with a tidal harbour. And the tide that afternoon is on the ebb, which means that the ships will have to anchor offshore until the water becomes deep enough for them to enter. By early evening some 250 vessels are converging on the great semicircle of Douglas Bay and dropping anchor only a couple of hundred yards offshore. They are close to safety, but far from safe. For already the strip of water between ships and shore is a no-go area, with heavy seas surging over the rocks that serrate the low-water line. As ill luck would have it, a recent storm has destroyed the lighthouse that marks the entrance to the harbour, and as darkness falls only a single lantern slung from a pole marks the way in.

But soon other lights begin to illuminate the curve of the bay. The people of Douglas realize the danger their fishermen are in. They want desperately to help. But because they lack even the most rudimentary means of mounting a rescue, all they can do is wait – wait and watch and hope that the light from their lanterns will point the way to safety.

Tynemouth's lifeboat on service to a vessel wrecked near the lighthouse and priory, *circa* 1840.

Before lifeboats provided a rescue-service, there was little hope of survival for the crew of vessels wrecked on the coast of Britain. A contemporary periodical depicts what was likely to be the fate of shipwrecked seamen.

Bows into wind, the fishing ships are able for a time to ride out the storm; but as the wind increases and the waves steepen, their anchors begin to drag or snap. Several vessels are driven ashore and pounded to fragments among the rocks. The others, although uncertain if the water is yet deep enough, head for the harbour entrance. One of the first ships in is flung by a wave against the end of the harbour wall, dislodging the pole and its lantern. The one guiding light to safety is snuffed out. In a maelstrom of darkness, shoal-water and surging and backing waves, some vessels collide, some capsize, some are battered to pieces by the rocks.

With dawn, the full horror of what has happened becomes apparent. The bay is strewn with shredded canvas, splintered timbers and bodies. Fifty-three (some reports say fifty-five) vessels have been wrecked; 161 fishermen have been drowned. There is hardly a family in the close-knit community of Douglas that hasn't lost a loved one: father or son; uncle or nephew; husband, brother or lover.

At the time, the loss of the Manx herring fleet was accepted with fatalistic resignation. Little effort was made to help the bereaved families, and little effort made to prevent the same thing happening again. For shipwreck, in those days, was thought of as one of the occupational hazards of seafaring, an accident waiting to happen – an attitude summed up in the words of a contemporary newspaper: 'Only God could have saved the fishermen. They were beyond all human aid.'

Why, one wonders, did a nation that prided itself on its seafaring reputation do so little to protect its seafarers? Why, when there was such an obvious need, wasn't an organization on the lines of the RNLI founded earlier?

The reason would seem to be that until the end of the eighteenth century, the lives of seamen were perceived to be 'nasty, brutish and short', and hence of little value. It is difficult for us today to realize just how squalid and brief life below deck was in the heyday of empire building. During the more or less continuous wars that dragged on throughout the second half of the eighteenth century, it was not uncommon for a ship of the line to lose seventy-five per cent of her crew on a single voyage, the casualties being due not to enemy action but to disease, brought about by the appalling living conditions on board, and shipwreck. No wonder the majority of seamen who fought in the Napoleonic Wars had been impressed – that is to say, they had been kidnapped and were serving under duress. Not until the early nineteenth century did the quality of a seafarer's life, and hence his status and the value attached to his life, improve.

This improvement was brought about partly by the conquest of scurvy (which had killed more seamen in the eighteenth century than enemy action, shipwreck and accident combined), partly by the end of the debilitating wars with France, and partly by a postwar boom in trade and trading profits. There was also an intangible and less easily definable reason for improvement. In the *Oxford History of England*, the volume that deals with the years immediately after the Napoleonic Wars is called *The Age of Reform*, and its author makes the point that during the nineteenth century England gradually became a better place to live in: 'The scales [became] less weighted against the weak, against women and children, and against the poor. There was less of the fatalism of an earlier age. The public conscience was more instructed.' This really was an age of reform, in which many people had a belief in progress and a desire to alleviate the lot of the underprivileged. In the early years of the nineteenth century seafarers were underprivileged, and the campaign to protect them from shipwreck had the same humanitarian roots as the movements that led to prison reform and the abolition of slavery.

And how urgent a need there was for such a campaign.

The end of the Napoleonic Wars ushered in an era of prosperity for Britain. It was not long before the mother country was sucking in raw materials from all over the world – timber and furs from Canada, cocoa and palm oil from Nigeria, tobacco and copper from Rhodesia, teak and jute from Burma, rubber and tin from Malaya, wood and beef from Australia – and spewing out in return the products of the Industrial Revolution – woollens and cottons, and a vast range of machinery and machine-made items. This huge increase in trade led to a corresponding rise in the number of ships that made use of British ports and British coastal waters. This in turn led to a huge increase in the number of shipwrecks.

An analysis of nineteenth-century wreck charts brings to light some horrifying statistics, the basic one being that there were on average more than 1800 wrecks a year on the coast of Britain. In other words, a ship was being driven ashore and battered to destruction about every six hours. If no lifeboat was at hand, the crews of these wrecked vessels often had little chance of survival. For no matter how brave and how determined potential rescuers might be, if they lacked basic equipment such as lifeboats their efforts were likely to be in vain.

What happened to the crew of the *Mary Stoddart* is evidence of this.

Late one April morning, the barque *Mary Stoddart* was seen to be in difficulties off the north-east coast of Ireland. Captain Bernard Johnston, who seems to have been the most committed of her would-be rescuers, reported her 'labouring in high winds and heavy seas, and flying her ensign union-down as a flag of distress'. Johnston stood by her for six hours until she appeared to be safely anchored in the approaches to Dundalk harbour; she was too heavily laden to enter the shallow harbour itself. During the night, however, the weather worsened, and next morning it was clear to the people of Dundalk that the *Mary Stoddart* was in serious trouble.

Johnston set out in the steamer *Independence* in the hope of towing the barque into the shelter of nearby Carlington Bay. Conditions were appalling. The wind had now increased to a near-hurricane, and sheets of spray were being driven horizontally off the crests of the waves. In the huge seas *Independence* came close to being swamped. However, she managed to close with the *Mary Stoddart* and, with great difficulty, Johnston was hoisted aboard. Then the weather deteriorated still further, leaving the luckless Johnston stranded on the vessel he had come to save. *Independence* did her best to stay in touch, but a tremendous sea burst flush on her bow, ripping open her deck and forcing her to limp back to Dundalk. The *Mary Stoddart*, meanwhile, dragged her anchors and, as darkness fell, was swept on to a sandbar. Half-submerged and pounded by heavy seas, she seemed likely to break up at any moment. Her crew took to the rigging.

It seemed unlikely that either ship or ship's company would survive the night. But at daybreak they were still there.

Although there was no lifeboat in Dundalk, there were a fair number of ship's (or rowing) boats. Three of these were launched; and one, led by Captain Kelly, managed to get to within hailing distance of the wreck before her crew, near-insensible from cold, exposure and exhaustion, were forced to give up. The other boats were equally unsuccessful. And as night fell, it seemed to those watching that 'all aboard the wreck were doomed, including the unfortunate Johnston, on whose behalf the most intense feeling of commiseration was felt'.

Yet at dawn the *Mary Stoddart* was still impacted on to the sandbar, and some of the figures in her rigging were moving, though others hung stiff as carcasses in an abattoir.

All day, a succession of would-be rescuers again tried to get to the stranded vessel. But the wind was still gusting to over sixty miles per hour, and the waves still curling to over twenty feet as they broke inshore. In such conditions the ship's boats were hard put to it to survive, let alone make headway, and a little before noon the inevitable happened. Captain Kelly was making his second rescue attempt when his rowing boat capsized. Some of his men managed to cling for a moment to the overturned keel, but a wave swept them away. Kelly and two of his crew were never seen again; another man was washed ashore insensible and a few hours later died of hypothermia. In the early evening a rescue boat did briefly get alongside the *Mary Stoddart*; but the men in the rigging were either too weak or too frightened to jump, and before they could be helped aboard a huge wave flung the rescue boat against the wreck and she was forced to return, near-foundering, to the shore.

It looked as though the crew of the *Mary Stoddart* were condemned to yet another night on the sandbar. But a little before dark, a rowing boat manned by coastguards managed to get alongside and take off the few of her crew who were still alive.

The survivors were close to death, barely able to speak or move, and suffering from a combination of hunger, thirst, cold, exposure and exhaustion. Of those who had clung to the rigging, three had fallen and been washed away and drowned; while of those who had lashed themselves to the rigging, four had died, literally frozen solid. Among the survivors was Captain Johnston. His report tells us that as he hung, barely conscious, in the rigging, the knees of the two men above and behind him kept knocking into his back. When he pleaded with them to move, there was no reply. And looking up, he saw that they were dead.

The loss of the *Mary Stoddart* could hardly be described as a major maritime disaster. In every decade in the nineteenth century there were shipwrecks that led to far greater loss of life. It was, however, the sort of disaster that would almost certainly have been avoided if a lifeboat had been at hand. It was to provide such lifeboats that the Shipwreck Institution came into being.

One would have thought that the idea of using special rescue boats would have occurred to people long before. And in one or two coastal regions where conditions were particularly dangerous and shipping particularly heavy, local rescue organizations had indeed been operating for some years. These local rescue services were the forerunners of the RNLI and their boats the forerunners of lifeboats.

One of the first ports where there are written records of such a service is Liverpool where, we are told, 'from about 1730 onwards a boat was kept stationed on the strand about a mile below Formby lower landmark'. Another, highly efficient service was provided at Bamburgh in Northumberland, overlooking the Farne Islands (where Grace Darling was soon to win fame by helping to rescue passengers from the *Forfarshire*). We are told that the Bishop of Northumberland, Dr John Sharp, was so distressed by 'the melancholy sight of persons wrecked on [these] islands and starving with cold and hunger, together with the savage plundering of goods . . . [that he] induced the lords of the manor to give every assistance to vessels in distress, and premiums for the saving of lives'. In bad weather, two men from Bamburgh Castle patrolled the coast on horseback. Bells gave warning when there was fog. The firing of a cannon gave warning of a vessel in distress. 'By these signals people are directed to the spot . . . and by this means they frequently preserve not only the crew but even the vessel; for machines of different kinds are always in readiness to heave ships out of their perilous situation.'

What, one wonders, were these 'machines of different kinds'? We know that Bamburgh Castle provided speaking trumpets for hailing ships, rooms for shipwreck survivors, and coffins for those who did not survive, but no details of the 'machines' are extant. We do, however, know that among them was an 'unimmergible' coble, designed by Lionel Lukin.

This might claim to be the first purpose-built, working lifeboat. Lukin, born in Essex in 1742, was an inventor. He designed rafts for rescuing people trapped under ice, beds for the disabled, and stoves for heating and ventilating vessels below deck. In 1785 he took out a patent for what he described as an 'unimmergible', a boat that would not sink. He based his design on a Norwegian yawl, to which he added a projecting cork gunwale, watertight buoyancy chambers, and a heavy false keel. After successful tests on the Thames – watched, we are told, by the Prince of Wales – he loaned his boat to a Ramsgate pilot who promptly 'lost' it, almost certainly on a

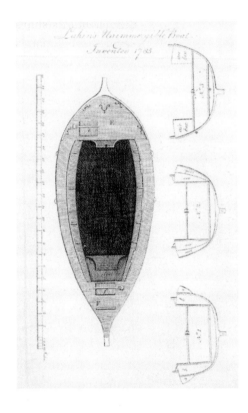

cross-Channel smuggling venture. Undeterred, Lukin built another boat, which he named the *Witch* because she 'performed prodigies of sailing in bad weather'. He tried to interest first the Admiralty, then Trinity House, in his invention. Neither showed much interest. But in 1786 he was approached by Dr Sharp, who asked him to apply his innovative design to a Northumberland coble (a flat-bottomed rowing boat). The result was a small, eminently seaworthy vessel, which is known to have been kept at Bamburgh for many years and is believed to have saved many lives.

In support of his claim that this was the first specially designed lifeboat, Lukin had his gravestone inscribed with the words 'This Lionel Lukin was the first who built a Lifeboat, and was the original inventor of that principle of safety, by which many lives and much property have been preserved from shipwreck.'

However, this claim was disputed. Another man who reckoned he invented the

Lionel Lukin (1742–1824). Using cork belting and buoyancy chambers, he designed an 'unimmergible', which was the prototype of future lifeboats.

lifeboat was William Wouldhave, a parish clerk from South Shields. Wouldhave's interest in lifeboats was brought to a head by a disaster that took place in 1789 when the collier *Adventure* was wrecked off the mouth of the Tyne. This tragedy had two things in common with the loss of the Manx fishing boats. It happened close inshore, and it happened in full view of thousands of onlookers, who could only watch helplessly as the crew of the *Adventure*, like the crew of the *Mary Stoddart*, were torn one by one from the rigging and swept to their deaths.

Among those watching was a group of South Shields businessmen who belonged to a club known as 'The Gentlemen of the Lawe House'. It seemed to these men that the *Adventure*'s ship's company might have been saved if only there had been a rescue boat stationed on the Tyne that was capable of surviving close inshore in heavy surf. They offered a prize of two guineas to whoever submitted the best model for such a boat, and one of the entries was by William Wouldhave.

Several stories have grown up around Wouldhave and his model. It is said that he got the idea for his design while watching a woman drawing

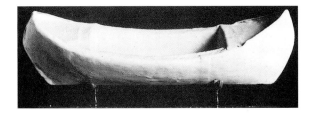

water from a well. She used a wooden dish shaped like a segment of an orange to scoop up the water, and Wouldhave noticed that this dish never stayed upside-down: every time it was immersed it turned over and floated the right way up. This is supposed to have given him the idea for a self-righting lifeboat. The committee judging the entries apparently liked and made use of Wouldhave's design, but offered him only half the prize money. This, it is claimed, he indignantly refused, saying, 'Never mind. I know they have sense enough to adopt the good points of my model; and, though I am poor, if they refuse to give me the reward, at least I shall have the satisfaction of being instrumental in saving the lives of some of my fellow creatures' – a mouthful that seems a bit too pat to be true.

Wouldhave's tombstone is inscribed with the words 'Inventor of that invaluable blessing to mankind, The Life-boat'. And history has been kinder than his contemporaries in recognizing the contribution he made to the design of the earliest lifeboats.

The fame and fortune that eluded both Lukin and Wouldhave were heaped in abundance on the man who built these early life-saving boats, Henry Greathead.

Greathead had also submitted a model to the 1789 competition. This was described as 'useless'. Nevertheless, he found favour with the adjudicating committee on two counts: he was a practising shipwright; and he worked in South Shields,

William Wouldhave (1751–1821). He designed a boat with a high bow and stern like 'the segment of an orange'. This would self-right if it capsized, a characteristic of many subsequent lifeboats.

where it was easy for his sponsors to keep an eye on him. Two members of the committee, Michael Rockwood and Nicholas Fairles, began a series of experiments in which they combined the best features of the various models they had been asked to judge. Fairles was a builder, and the clay in his brickyard was used to fashion a 'model with all the virtues'. This was then given to Greathead, and he was told to build a vessel to its specification.

The result was the *Original* – not the first ever purpose-built lifeboat, for that niche in history surely belongs to Lukin's Northumberland coble – but the first of a class of lifeboats, a design that was replicated many times, was in use for many years, and saved many lives.

The *Original* was a hybrid, combining Lukin's extensive use of cork, with Wouldhave's orange-segment shape. In his *Lifeboat Design and Development*, Eric Fry writes:

> She was 30 ft. overall in length, with a beam of 10 ft. and a draft of 3 ft. Her most outstanding features were her sharply curved keel . . . and her extremely high stern-post and stemhead. She pulled ten oars, double-banked and, having no rudder, was steered by a sweep oar. A completely open boat, she had no end boxes or air cases, but Greathead made much use of cork beneath the side benches and in a large outboard belting below the gunwale. Massively built, she was fitted with a pair of timberheads or bollards on each side of her bluff bow, and single posts on each quarter. Being without any automatic means of being relieved of water, hand baling was the order of the day.

The *Original* was to prove a sturdy if cumbersome boat. And Greathead was to prove a highly successful shipwright. Within a couple of decades he had built no fewer than thirty-one Originals, eight for use on the continent and twenty-three for the British Isles. For this he was more than adequately rewarded. As well as making a sizeable profit on each of his boats, he was awarded honoraria from Parliament, Trinity House and Lloyd's, and showered with a cornucopia of gifts

Henry Greathead (1757–1816) a South Shields shipwright. He combined Lukin's and Wouldhave's designs to build the *Original*: a class of sturdy but cumbersome boats which were the work-horses of the fledgling RNLI.

including a gold medal from the Society of Arts and a diamond ring from the Emperor of Russia.

One wishes Lukin and Wouldhave could have shared in this bonanza, but it would be churlish to carp at Greathead's financial success for his boats were the workhorses of the embryonic RNLI. Records show that between 1789 and 1804 Originals were sent to harbours as diverse as North Shields, St Andrews, Montrose, Lowestoft, Bawdsey Haven, Ramsgate, West Whitby, Redcar, Holy Island, Douglas (Isle of Man), Aberdeen, Ayr, Hoylake, Christchurch, St Peter Port (Guernsey), Newhaven, Plymouth, Arbroath, Exmouth, Rye, Penzance and Whitehaven. The records also provide evidence of the many rescues they carried out. A typical operation by an Original is described by Mr Hinderwell of Scarborough:

> On Monday the 2nd of November 1801, we were visited with a most tremendous storm from the eastward. I scarcely ever remember seeing a more mountainous sea. The *Aurora* of Newcastle, in approaching [Scarborough] harbour, was driven ashore to the southward, and, as she was in the most imminent danger, the life boat was launched. The place where the ship lay was exposed to the whole force of the sea, and she was surrounded with broken water, which dashed over the rocks with considerable violence. In such a perilous situation the life boat adventured, and proceeded through the breach of the sea, rising on the summit of the waves without shipping any water, except a little from the spray. On going upon the lee quarter of the vessel, they were endangered by the main-boom, which had broken loose, and was driving about with great force. [In spite of these difficulties, the whole crew was taken onboard.] Thus by means of the life-boat . . . and the exertions of the boatmen, seven men and boys were saved . . . I must add it was the general opinion that no other boat of the common construction could have possibly performed the service, and the fishermen, though very adventurous, declared they would not have made the attempt in their own boats.

It should, however, be pointed out that such lavish praise for the Originals was by no means universal. They were suitable for working in shallow waters off the east coast, but in small and open harbours they were not popular. This was partly because their weight made them difficult to launch, and partly because they needed to be manned by so large a crew. Indeed, some of the harbours to which they were sent described them as 'unfit for service', and more than one of Greathead's boats suffered the indignity of quietly rotting away because no one was willing to spend money to keep it serviceable.

It would therefore be fair to say that although there was a dramatic increase in the years after the Napoleonic Wars in the number of vessels using British coastal waters, there was no corresponding increase in the efficiency of measures to help these vessels in the event of shipwreck. One or two ports did have well run, privately owned rescue services; but along huge stretches of coastline there were either no lifeboats at all, or the boats that were available were ineffective. Each year, more and more ships were being wrecked, and more and more lives lost.

What was needed was a white knight, a charismatic figure who would meld the various local services into a national organization. A somewhat unlikely white knight was found in Lieutenant-Colonel Sir William Hillary.

The founding
of the

Shipwreck Institution

t is the night of 12 December 1822, and the brig of war HMS *Racehorse* is on passage from Milford Haven to Douglas. There is no moon and ten-tenths cloud. The wind is rising, and the barometer falling.

Naval officers are usually meticulous in their navigation, but *Racehorse*'s commanding officer, Captain Suckling, decides to trust his local pilot rather than his dead-reckoning plot. When the pilot tells him the lights on his starboard bow are those of Douglas, he turns towards them. It is a mistake. The lights are those of Castletown, in those days the island's capital, and before Suckling realizes his error there is a lurch, a shudder, and *Racehorse* is impaled on the reef of the Skirranes.

HMS *Racehorse*, wrecked off Castletown, Isle of Man, 12 December 1822: a disaster that prompted Willian Hillary to campaign for the founding of the RNLI.

The situation doesn't at first seem all that serious. *Racehorse* fires distress rockets and flares, then lowers her cutter, with orders to its crew to row to nearby Castletown for help. The local fishermen are quick to respond, and as dawn is breaking five rowing boats are heading for the Skirranes. However, by the time they get there, the wind has increased to a full gale, the waves have heightened, and *Racehorse*, swept by heavy seas, is in danger of breaking up. Initially, none of the rowing boats can get close to her for fear of being swept on to the reef. Eventually the largest of them manages to get near enough for some dozen of the brig's crew to jump aboard. They are ferried through heavy surf and landed, with no little difficulty, on a nearby beach. There they are left to fend for themselves while the men from Castletown go back for more.

The rescue that follows demands perseverance, fine seamanship and courage. Again and again the fishermen manage to bring their rowing boat close enough to the brig to enable some of the crew to jump, scramble or be hauled aboard – no easy job with the rescue boat now being flung up to the level of *Racehorse*'s rail, now

plunged deep into a trough beneath her keel. Time after time the rescuers are within an ace of being dashed to pieces on the reef or crushed by the weight of the brig. By mid afternoon four successful runs have been completed. One final sortie, and *Racehorse*'s captain and the last of her crew are taken aboard, and the rescue boat is heading for the beach.

But in the moment of triumph comes tragedy. As the boat nears shore for the last time it is overturned by a huge wave. Rescuers and rescued are flung into a turmoil of breaking waves and scouring undertow. Some are saved, dragged ashore half-sense-less by their companions on the beach; but six of *Racehorse*'s crew and three of the Castletown fishermen are drowned.

To William Hillary, as he reads the report of what happened in his home in nearby Douglas, it seems monstrously unfair that the families of the Castletown fishermen who have died should now be faced with penury because their menfolk gave their lives to save others. One of the men who has drowned, Norris Bridson, had just taken on the job of looking after his sister and her two young children. Another, Thomas Hall, has left a widow and daughters aged one and two. The third man, Robert Quale, has left a widow and eight children. Why, Hillary asks himself, should these innocent people now have to face not only the sorrow of bereavement but the threat of the poorhouse? The same day that the Castletown fishermen are buried, he writes on behalf of their families to the Admiralty.

One wonders why a man who has never served at sea and whose family has no seafaring tradition should be so concerned with the plight of the shipwrecked.

William Hillary was born in the Yorkshire Dales in 1771, the youngest son of Hannah and Richard Hillary who farmed a none too fertile area of moorland along the upper reaches of the Ure. His distant ancestors are thought to have been Huguenots, his not so distant ones are known to have been Quakers, and his subsequent championship of the shipwrecked probably had its roots in his Quaker upbringing with its tradition of concern for the underprivileged.

His parents were not wealthy. However, several members of the Hillary family had emigrated to the Caribbean where they had made their fortunes from the sugar-cane plantations; and it was this family money that first gave young William a sound education, then launched him into the fashionable world of London society. His biographer, Robert Kelly, tells us that in his early twenties he was 'a handsome man . . . with the gift of ready and intelligent wit', and that his whole demeanour was that of an aristocrat. This may be pushing it a bit; but Hillary certainly moved in aristocratic circles, and in 1794 was appointed equerry to Prince Augustus Frederick, ninth child of George III.

During the next few years, the Prince and Hillary did a fair amount of travelling together, mostly in Italy, Sicily and Malta, and it was then that Hillary acquired the interest in seafaring and the penchant for spending more money than was prudent that were to shape the course of his life. The Prince was a dedicated patron of good

(and often lost) causes, and Hillary became involved with several of these. In particular, during their visits to Malta, he became involved in the affairs of the Knights of St John. When the latter surrendered their Maltese stronghold to a French fleet – rumour had it, after a bribe of 600,000 francs – Hillary was disillusioned, resigned his position as equerry, and went to live with his brother in Liverpool.

It was at this somewhat low point in his fortunes that he fell in love.

The Quaker philanthropist William Hillary. In 1824 he founded an 'Institution for the Preservation of Life from Shipwreck'. He personally helped to save over 300 lives, and was three times awarded the Institution's Gold Medal for gallantry.

Frances Elizabeth Disney Ffytche was young – six years younger than William – attractive and very, very rich. Her parents owned 'the resplendent Danbury Place, the largest estate in Essex ... surrounded by parkland stocked with deer and reputed to have the best sweet chestnuts in the county'. Frances's father didn't care for William, who, he reckoned, was after his daughter's money, and he made it clear there would be neither parental approval nor marriage settlement. The couple therefore eloped, and in February 1800 were married by special licence. Later that year Frances gave birth to twins, a girl and a boy, and her father relented a little and agreed to let them live in Danbury Place. This, from the point of view of the Ffytche family, was a mistake, because William now proceeded to spend all his wife's money.

The first few years of the nineteenth century, before Trafalgar, saw the nadir of British fortunes in the war with France. There was believed to be a real danger of invasion and landowners were asked to raise a volunteer militia, a sort of cross between the Territorials and the Home Guard. Hillary, never one to do things by halves, responded with more enthusiasm than prudence. To quote his biographer:

Placing his country above all else and throwing financial discretion to the winds, he plunged blindly into the formation of the biggest private army in Britain. Within weeks the parkland around Danbury Place echoed to the sounds of galloping horses and the shouts of men in training ... There were troops of infantry, a cavalry corps of five-hundred horses, and a detachment of light artillery with two brass field pieces ... The Hillary purse seemed limitless.

However, 'the Essex legion', as it came to be called, soon proved an unbearable strain not only on Hillary's finances but also on his marriage. To maintain his army he was forced to sell first his own home and then the sugar plantations he had inherited from his brother, while the once stately Danbury Place, deprived of funds, fell into disrepair. Frances saw all that her father had warned her of coming true. The

marriage broke up, and Hillary, to all intents and purposes bankrupt, sought refuge in the Isle of Man – a haven he chose because, in those days, residents on the island could not be held responsible for debts they had incurred on the mainland.

In this scenario of disaster there was, for Hillary, one bright spot. On 8 November 1805, in recognition of the contribution he had made to the defence of his country, he was made a baronet. This meant a lot to him. And the motto he chose for his coat of arms, '*Virtute nihil invium*' ('With courage nothing is impossible'), gives us a clue to his character. Profligate he may have been, but not even his enemies would deny he had courage.

He settled into rented accommodation in Douglas, a town being transformed from a jumble of fishermen's cottages into a haven for tax-exiles, debtors and retired members of the services, all of whom were attracted to the Isle of Man by its cheap cost of living and exchange rate of fourteen pence to the shilling. Hillary remarried, put what little money he had into an unsound local mining venture, and gradually became accepted as a somewhat eccentric 'come over' – that is, one who had come to the island from the other side of the sea.

Firing a maroon – in the old days the signal for lifeboat crews to assemble. Howth lifeboat station, 1944.

He was forever championing good causes. In particular, year after year he campaigned for improvements to Douglas harbour, and for the maintenance there of a lifeboat. Bearing in mind what had happened a generation earlier to the Manx herring fleet, one would have thought his advice would have been heeded. However, it was not. And when, inevitably, there was another shipwreck off Douglas, there was once again no way of mounting a rescue.

Early in the morning of 6 October 1822, Hillary was woken by the roar of the wind and the staccato crack of maroons. Looking out of his bedroom window, he saw that, once again, ships were in trouble in Douglas Bay.

The maroons were being fired by the Royal Navy cutter *Vigilant*. The previous evening, together with half a dozen other vessels, *Vigilant* had run for shelter into Douglas Bay. However, the wind had suddenly backed from north-west to south-west and Douglas Bay, as in 1787, was transformed from haven to death-trap. *Vigilant*'s captain, Lieutenant Reid, decided to run for the open sea. However, another vessel, a heavily laden sloop, had the same idea at the same time, got out of control and yawed across *Vigilant*'s bows. Trying to take evasive action, the cutter ran aground on St Mary's Island, close to the harbour entrance. Impacted into the rocks, unable to move, and battered by heavy seas, she was in danger of breaking up.

St Mary's Island is only a few hundred yards from the shore. But with no lifeboat available, it seemed that once again there was no way of rescuing the crew. However, Hillary and a handful of retired naval officers had other ideas. The owner of the York Hotel had a number of rowing boats, used for pleasure trips by his guests; these, he said, could be used for an attempted rescue, if anyone was prepared to take the risk.

About a dozen fishermen volunteered, and under the command of two retired naval officers, Lieutenants Burbridge and Graves, two rowing boats were launched. Hillary, although he was fifty-one and unable to swim, took an oar.

The rescue that followed has many of the hallmarks soon to become synonymous with the work of the RNLI: physical endurance, fine seamanship, and the willingness of the crew of the rescue boats to risk their lives to try to save others. The plan was for the boats to bear out to sea, then allow wind and wave to carry them back towards the *Vigilant*; as they passed her, hawsers would be thrown aboard, and the boats would then attempt to pull the cutter clear of the rocks. However, the seas were so heavy and the wind so strong that, to those watching from the shore, it seemed impossible that the tiny rescue boats would survive, let alone make headway. But make headway they did, and they managed to pass hawsers to the *Vigilant*. Lieutenant Reid saw what was needed. He set about lightening his vessel, cutting down his mainmast and heaving it over the side, and rolling his cannon and the better part of his stores into the sea. Then, as the hawsers tautened, came the first moment of truth. The rowers heaved with all their strength. There was a creaking and groaning of timbers, and *Vigilant* shuddered. Another heave. And another. And another. And, with a splintering of timbers, she slid free. Now came the second moment of truth. Would she founder or float? Her rudder had been torn away, her stern-post was split open, and the after part of her keel had been holed. But she floated. And slowly and painfully the rowing boats towed her to safety. About the time that behind the storm clouds the sun was rising out of the Irish Sea, *Vigilant* was beached in Douglas harbour.

The rescuers collapsed in the shelter of the York Hotel, where they were covered with blankets and revived with hot tea. One would have thought they had done all – and more – that could be expected. But although one ship had been saved, others were still at risk. That morning the storm increased in violence. One of the vessels trying to shelter in Douglas Bay, the *Merchant of Fraserburgh*, was driven ashore and battered to destruction. Another five vessels (two schooners, two sloops and a brig) seemed likely to follow her on to the rocks. Hillary called for more volunteers to go to their aid.

No one stepped forward. The naval officers had risked their lives once to save their fellow servicemen; they reckoned they had done enough. The fishermen were reluctant to risk their lives a second time because, apart from anything else, they had their families to consider. We are so cosseted today by the welfare state that it is hard for us to realize just how terrible poverty could be 175 years ago. It was not unheard of in those days for a mother to murder her newborn child because she knew she would not be able to afford to feed it. If a fisherman died and his wife and children were left without a breadwinner, their future might be truly harrowing. So Hillary's call went unanswered.

It is now that he emerges out of the debris of a none too satisfactory life towards a niche in history. Although he was not a rich man – he was soon to go bankrupt and die in poverty – he promised personally to give a cash reward to anyone who volunteered to man a rescue boat. The fisherfolk of Douglas had, over the years, come to trust him. Slowly men came forward.

That afternoon the overworked rowing boats put out again. They went first to the sloop *Eliza* and the schooner *Content*, took them in tow, and brought them safely back to harbour. Hillary led one rescue, and helped to organize the other. Then it was the turn of the sloop *Dove*, the schooner *Fame* and the brig *Two Sisters*. Lines were attached to them and they were hand-hauled by teams of men and women on to the beach. Again Hillary played a leading role in the rescues.

As he relaxed that evening in his home on Prospect Hill, he was conscious of a job well done. But he couldn't help thinking how much easier things would have been if a lifeboat had been at hand, and that he himself wouldn't be so seriously out of pocket if financial help had been on offer to those who had volunteered for rescue work. A few weeks later the same issues were raised by the wreck of the brig *HMS Racehorse*. And this time there was loss of life; this time the tragedy was compounded by the fact that the families of those who had died were threatened with penury.

It was October when Hillary wrote on their behalf to the Admiralty. On Christmas Eve he received a reply. The Sea Lords agreed to award life pensions to the bereaved. Hillary was delighted. However, it worried him that the pensions had been awarded not as a right but as a gesture of goodwill, and if *Racehorse* had been a privately owned vessel rather than a warship of the Royal Navy the odds were that no pensions would have been forthcoming at all. So, during the first few weeks of 1823, he devoted his very considerable energy to preparing a pamphlet: 'An Appeal to the British Nation on the humanity and policy of forming a national institution for the preservation of lives and property from shipwreck.'

It is easy today to smile at the verbosity of this appeal, but its message still comes through loud and clear:

> For many years and in various countries, the melancholy and fatal shipwrecks which I have witnessed have excited a powerful interest in my mind for the situation of those who are exposed to this awful calamity; but the idea of the advantages which would result from the establishment of a national institution for the preservation of human life from the perils of the sea, first suggested itself to me during my residence on a part of the coast often exposed to the most distressing scenes of misery, and where the dreadful storms of the last autumn prevailed with unusual violence.
>
> On some occasions it has been my lot to witness the loss of many valuable lives, under circumstances where, had there been establishments already formed for affording prompt relief, and encouragement given to those who might volunteer on such a cause, in all probability the greater part would have been rescued from destruction. At other times I have seen the noblest instances of self-devotion; men have saved the lives of their fellow-creatures at the peril of their own, without a prospect of reward if successful, and with the certainty that their families would be left destitute if they perished.
>
> From these considerations I have been induced to [suggest] the formation of one great Institution, which would in itself embrace every possible means for the preservation of life from the hazards of shipwreck.

He went on to propose:

> a national institution should be formed, important to humanity, and beneficial to the naval and commercial interests of the United Empire, having for its objects:

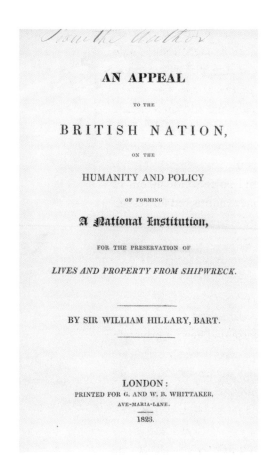

AN APPEAL

TO THE

BRITISH NATION,

ON THE

HUMANITY AND POLICY

OF FORMING

A National Institution,

FOR THE PRESERVATION OF

LIVES AND PROPERTY FROM SHIPWRECK.

BY SIR WILLIAM HILLARY, BART.

LONDON:
PRINTED FOR G. AND W. B. WHITTAKER,
AVE-MARIA-LANE.

1823.

FIRST: The preservation of human life from shipwreck, which should always be considered as the first great and permanent object of the Institution.

SECOND: Assistance to vessels in distress, which often immediately connects itself with the safety of the crews.

THIRD: The preservation of the vessels and property, when not so immediately connected with the lives of people, or after the crews and passengers shall already have been rescued.

FOURTH: The prevention of plunder and depredations in case of shipwreck.

FIFTH: The succour and support of those persons who may be rescued; the promptly obtaining medical aid, food, clothing and shelter for those whose destitute situation may require such relief, with the means to forward them to their homes, friends or countries. The people and vessels of every nation, whether in peace or war, to be equally objects of the Institution, and the efforts to be made and the recompenses to be given to their rescue, to be in all cases the same as those for British subjects and British vessels.

SIXTH: The bestowing of suitable rewards on those who rescue the lives of others from shipwreck, or those who assist vessels in distress; and the establishment of a provision for the destitute widows or families of the brave men who unhappily lose their lives in such meritorious attempts.

Facsimile of Hillary's first and unsuccessful 'Appeal to the Nation', printed privately in 1823.

Most of these remain, to this day, the objectives of the RNLI.

Seven hundred copies of the appeal were printed at Hillary's expense and distributed to the Admiralty, members of parliament and 'the most eminent characters in the country'.

Everyone was sympathetic. No one was prepared to do anything.

The response from the Admiralty was typical: 'I have wrung this over and I think what it advocates is worthy at least of consideration,' wrote one of the Sea Lords, '. . . [but] I should not deem it necessary for the Admiralty to take any immediate lead with respect to it.' However, in the autumn of 1823 one or two institutions and individuals began to offer support. Lloyd's agreed to finance the building and maintenance of a lifeboat; and George Hibbert, chairman of the West India Merchants, and Thomas Wilson, an energetic Member of Parliament for the City of London, agreed to use their influence to try to get Hillary's scheme off the ground.

It is claimed on Hillary's tombstone that 'He founded the Royal National Lifeboat Institution,' and this is now widely accepted. The truth, though, is a little more complex. Hillary was an ideas man, but he lacked the tact, patience and perseverance that were needed to transform his ideas into reality. These characteristics, however, were possessed in abundance by Thomas Wilson, whom contemporaries describe as

'a man of discriminating judgement and sterling integrity'. And it was the unsung and almost unheard of Wilson who not only did the spadework that led to the founding of the RNLI, but ensured that it came into being not as an ancillary of the Navy, and not as an adjunct of the government, but as a charity.

OPPOSITE
The London Tavern,
Bishopsgate,
where the proposal
to found a
'Shipwreck
Institution' was
passed.

For it was Wilson who now pointed out to Hillary that whereas the government and the services were likely to be reluctant to finance new projects (especially when there was going to be continuous expenditure and little tangible benefit), wealthy philanthropists would be more likely to sponsor a good cause. So, early in 1824, another and better targeted appeal was launched. Hibbert lobbied his commercial friends, Wilson lobbied his political friends, Hillary lobbied his friends at court. And this time the response was more encouraging. A list of those who promised support for the embryo charitable Institution reads like an extract from *Who's Who*: King George IV; Prince Leopold, soon to be King of the Belgians; five royal dukes; two archbishops; six bishops; many eminent politicians, including arguably the two most influential of the day, Canning and Peel; many serving officers, including Captain Marryat, the popular novelist; the Lord Mayor of London; the Governor of the Bank of England; the chairman of Lloyd's; the chairman of the East India Company; and a number of radical Christian reformists, including William Wilberforce, founder of the Society for the Abolition of the Slave Trade.

Thomas Wilson, chairman of the National Institution for the Preservation of Life from Shipwreck from 1824 to 1849.

On 4 March 1824 a meeting was held at the fashionable London Tavern in Bishopsgate, with the Archbishop of Canterbury in the chair, and in an atmosphere of almost fervent enthusiasm the resolution was passed: 'That an Institution be now formed for the Preservation of Life in cases of Shipwreck on the Coasts of the United Kingdom, to be supported by donations and subscriptions, and to be called the National Institution for the Preservation of Life from Shipwreck'. The man elected chairman of this fledgling charity was not Hillary but Wilson.

Initially there was no lack of financial support. Money fairly poured in, and by the end of the year almost £10,000 (the equivalent in today's money of some £8,000,000) had been donated. The Institution chose a prestigious headquarters – 12 Austin Friars, not far from the Bank of England – and set up committees and sub-committees to define its objectives and carry out its work.

The age of oars

On the evening of 6 September 1838, a new and luxurious paddle steamer, the *Forfarshire*, is on passage from Hull to Dundee. Aboard her are sixty-three passengers and crew. The weather is bad; but the *Forfarshire's* master, Captain Humble, has orders that for the sake of his VIP passengers he is to keep as close as possible to schedule. He therefore holds course, confident in the seaworthiness of his ship. However, a little before midnight the *Forfarshire* springs a leak in her boilers, and at almost the same moment the weather takes a sudden turn for the worse; the wind increases to a hurricane, visibility is reduced to a few yards, and just when she needs full power the *Forfarshire's* engines falter and die.

Grace Darling and her father William row through heavy seas to rescue survivors from the *Forfarshire*, wrecked off the Farne Islands, 6 September 1838.

Storm sails are hoisted, but within minutes they are ripped apart, and bludgeoning winds, huge seas and a flood tide combine to sweep the helpless vessel towards the shore. Her anchors fail to hold and she piles up on the Harcar Rocks in the Farne Islands. Her end is sudden and violent. Pounded by heavy seas, she breaks in half. Her stern section sinks, drowning forty-two of her passengers and crew. The survivors cling despairingly to the forward section of the ship, which is wedged into the Harcars and swept by huge seas. Eight of the crew and one passenger manage to lower and clamber into a ship's boat; they are swirled away into the darkness, and twenty-four hours later are picked up, close to death from hypothermia and exhaustion. The thirteen people still on the *Forfarshire* are not all so lucky. Among them are a woman and her two young children, and several passengers who are injured. During the night, the two children and two of the adult passengers freeze to death. At daybreak, the nine people still alive manage to clamber out of the wreck and on to the Big Harcar. But this is no safe haven. The Harcars are swept by spray and waves, far from the shore, and surrounded by dangerous reefs. There seems little hope of rescue.

Then, a couple of hours after daybreak, the survivors see what they think at first must be a mirage. Dwarfed by an immensity of sea and sky, now poised on the crest of a wave, now out of sight in the depths of a trough, a tiny rowing boat is edging towards them. As it comes closer, they see that the rowers are a middle-aged man and a young woman.

About a quarter of a mile from the Harcars, the Longstone lighthouse rises out of a mosaic of reefs. Most of the time the keeper, William Darling, has at least one of his sons with him. However, on the night the *Forfarshire* is wrecked his sons are ashore on the mainland, and the only other people in the Longstone are his wife and his twenty-three-year-old daughter Grace. As soon as it is light the Darlings spot the wreck on the Harcars. They reckon the seas are too heavy for a boat from the mainland to go to the rescue, so it is up to them. Grace stows blankets under the thwarts of their coble, takes off her petticoat, and helps her father with the launch.

It is a little after six a.m. as father and daughter set out for the wreck. The hurricane by now has subsided to a gale, but the wind is still blowing at thirty knots and the seas are mountainous. As the crow flies, it is only about a quarter of a mile from the Longstone to the Harcars; but to reach the rocks the Darlings have to head almost a mile out to sea to avoid a succession of reefs. Grace is no more than five feet tall and not strong – she is to die only a few years later of consumption – so the passage to the Harcars is, to say the least, physically demanding. When they get there, they find there are too many survivors for them all to be taken back to the lighthouse in one journey. So William scrambles on to the rocks to assess the situation, leaving Grace to man the coble alone. Eventually five people, including those who have been injured and the woman who has lost her children, are helped into the coble, and father and daughter row them back to the Longstone. Grace then remains in the lighthouse to care for the bereaved woman and the injured, while her father and another man go back for the rest of the survivors.

This was a brave, well-executed rescue, in which Grace played a major part. But it is hard to see why it should have aroused in the public the sort of near-hysterical adulation that is nowadays accorded to pop stars. However, this is what happened. The nation went overboard for Grace Darling. Well-known artists queued up outside the Longstone to paint her portrait. Fragments supposedly cut from her dress and her hair were sold in huge quantities all over the country. Her heroics were acted out, with ever increasing inaccuracy, in music hall sketches and plays. Poems were written in her honour, including one by Wordsworth, and one containing the immortal lines 'And through the sea's tremendous trough / The father and the girl rode off'. A trust was set up to collect money for her. The Shipwreck Institution gave her a silver medal. And in the words of her biographer, 'She became Britain's first national heroine'.

Grace reacted to all this with a modesty that, one can see in retrospect, helped raise her to icon status. Declining invitations to take money, speak in public, or appear on the stage, she continued to lead the reclusive life of a lighthouse keeper's daughter for as long as she could. This was not for long. She died of consumption at the age of twenty-six.

Grace Darling had no connection whatsoever with the Shipwreck Institution, apart from the fact that it gave her a medal. Yet more than 150 years after her death she is still widely regarded as *the* personification of the sort of gallantry one associates with lifeboat crews; and one can still find in erudite books published in the 1990s such amazing claims as: 'Her rescue of the nine passengers from the *Forfarshire* led to the founding of the Royal National Lifeboat Institution'.

Why, one wonders, did she achieve this icon status? One reason perhaps is that her rescue stirred up the latent feminism that was soon to manifest itself in the campaign for women's rights. Another reason could be that her youth, her lack of physical strength, and her femininity made people realize that *anyone* – if they had enough courage – could help to save lives at sea. We tend nowadays to equate the rescue of seafarers with lifeboat crews. However, in the early years of the Shipwreck Institution, the vast majority of rescues were carried out by ordinary members of the public – by people who, like Grace Darling, were connected with the sea but had no connection with the RNLI. The table below shows that, in its first decade, the Institution gave medals for rescue work to people of many different callings. Among the 'others' awarded medals were bailiffs, water-bailiffs, steam packet agents, Lloyd's agents, customs officers, surveyors, farmers, 'gentlemen', clergymen and doctors, not to mention those whose occupation is not specified.

Medals awarded by the Shipwreck Institution 1825–35

To Coastguards	To Seamen/ fishermen	To Officers of the Royal Navy	To Lifeboatmen	To Others
25 gold	1 gold	7 gold		9 gold
64 silver	65 silver	8 silver	6 silver	27 silver

So perhaps having a lighthouse keeper's daughter as a role model is not all that surprising.

When the Institution's general committee met for the first time in the summer of 1824, it set itself three objectives:

i. To award medals and/or cash to those involved in rescuing people from shipwrecks
ii. To provide Captain Manby's line-throwing mortars to all coastguard and lifeboat stations
iii. To provide lifeboats to as many places on the coast as possible.

Giving rewards, and especially pecuniary rewards, for acts of heroism may seem today to be debasing the value of the heroic act; one of the reasons why so many people nowadays support the RNLI is that its personnel are mostly unpaid and, more

William Darling – Lighthouse Keeper

William Darling (above) was keeper of the Longstone light for thirty-three years. It was from this remote lighthouse that he and his daughter Grace rescued nine passengers from the *Forfarshire*.

Longstone is one of the bleakly beautiful Farne Islands off the coast of Northumberland, a notorious place for shipwrecks: 'On one night alone [in 1774], no less than 6 ships and 100 souls perished there'. However, it was not until 1826 that a lighthouse was built on the island: a circular tower of dark-red local stone, designed by Joseph Nelson, with twelve coal-burning lanterns in its gallery. The Darling family (father, mother, three sons and two daughters) were its first occupants.

Their life was hard. In those days, only the lighthouse keeper was paid a salary, his family being allowed to live with him on the understanding that they worked as unpaid assistants. William's diary records everyday events. 'Tremendous sea came in, passing over the island and entering into the kitchen ... Codling very plentiful, caught four score [on] New Year's Day... Severe weather, the garden seeds totally blown off or destroyed... Signalled for

doctor. Our five children all sick of measles... Severe winter, frost and snow lying full three months ... Great gale with NE swell. Sea broke open the gateway and flooded the lower building. Got all the family into the Tower.'

In spite of the warning light from the Longstone, there were over fifty serious wrecks in the Farne Islands during William's time as keeper. Most famous was the wreck of the *Forfarshire* on 7 September 1838.

However, William never thought the *Forfarshire* rescue particularly noteworthy – he was several times involved in more hazardous operations. Nor did he think the part played in it by his daughter was in any way noteworthy – he loved Grace dearly, yet when he wrote up the *Forfarshire* rescue in his diary he never even mentioned her. (His entry reads simply: 'Nine others held on by the wreck and were rescued by the Darlings.') He took it for granted that any member of his family, any time, would do whatever was needed to save life at sea.

Grace Darling. After helping her father rescue nine people from the wreck of the *Forfarshire* she became 'Britain's first national heroine'.

A dramatic representation of survivors being rescued from the wreck of the *Forfarshire*. Such paintings helped to publicise Grace Darling's bravery.

The commemorative gold locket awarded to Grace Darling for her rescue.

William Darling retired at the age of seventy-five. One of the last entries in his diary reads: 'Oct 3rd, 1860. Wind a hurricane, the sloop *Trio* of Arbroath was run onto Harker's west point. The crew got on the rock. The vessel became total wreck and drifted to sea in fragments. My son, my two grandsons and me succeeded in bringing the crew safely to Longstone in our boat.'

The Darlings were typical of that small coterie of families who, in the nineteenth and early twentieth centuries, spent the better part of their lives on what were sometimes little more than wave-swept outcrops of rock, not infrequently in danger, often in discomfort, always in isolation. The debt that generations of seafarers owe to them is incalculable.

often than not, unrewarded. However, the situation was different in the 1820s. In those days people needed a specific inducement to go to the aid of the shipwrecked. This was partly because if rescuers lost their lives their families might suffer poverty, and partly because wrecks were still widely regarded as legitimate sources of plunder. Indeed, far from rescuing people from a shipwrecked vessel, it was not unheard of for onlookers to murder them, because if there were no survivors there would be no chance of plundered goods having to be returned. In 1829, for example, when the Spanish brig *Capricho* was wrecked off Ballycotton, County Cork, 'A boat was seen to put out from the shore with armed men intent on plunder'. If it had not been for the efforts of the Ballycotton coastguard officer, Samuel Lloyd, who 'for six days had to protect the vessel's remains from thousands of locals intent on plunder', none of the *Capricho*'s cargo, and maybe none of her crew, would have survived.

It was therefore highly desirable that the Institution should bring about a change in the attitude of the public towards those who had been shipwrecked. One way of doing this was to give medals to those who took part in rescues. And this accounts for the large number of gold and silver medals initially awarded by the Institution, sometimes 'with the view of exciting others to follow the example of the parties herein referred to... [rather] than from any particular risk incurred by them'. Generally speaking, the Institution's medals were received gratefully; but on a couple of occasions the awards led to a furore.

In November 1824, the *Admiral Berkeley*, a transport bound for South Africa, was wrecked in a violent gale off Portsmouth. Attempts to get her crew and passengers ashore via her lowered jib boom were unsuccessful, and for several hours the luckless vessel was driven along the beach and pounded by heavy seas, with her ship's company despairing of their lives. Eventually, however, her masts were cut away, hawsers were passed between the ship and the beach, and passengers and crew were floated ashore on rafts. Miraculously all 195, including many women and children, were saved.

This was clearly a major rescue operation, but it was far from clear who contributed most to it. Was it Captain Peake, commander of the *Berkeley*, who 'was for six hours wholly exposed on the beach to the violence of the storm, drenched by the sea ... and who deserved the best thanks of all concerned'? Or was it Lieutenant Grandy of the coastguards, who, 'at the risk of his own life, crossed from Portsmouth to Haslar in a six-oared boat ... and afforded the greatest assistance in landing the troops, baggage etc.'? Or was it the seamen James Torrible and Thomas Godfrey, who 'rushed boldly into the surge and extricated a man from the rigging of the mast who had brought a hawser on shore'? Or could it be that the real heroes were Lieutenants Festing and Walker of the nearby HMS *Brazen*, who 'manned the whaleboat of the *Brazen* and after considerable fatigue and great risk to their lives, succeeded in crossing the harbour's mouth and getting to the *Berkeley* where [they] suggested a raft to be made, which with their united exertions was done by their own hands, after which these two officers, aided by the whaleboat's crew, succeeded in landing the troops, women etc.'?

After studying a mass of conflicting reports and recommendations, the awards committee decided to give gold medals to Peake and Grandy, silver medals to Festing

The *Admiral Berkeley* aground near Portsmouth, November 1824; all 195 of her passengers and crew were saved. One of the first services for which the RNLI awarded Gold Medals.

and Walker, and two guineas apiece to Torrible and Godfrey. However, Festing and Walker returned their medals in a fit of pique, claiming, perhaps with some justification, that their exertions had been more meritorious than those of a man who had conducted rescue operations solely from the beach. It was clear that the Institution would need to be circumspect when it came to quantifying acts of bravery.

This was confirmed a few months later by the correspondence that followed the wreck of the *Fanny*. On the evening of 9 January 1825, the De St Croix brothers, Francis, Jean and Philip were at 'a convivial party' in St Helier when they heard the sound of gunfire. Realizing there must be a vessel in distress, they ran to the beach. It was a dark night, with low cloud, swirling mist and a heavy swell rolling in from the Atlantic. There was no lifeboat in St Helier, but the brothers found a ship's whaler hauled up on the sand. They were now joined by three other men, and the six of them launched the whaler and headed into the murk in the direction of the gunfire. After about fifteen minutes' hard pulling, they sighted the yacht *Fanny* aground on the rocks at the approaches to Elizabeth Castle. It was a dangerous place, now made doubly so by the darkness and the huge swell breaking over the reef. Threading their way through the rocks, as much by sound as by sight, they managed to close with the sinking yacht, and seven people (as many as the whaleboat could carry) leapt to safety. The survivors were rowed ashore. The brothers and their helpers then made a second sortie, this time taking off another six people and landing them on the beach. They were on their way to the wreck a third time, when the *Fanny* gave a sudden lurch and disappeared. The six people still aboard her, including a young girl, were drowned.

After careful consideration, the awards committee decided to give gold medals to the three brothers, who were described as 'gentlemen of property', while the other rescuers, who were said to be 'persons in a humble sphere of life', were given three sovereigns apiece.

It was standard practice in those days for officers and gentlemen to be given medals, while those perceived to be children of a lesser god got cash – a discrepancy that persisted well into the twentieth century. Two of the three rescuers were happy enough with their sovereigns, but the third, Philip Nicolle, wrote to the Institution to say that although he was 'highly sensible of the compliment intended him [the taking of] pecuniary reward was foreign to his feelings'. This triggered off a lengthy and at times heated correspondence, before the Institution tactfully reclassified M. Nicolle as a gentleman and sent him a silver medal.

The Gold Medal of the RNLI, the equivalent to the Serviceman's VC. Only one has been awarded in the last twenty-five years.

The second objective of the Institution was to encourage the use of Captain Manby's line-throwing mortars. These were derived from the Congreve rockets which had terrified the cavalry – and a good many of the combatants – at Waterloo. They consisted of an iron mortar mounted on one trolley and a lightweight rope coiled up on another. The mortar fired a leather-clad shot to which the rope was attached, so that (hopefully) it fell over the wrecked vessel. Once contact had been made between rescuers and rescued, heavier ropes could be passed between the ship and the shore, and there was a chance that the wrecked vessel could either be pulled clear of the rocks or its passengers and crew brought ashore by sling life-buoy.

There are two schools of thought about these mortars and the man after whom they are named, Captain George William Manby. One says that Manby served with distinction during the Napoleonic Wars, that on his retirement he invented and patented the design of his mortar, and that the Shipwreck Institution saw the potential of his invention and campaigned for his mortars to be held as standard equipment at all lifeboat and coastguard stations. The other school says that Manby was a con man, that his mortars were little more than replicas of those patented in the previous century by Sergeant Bell, and that after the war Manby bought up Bell's surplus mortars, claimed they were his own invention and sold them at a huge profit.

The anti-Manby lobby also point out that his mortars were 'heavy, clumsy and unreliable', and were soon superseded.

The truth seems to be that Manby was indeed an abrasive character – he fell out in a big way with Hillary, and the two of them were forever bickering like Tweedledum and Tweedledee – and he did make a fortune out of an 'invention' that, to say the least, was highly derivative. On the other hand his apparatus was sent to well over a hundred lifeboat and coastguard stations all over the British Isles. Barry Cox, in his *Lifeboat Gallantry*, gives details of two occasions when these mortars were put to good use off the east coast of Scotland:

2 January 1827: The weather was the most serious it had been for many years when the ship *Rose* was wrecked near Fraserburgh, Aberdeenshire. Lieutenant Bowen and a Coastguard team set up the Manby rocket apparatus. The third shot pitched alongside the mainmast, and a hawser was sent from the wreck enabling the exhausted survivors – three men, two women and a child – to be rescued. The rescuers worked for seven hours up to their waists in freezing water.

8 March 1827: The vessel *Alice* of Garthwaite was driven ashore near Arbroath at 2 a.m. in a severe gale accompanied by snow. The Manby apparatus was got down, but as the vessel was 300 yards away 10 or 12 oz charges were used which caused the line to break several times . . . [At last] a discharge laid a line over the main boom, but the crew of two men and one boy were so exhausted they could not help and the line slipped off into the water.

Eventually they were able to rescue the Master. The other man drowned and the boy died of cold.

Whatever one may think of Manby, his mortars saved many lives.

The third and undoubtedly the most important objective of the Institution was to provide lifeboats. The question at once arose – what type of lifeboat was best? A committee was formed to look into this, and one of the shortcomings of the new Institution at once became apparent. Royal dukes, bishops and archbishops are not renowned for their knowledge of seamanship; several committee members did not know the blunt end of a boat from the sharp end, and deliberations tended to be

lengthy and conclusions not always the best. For example, the type of lifeboat sent to a particular station was not always suited to local conditions, and more often than not no provision was made for its maintenance. However, the Institution did get the basics right in ruling out a number of cranky and unduly innovative designs (like Hillary's proposed steam boats) and settling for the types of lifeboat that had been tried and tested: the Lukin-style 'unimmergibles', and the boats based on the Greathead design.

The unimmergibles, built by the brothers Pellew-Plenty at Newbury, were twenty-four feet long, eight feet in the beam, and weighed thirty hundredweight (one and a half tons). They had a great deal of cork casing, a small number of buoyancy chambers, pulled eight oars double-banked, and were rigged with a single but seldom used sail. They were expensive to build – £160 each – but were described as 'good, seaworthy if rather cumbersome boats, pulling moderately well in all weathers'.

The other boats, built to an improved design by George Palmer, were usually about twenty-six feet long, six feet in the beam, and

A great rescue by a great coxswain. Henry Blogg of Cromer (inset and at the tiller) and his ageing wartime crew launch through surf to go to the aid of the Swedish SS *Fernebo*, split in half by a mine and aground off the Norfolk coast, January 1917.

weighed no more than fifteen hundredweight (three-quarters of a ton). They had less cork than the unimmergibles but more buoyancy chambers, pulled five or six oars single-banked, and had no sail. Their plus points were that they were easy to launch, and cost only about £60 to build. We are told that 'they pulled well, thanks to their shallow draft and light weight'.

These boats were the workhorses of the Shipwreck Institution for the next twenty-five years. Between 1825 and 1850 some forty-five of them were sent to stations as disparate as Wexford and Arklow in Ireland; Campbeltown, St Andrews and Thurso in Scotland; Stromness in the Orkneys; St Mary's in the Isles of Scilly; Douglas in the Isle of Man; Barmouth, Holyhead and Swansea in Wales; and the Lizard, Ramsgate and Holy Island in England. Records held in the archives tell us that in these twenty-five years they were launched well over two thousand times and saved 7186 lives.

These early lifeboats were basically rowing boats; if they did carry sails they were only lug or storm sails, for use in emergency. And it is the image of these oar-pulled boats cresting the waves that for many older people still evokes most powerfully the ethos of the RNLI. Tim Thompson's painting of Henry Blogg and his crew launching through heavy surf to go to the aid of the *Fernebo* says it all. Here are the survivors lining the deck of the doomed vessel, the lifeboatmen heaving desperately at their oars, the huge wave about to engulf the lifeboat, and the coxswain's outflung, sea-ward-pointing arm. This is the stuff of legend.

However, oar-pulled boats had one great disadvantage. Because there is obviously a limit to the distance a crew can row, especially in the high winds and heavy seas often associated with shipwrecks, they had a very restricted range. They therefore needed to be launched as close as possible to the scene of the wreck. This meant that a lifeboat often had to be hauled for several miles along the coast before it entered the water. A few lifeboat stations did have slipways, enabling their boats to be launched straight from boathouse to sea; but for most of the nineteenth century the majority of launches were from the beach, with the lifeboat being hauled along the shore on its carriage and not floated until it was near the wreck. As lifeboats became heavier so, by necessity, did the carriages on which they were transported, until by the 1870s the average oak-built carriage weighed a good three tons. Men and women did not have the strength to haul such a deadweight along the shore, maybe for several miles through soft sand, so horses were called into service.

The role of these willing and patient animals in the work of the RNLI has never been given the recognition it deserves. From the middle of the nineteenth century onwards, horse-owners were required by law to make their animals available if they were needed to help with launching a lifeboat. However, the law was not often called into play. Most farmers were happy for their horses to be used, partly out of human-ity, and partly because they were paid for the loan of their animals and given gener-ous compensation if they were injured or killed. In areas where wrecks were frequent, the local horses soon got to know what was expected of them. When they heard the maroons, they would go and wait by the gates to their fields; and there are several instances of horses that heard the maroons making their way unattended to the boathouse. Without the help of these seldom appreciated animals, many lifeboats could never have been launched, and hundreds, possibly thousands, of lives would not have been saved.

A typical rescue involving horses and the beach launching of a Greathead unim-mergible took place near Bridlington in 1828. On Thursday 10 January the north-east coast of England was hit by a storm of terrifying violence. The wind was fifty knots, gusting to seventy; great waves pounded the shore, and for hour after hour snow poured endlessly out of a slate-grey sky. There was so much snow that when the tide fell, it lay on the uncovered sand two feet deep. At about half past three in the afternoon, the clouds lifted for a moment to reveal a schooner in obvious difficulty off Bridlington, to the north of the Humber. We are told that 'the whole town of

Bridlington Quay was in alarm . . . with people crowding down to the beach'. For shipwrecks in those days were a spectator sport, often watched by thousands with the avidity of those who, a couple of millennia earlier, had crowded into the Colosseum to watch the 'games'. The ship was seen for only a few minutes, then the weather closed in; and when, in the twilight, the clouds again lifted, the schooner was observed to have gone ashore about three miles south of Bridlington. Pounded by huge seas, she looked as though she was breaking up.

The ship was the 120-ton *Fox*, on passage from the Baltic to Yarmouth with a cargo of linseed. As she grounded, her three young apprentices, against the advice of her master, lowered and tried to scramble into their ship's boat. The boat was almost at once swamped by huge waves and, together with the apprentices, 'sank to rise no more'. It seemed to the rest of *Fox*'s crew that they were likely to suffer the same fate. But help was at hand.

Back in Bridlington it was getting dark. The roads were knee-deep in snow and parts of the beach, scoured by huge waves, were impassable. However, the lifeboat coxswain and landlord of the Tiger Inn, John Usher, was determined to attempt a rescue. He got together a crew of fourteen experienced oarsmen and six horses, and set out to try to haul the lifeboat as close as possible to the wreck. It was a nightmare journey, made possible only by the exertions of about half the population of Bridlington, who with lanterns, spades, ropes and muscle power, half-carried, half-dragged the lifeboat to within a quarter of a mile of the wreck. The launch and rescue were almost an anticlimax. With the aid of the horses, the lifeboat was fairly catapulted into the water. We are told that 'she rose beautifully above every sea, and in twenty minutes returned in safety with the master, mate and one seaman . . . who were conveyed to the nearest farmhouse, where every care was taken of them that humanity could suggest'.

It was the local Lloyd's agent, William Bramble, who reported the loss of the *Fox*.

In those days Lloyd's had a virtual monopoly in insuring ships and ships' cargoes, and their ubiquitous agents often recorded details of wrecks. Bramble ends his report, 'as we have no funds at present, we beg the parent Institution will take [this] into consideration, and will allow us something for the encouragement of the men who volunteered their services to save the crew' – an entry which spotlights the threat ever hanging like the sword of Damocles over the newborn RNLI.

They were always short of money.

By and large, the Institution did not do a great deal wrong in its early years as regards distributing medals, providing line-throwing mortars, or building lifeboats. But it was a different story when it came to fundraising.

In 1824 the income of the Shipwreck Institution was £9706 6s. 6d. By 1826 its income had dropped to £2392 7s. 5d. By 1849 it had dropped to £354 17s. 6d. Early historians of the RNLI attributed this decline to 'the general unrest prevailing in the country during a period of riots'. This is not a view that many people would subscribe to today. More likely reasons are a lack of dynamic leadership, and too great a dependence on funds from elite sources.

Animals to the Rescue

Lifeboat crews often rescue animals. Not so often animals help to rescue people. Horses used to play an important role in the work of the Institution, dragging lifeboats along clifftops or beaches to their launching sites. For the launch itself they were usually divided into two teams, one on either side of the carriage on which the lifeboat was transported; they were then driven into the sea, until they had manoeuvred the carriage into deep enough water for the lifeboat to float. In heavy seas this was dangerous work: quite a few horses were injured; some were drowned. There are also many instances of horses being ridden into the sea and swimming to the aid of the shipwrecked. Most famously, a sixty-five-year-old farmer, Wolraad Woltemade, and his horse swam out no fewer than eight times to the wreck of the *De Jonge Thomas*. On each of the first seven occasions the farmer and his horse brought two of the crew to safety. Sadly, on their eighth attempt, so many of the crew tried to climb on to the horse's back that both it and its rider were drowned.

Dogs have never been used officially by the Institution. However, organizations such as Casualty Search Dogs train animals which occasionally work with inshore lifeboat crews. Amazing claims have been made for these dogs – 'They can smell humans two miles away ... and can trace 200 different scents'. However, only one breed, the Newfoundland, has carried out rescue work of note. Some say that Newfoundlands are descended from the 'big black bear dogs', taken to the New World by the Vikings. Their webbed feet and double coat of oil-impregnated fur make them excellent swimmers, and for many years they have been used as working dogs by the fishermen of Newfoundland and St Pierre et Miquelon. There are many well-documented accounts of their rescue work. In 1828 the passenger ship *Despatch* was driven ashore by storm on the south coast of Newfoundland. The wreck was spotted by the Harvey family, who tried to row to the rescue but could make no headway in the heavy seas. We are told that 'their faithful dog "Watch" leapt overboard and managed to swim to the wreck. A rope was attached to the dog, which then swam

WORTHING LIFEBOATS RETURN FROM RESCUE WORK.

OPPOSITE AND ABOVE When lifeboats became too heavy to be manhandled, horses were used to help with beach-launching. RIGHT Carrier pigeons, tagged with a message, were sometimes 'flown off' from vessels, lighthouses and aircraft.

back to its master. A bosun's chair was rigged up, and all 163 passengers and crew were saved.' In 1919 another dog, 'Tang', carried out a similar rescue in North Newfoundland, saving 119 people.

Carrier pigeons were taken to Sable Island (off Nova Scotia) in the 1890s and used to carry messages between the island, ships in distress and lighthouses. This experiment ended when it was found that although many pigeons were released, few got to their destinations. They were being mobbed and killed by the local seagulls! In the First World War homing pigeons were often carried in the Royal Navy's airships, seaplanes and flying boats. In 1917 a Curtiss H12 flying boat landed in the North Sea to rescue the crew of a ditched aircraft, but found it was unable to take off again. Its four pigeons were released with the message, 'Have landed to pick up crew about 50 E by N of Yarmouth. Sea too rough to take off. Please send for us as soon as possible.' Only one pigeon reached land, where it was found dead from exhaustion. However, its message got through, and the crew of both aircraft were rescued. Royal Naval Air Service officers recovered the body of the pigeon and had it stuffed and mounted on a silver plinth with the inscription:

His Majesty's Pigeon Number NURP/17/F/16113
A Very Gallant Gentleman.

The man who might perhaps have been expected to take control of the emergent RNLI was William Hillary. However, he lived in the Isle of Man and was no good with money. The man elected as chairman, Thomas Wilson, was universally liked and respected. However, like nearly all his colleagues, Wilson had a host of other commitments and was never able to devote himself full-time to the affairs of the Institution. He was fifty-six when he was elected chairman, and remained in office until the day he died at the age of eighty-four. For all his many admirable qualities, one cannot help feeling that the Institution would have benefited from new blood, and that Wilson was neither the first chairman nor the last to cling too long to office because nobody was keen to take over his job.

Another stumbling block to the Institution was that it drew support from only a small and exclusive section of the public. It had come into being as the protégé of aristocratic patrons, most of whom had been happy to make a one-off donation but were unwilling to pledge continuous financial aid. The committee did their best to attract new patrons: the Duke of Wellington was invited to become president, but declined; Lord John Russell was asked to provide help from the government, but declined; the Lords of the Admiralty were repeatedly asked for help, and repeatedly declined. One wonders why the Institution did not seek help from the general public. For the wave of enthusiasm that greeted Grace Darling's exploits is evidence that there was considerable interest in the work of saving life at sea. However, the opportunity was missed, and the Shipwreck Institution soon found itself in ever increasing difficulties, so short of funds that it could neither build new lifeboats nor maintain those it already had.

Richard Lewis (for many years secretary of the Institution) tells us in his *History of the Life-boat and its Work* (published in 1874) that between 1841 and 1850 no appeal for money was made to the public, and by 1849 the lifeboat work was in a very depressed state, the public having apparently lost all interest in it:

Some of the Local Life-boat Associations had ceased to exist, and many of the Life-boats had been allowed to fall into decay; and in places where shipwrecks were rare, the boats had remained many months out of the water; so that when wrecks did occur the boatmen had no confidence in them, and preferred going off in their own craft to a wreck ... Funds, too, were often wanting to pay these brave men for their services, and the whole system was in such a low state that among all the Life-boats in the United Kingdom there were perhaps not a dozen really efficient boats. The National Shipwreck Institution, with diminished funds, had been exciting less interest from year to year, while the great increase of our commerce was constantly occasioning an increased number of casualties at sea ... The Committee were not insensible to [their] deficiencies in the means of saving life, but the support they received was not sufficient to enable them to overcome these difficulties.

It was at this low point in the Institution's fortunes that its founder, William Hillary, died.

His fortunes were also at a low ebb. In poor health, bereaved and bankrupt, he died in 1847, in the words of his biographer, 'enfeebled by the exertions he had made on behalf of his fellow men'. It is said that his creditors had so little regard for him that to settle his debts they tried to seize and sell his body as it was about to be buried. It was not until 1924 that his achievements were recognized by a valedictory plaque in St George's Churchyard in Douglas, inscribed:

To the Honoured Memory of

Lieutenant-Colonel Sir William Hillary,

Baronet, of Yorkshire, Essex and the Isle of Man.

Lieutenant Turcopolier of the Order of the Knights of St. John of Jerusalem.

Born 1771. Died 1847.

Soldier. Author. Philanthropist.

He founded in the year 1824 the Royal National Lifeboat Institution

and in 1832 built the Tower of Refuge in Douglas Bay.

Fearless himself in the work of rescue from shipwreck he helped to save 305 lives

and was three times awarded the Gold Medal of the Institution for great gallantry.

'What his wisdom planned and power enforced

More potent still his great example showed.'

THOMSON

It must have saddened Hillary as he lay waiting for death in 'a small but gentlemanly house' on Falcon Cliff that the Institution he had founded amid such euphoria only twenty-three years earlier should now seem, like himself, to be in terminal decline. No one doubted that lifeboats were needed. Yet all over the British Isles, with no funds available to keep them seaworthy or reward their crews, the unimmergibles and self-rightings were falling into decay. A couple of years after Hillary's death, the Institution's records contain a sad little entry: 'It is grievous to be obliged to record that barely a vestige of them (the lifeboats) exists, and what may remain is quite unfit for use'.

It seemed that nothing short of a miracle would enable the ailing charity to survive.

The age of sail

ine-tenths cloud, a fifty-knot wind, and huge seas pounding the shallow approaches to the Thames estuary. Soon after dark, star-shells bursting over the Tongue lightship tell of a vessel in distress. In such terrible conditions it seems impossible even to attempt a rescue, but a little before nine p.m. a steam tug from Ramsgate heads out to sea with the lifeboat *Northumberland* in tow.

It takes them three hours to reach the lightship. When they get there, they are told that a vessel has gone aground on the nearby Shingles. They search for more than an hour, but can find no trace of her. They are about to give up when they sight the flicker of burning tar-barrels – another sign that a vessel is in trouble. Closing with the lights, they find a ship, swept by heavy seas, aground not on the Shingles but on another part of the shallows known as the Girdler Bank. The tug tows *Northumberland* upwind of the casualty, slips her cable, and the lifeboat bears down under storm sails on the wrecked vessel.

Beach-launching the Brighton lifeboat, 1875.

The wind by now has increased to a hurricane from the west-north-west. It is pitch dark and raining heavily. The seas are mountainous and made doubly dangerous by the shallow water. Getting alongside is a tricky business. Two of the lifeboat's crew half-leap, half-scramble aboard the wreck, and find themselves faced with about as difficult a rescue operation as it would be possible to imagine.

The casualty is the *Fusilier* of the Black Ball Line, an emigrant ship bound for Melbourne. More than half her hundred-odd passengers are women, some pregnant, some breast-feeding and some with young children. Many of them feel that to leave the solid deck of the *Fusilier* for the tiny, corkscrewing, wave-swept lifeboat is jumping from frying pan to fire; but the order is given to abandon ship. Two seamen are lashed in bowlines and slung out from the side of the emigrant vessel. The passengers, women and children first, are then passed one by one to the seamen, who cling on to them until they think it safe to drop them into the lifeboat, where crewmen cushion their fall and haul aboard those whose mistimed drops have ended in the sea. It is a hazardous transfer, with the lifeboat now poised on the crest of a wave above the *Fusilier*'s deck-rail and now twenty feet lower beneath her keel, now close alongside and now tossed clear by the surge of the sea. Some mothers, unable to cling to their children during the drop, are separated from them; but their babies are wrapped in blankets and thrown down to the waiting lifeboatmen. When some twenty-five emigrants have been dropped – miraculously with no casualties – into the lifeboat, it casts off and heads for the steam tug, which has now manoeuvred into a position where the *Northumberland* can run to it downwind. The survivors are transferred to the tug, and the lifeboat goes back for more.

Three times *Northumberland* returns to the emigrant ship, on each occasion taking off as many passengers as she can carry and transferring them to the tug. She offers to take off the crew as well, but with daylight in the offing and the storm if anything decreasing, they decide to stay on board in the hope of salvage. *Northumberland* agrees to stand by, while the tug, jam-packed with over a hundred traumatized but thankful emigrants, heads for Ramsgate.

The lifeboat crew have now been at sea for nearly twelve hours. They are wet, cold and exhausted; but their work is not yet finished. After they have been standing by the *Fusilier* for about an hour and a half, much to their surprise they see the steam tug returning, making urgent signals. She tells them that on her way back to Ramsgate she has sighted another wreck, this time on the Shingles – almost certainly the distressed vessel reported the previous evening by the lightship. The tug signals that this second casualty is on her beam ends and swept by huge seas, with survivors clinging to the rigging.

Again the tug tows *Northumberland* into a position upwind of the wrecked vessel, the *Demerara* of Greenock, and again the lifeboat bears down on her under sail. But the *Demerara* is in a difficult place, surrounded by shoal-water, scoured by a fast-ebbing tide, and with the waves breaking clean over her. The copper sheathing has been ripped from her keel; the cargo has been washed out of her shattered hold; she is dismasted, and only a few feet of her mainmast remain above water, with her crew clinging desperately to what is left of the shrouds. The lifeboat coxswain, Isaac Jarman, realizes their only hope is to plough straight in through the wreckage, and make fast to a half-submerged windlass at the foot of the mast. It is a risk. *Northumberland* is all but stove in, and is saved only by her cork belting; but at last she comes to rest beneath the mast. One by one the crew of eighteen, including an eleven-year-old boy, drop thankfully to safety. They are in the last stages of exhaustion and hypothermia, having been clinging to the wave-swept mast for more than fifteen hours.

Jarman ends his report: 'We returned to harbour, where we arrived at 12.15 after an absence of about sixteen hours, the chief part of the time being drenched by the sea. We landed in all about 120 souls'.

The rescues from the *Fusilier* and the *Demerara* are typical of the work carried out in the second half of the nineteenth century by the Institution's new Beeching class lifeboats. Beechings and similar sailing lifeboats were soon working from more than a hundred stations all round the British Isles. How, one wonders, did the ailing charity of the 1840s, with its dozen or so rowing boats, become metamorphosed into the burgeoning organization of the 1860s with its hundred-plus sailing boats?

It was a case of new brooms making a clean sweep. The year 1849 had marked the lowest point in the Institution's fortunes. Its founder had just died in poverty. Its chairman and secretary were both approaching their eightieth birthdays. And at the end of the year it suffered a tragic loss. The South Shields lifeboat had gone to the aid of a vessel aground on Herd Sands. They were lying alongside her when 'a heavy sea turned the lifeboat up on end, throwing the crew into the stern sheets. Before she could recover, a second sea threw her completely over, and she drifted on shore bottom up.' Twenty out of her crew of twenty-four were drowned.

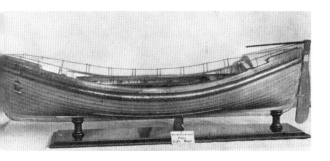

A Beeching lifeboat. James Beeching's design was characterised by high end-boxes, fore and aft; these helped his boats, like Wouldhave's, to self-right.

Such disasters have occurred at fairly regular intervals during the RNLI's history. They trigger off considerable interest among the public, and considerable heart-searching by the Institution. This is what happened in 1849. And in the spotlight of public sympathy and private misgivings, the Shipwreck Institution was obliged to account for its stewardship, and to admit the need for change.

The middle of the nineteenth century was a propitious time for change. When the Institution was founded in 1824 England was still in the aftermath of the Napoleonic Wars. Increasing trade was certainly beginning to generate wealth, but the country was nothing like as stable or as prosperous as it was twenty-five years later, in mid-century. The Great Exhibition took place in 1851, when 'all the world came to admire England's wealth, progress and enlightenment'. There was a feeling of confidence in the country – a feeling that with science at last being harnessed to meet human needs all things were possible. So even when the Shipwreck Institution was virtually bankrupt, a report by one of its committees could claim, 'there need be no misgiving for want of funds. No work of real benevolence in this country was ever allowed to languish for lack of means.' Events were to prove this optimism justified, although it took a lot of hard work by a handful of dedicated men before the moribund charity was resuscitated.

Historians of the RNLI tell us that in 1850 'a noble band of men formed themselves into a Committee to make renewed efforts on behalf of the shipwrecked sailor'. The best-known of this committee was probably 'the Good Sailor Duke', Algernon of Northumberland; but the most influential was Richard Lewis. In great undertakings there is often an unsung hero. In building the Panama Canal such a hero was John

Stevens, the little-known engineer who organized the railway system that carried away some 388,000,000 tons of soil. In rejuvenating the RNLI the unsung hero was Richard Lewis, the administrator whose work behind the scenes laid the foundations of the organization we are so proud of today.

Early in 1850, Lewis was appointed Secretary 'at a salary of £120, to be increased annually ten pounds till it shall amount to £150, provided he continues to give satisfaction'. This he obviously did. For the next thirty-three years he remained in office, using his considerable skill as a barrister to plead the Institution's need for financial support, filling thousands of pages with minutes of its committee meetings, travelling thousands of miles all over the British Isles to inspect and advise on its lifeboats, and giving hundreds of lectures to further its work. The graph below testifies to the astuteness of his stewardship. When he died, the Institution took the unprecedented step of awarding pensions to his widow and children, 'having regard to his very exceptional services'.

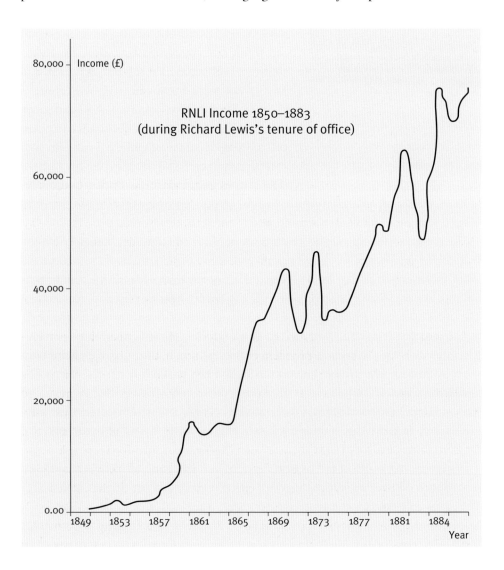

RNLI Income 1850–1883
(during Richard Lewis's tenure of office)

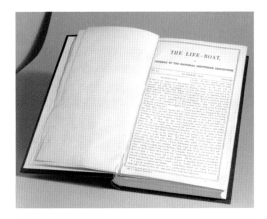

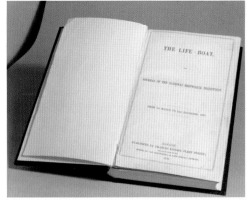

Facsimile of the first bound copy of *The Life Boat*. For 150 years this journal has provided a record of acts of courage and fine seamanship.

It would, however, be mischievous to suggest that Lewis resuscitated the Institution by his own unaided efforts. His colleagues on the RNLI committees of the 1850s, '60s and '70s were a great deal more hard working and a great deal more knowledgeable than their predecessors. Among the regular attenders were Algernon, Fourth Duke of Northumberland, Sir Edward Perrott, Thomas Chapman the (chairman of Lloyds), Thomas Baring, MP, Captain (later Rear-Admiral) John Washington, RN, Captain George Davies, RN, Captain J. R. Ward, RN, and Captain David Robertson, RN. Part-time dukes and archbishops were being replaced by full-time naval officers, men who brought to the Institution that practical knowledge of seamanship previously lacking. And because several members of the new committee worked exclusively for the Institution and were paid salaries, not only was more work done, but there was more accountability. In a word, the new men were more professional; and each year, in their first decade in office, they initiated changes that helped the ailing charity first to survive and then to prosper.

In 1850, they persuaded the Prince Consort to become a vice-patron and Queen Victoria to become an annual subscriber, thus creating links between the Institution and the royal family that continue to this day. More importantly, they tackled the problem of how to keep their lifeboats serviceable. It was agreed that each boat should have a coxswain who was to be paid a fixed salary. It was also agreed that full-time officers of the Institution should make regular inspections of lifeboats to ensure they were kept seaworthy and ready to be launched.

The year 1851 saw the first awards for the Duke of Northumberland's competition. Shortly before he became president of the Institution, the Duke 'offered the sum of one hundred guineas for the best model of a Life-boat . . . sent to the Surveyor's Department of the Admiralty'. This competition aroused great public interest, and one of the main tasks of the new committee was to decide not only which were the best overall designs, but which were best suited to the needs of individual stations. Towards the end of the year the Institution published its first official wreck chart, giving details of every vessel wrecked during the previous twelve months on the coast of the British Isles. This helped to keep the need for lifeboats in the public eye.

The Life-Boat, the official journal of the Institution, was first published in 1852, with the aim of 'laying before the public all the information respecting the construction and establishment of Life-Boats, the number of Shipwrecks, the exertions made

to save Life and Property, and the prizes and medals awarded to those who have been most active in that noble service'. It was priced at only 1½d, 'so as to place it within reach of every boatman around our shores', and for some 150 years it has provided the public with a record of acts of courage and fine seamanship that have seldom been equalled and never surpassed.

In 1853 the journal records that 'the Duke of Northumberland has committed the charge of his Life-Boats to the Institution'. In its early years the Shipwreck Institution had often found that local communities were reluctant to hand over control of their lifeboats. This was because local people felt, with some justification, that they were better judges of the sort of rescue services their area needed than landlubbers in London. The Northumberland coast had always had a particularly proud record of local, privately run rescue services, predating Lukin's coble; and the fact that the Duke of Northumberland now had sufficient confidence in the Institution to give them control of his lifeboats encouraged other organizations to do the same. Slowly the Institution began to draw under its mantle the dozens of lifeboats and lifeboat stations that for years had been operating independently.

In 1854, this assimilation was given momentum by a takeover. For some years the Institution had operated in tandem with a sister charity, the Shipwrecked Fishermen and Mariners' Benevolent Society. There had been duplication of duties

The Liverpool-class *Samuel Lewis*, on service at Skegness, 1906–1932. She launched twenty-one times and saved twenty-one people.

The 'sailing and pulling' lifeboat *William Arthur Millward* on service at Dunbar, 1901–1931. She launched thirty times and saved thirty-four people.

and confusion as to exactly what each organization did. It was now agreed that the Institution should concentrate on bringing people safely ashore, and that the Benevolent Society should concentrate on caring for them after they had been landed. As part of the deal, the Benevolent Society agreed to hand over its nine lifeboats and boathouses, and the Institution agreed to drop the word 'Shipwreck' from its title, becoming known from then on simply as the Royal National Lifeboat Institution. Later that year the Institution felt obliged to take what many people thought was a step in the wrong direction. It accepted an annual subsidy from the government – £2000 from the Mercantile Marine Fund, to be administered by the Board of Trade. This money was needed to give stability to the Institution's pro-gramme of increasing and efficiently maintaining its fleet. The government, need-less to say, expected a quid pro quo, and was soon trying to exert an ever increasing degree of control. In particular, it insisted that all local RNLI committees should include at least one representative from the Board of Trade. This frequently led to friction. So as soon as the Institution felt it could do without the subsidy, which was in 1869, it thankfully terminated it and reverted to its original charitable status, which it has maintained ever since.

The year 1856 saw the building of ten new lifeboats, including a veritable giant of a boat for the east coast. Big, heavy rescue boats had always been favoured by the people of East Anglia, and the building of a huge forty-footer to replace the old, privately owned boat at Southwold is evidence that the Institution was, at last, tailoring its lifeboats to satisfy local needs. The same year saw the first major bequest to the RNLI. In his will, Captain Hamilton Fitzgerald, RN, left the Institution £10,000 (the equivalent in today's money of nearly £8,000,000). It would be difficult to overstate the importance of this bequest, which more than doubled the Institution's annual income at a time when cash was badly needed. From then on a steadily increasing number of people remembered the RNLI in their wills, and funds derived from legacies now amount to over fifty per cent of the Institution's annual income.

In 1858 the Institution made another successful takeover, gaining control of the privately run lifeboats of the Norfolk Association. To quote the journal:

> This was a 'red letter year', because the Norfolk Association had the management of all the boats on the Norfolk coast, and it is well known that more lifeboat work is done there than in any other part of the coast of Great Britain, and the experience of the men who worked these boats [would be] invaluable. The boats handed over were at Cromer, Mundesley, Bacton, Palling, Winterton, Caister and Yarmouth.

Admiral Robert Fitzroy (1805–1865) recognised the importance of accurate weather forecasting. He recommended the introduction of barometers in all RNLI stations.

In 1860 Barometers were introduced in selected lifeboat stations. This came about largely through the efforts of Admiral Fitzroy (formerly Darwin's commanding officer on the *Beagle*), who was one of the first people to appreciate that instruments such as the barometer could help accurate weather forecasting, and that accurate weather forecasting could reduce the risk of shipwreck. Fitzroy wrote a number of technical papers on this subject; and in 1859 his point was tragically proven when the *Royal Charter* was wrecked off Anglesey with the loss of some 450 lives, largely because her captain had no warning of the hurricane that for the previous twenty-four hours had been devastating southern England. It was hoped that the more general use of barometers and the warning of storms by the Meteorological Office would make people realize that getting the weather right could be a matter of life or death.

These measures put the RNLI on the road to recovery. However, increased efficiency at headquarters would not by itself have been enough to sustain this recovery. When it came to the crunch, the Institution lived or died by the quality of its lifeboats and the dedication of its crews; and it is worth making the point that the crews would not give of their best unless they were happy with their boats. It was therefore of some importance that the committee got it right when they met to decide what sort of lifeboats to build to replace their ageing rowing boats.

They decided to go for sail, oar-pulled boats being thought to have too short an operating range and steam boats to be too innovative. When it came to deciding what type of sailing boat, the situation in 1851 was in some ways similar to that in 1789: there was a reward on offer for the best design of a lifeboat; many designs were submitted; and the Institution combined the best points of the various entries into a 'boat with all the virtues'.

The Duke of Northumberland's competition had attracted 280 entries. One or two were more esoteric than practical, including 'a boat of whimsical construction, open to the sea at the bottom,' and one built of dried rushes and gutta-percha (Malaysian latex); but the majority were serious contenders. Fifty were put on display at the Great Exhibition, where they attracted much interest and helped to publicize the work of saving life at sea.

One big difference between the 1789 and 1851 awards was that in the eighteenth century the committee had put all their eggs in one basket. They had decided the best boat was the *Original*, had commissioned more boats built to the same design, and had sent them to stations all over the British Isles irrespective of whether or not they measured up to local requirements. In the nineteenth century the RNLI took a more flexible approach. They decided the best design was that submitted by James Beeching. However, they saw Beeching's boat not as the last word in lifeboat design but rather as the starting point from which even more could be achieved. They commissioned the building of improved versions, incorporating innovative features from other entries. And, perhaps even more importantly, they commissioned the building of a number of specialist lifeboats for use on those parts of the coast that had special requirements. Throughout the second half of the century many different types of lifeboat operated from different parts of the country. Perhaps the most successful were the Beechings, the Peakes, the Richardson tubulars, the Norfolk and Suffolks, and in later years the Watsons.

James Beeching was an accomplished shipwright. When he lived in Yarmouth he designed and built fishing boats. When he moved to Flushing he designed and built smuggling cutters. His entry for the Northumberland award was considered the best design submitted, the adjudicating committee giving it eighty-four marks out of a possible 100. His boat was thirty-six feet long, nine feet six inches in the beam, and weighed almost three and a half tons. It pulled twelve oars double-banked, and was rigged with fore sail, lug and mizzen. The boat was self-righting, a characteristic made possible by a heavy iron keel, huge air cases fore and aft, two and a half tons of water ballast, and a plethora of relieving tubes which ensured the rapid discharge of whatever water was shipped. Additional plus points were that it was robust, seaworthy and could carry some fifty people. Minus points of the Beeching design were that it was heavy (which made it difficult for the boat to be carried overland and beach-launched), the water ballast system was unpredictable, and the huge fore and aft air cases made it impossible for survivors to be hauled aboard over the bow or stern. Beeching boats remained in service until the turn of the century. A good example of their work is the rescue of the passengers of the *Fusilier* and the crew of the *Demerara*.

James Peake was a member of the Northumberland award adjudicating committee; he was also a master shipwright at the Royal Dockyard, Woolwich. In the summer of 1851 he was invited to design a boat that combined the best features of those submitted for the competition. What he came up with was basically a lightweight Beeching. Peake's lifeboat was thirty feet long, eight feet six inches in the beam, and weighed thirty-eight hundredweight (nearly two tons). It pulled ten oars double-banked, and was rigged with fore and mizzen lug sails. It, too, was self-righting; in its trials off Brighton the prototype Peake righted within five seconds of being capsized, and emptied itself within fifty-five seconds of being swamped. This was achieved by a heavy keel, extensive use of cork ballast (which proved more reliable than Beeching's water ballast), and eight draining tubes and six scuppers. The plus points of Peake's design were that it was comparatively cheap to build and comparatively light; not only was it a smaller boat than a Beeching, it was built not of oak but of lightweight copper-fastened elm. Richard Lewis claimed that the Peake was 'pronounced by our hardy boatmen and fishermen who go afloat in her as the best and safest boat ever launched from our shores'. This is substantiated by the fact that Peake lifeboats were the workhorses of the RNLI for the next thirty or so years. Two rescues, one off Carnsore and one off Penzance, provide evidence of their versatility.

Peake lifeboats –
'the best and
safest ever
launched from
our shores' –
were the mainstay
of the RNLI fleet
in the 1850s,
1860s and 1870s.

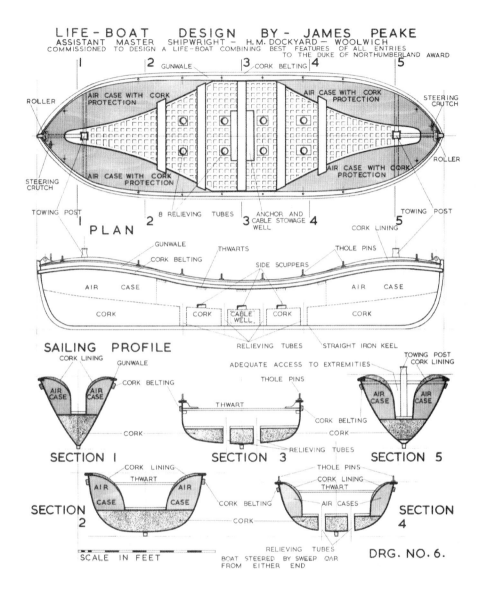

LIFE - BOAT   DESIGN   BY - JAMES   PEAKE
ASSISTANT   MASTER   SHIPWRIGHT –   H. M. DOCKYARD –   WOOLWICH
COMMISSIONED   TO   DESIGN   A   LIFE-BOAT   COMBINING   BEST   FEATURES   OF   ALL   ENTRIES
TO   THE   DUKE   OF   NORTHUMBERLAND   AWARD

PLAN

SAILING   PROFILE

SECTION 1   SECTION 3   SECTION 5

SECTION 2   SECTION 4

SCALE   IN   FEET   BOAT   STEERED   BY   SWEEP   OAR   FROM   EITHER   END   DRG. NO. 6.

The little fishing village of Carnsore, on the south-eastern tip of County Wexford, owes its lifeboat to an unknown lady benefactor who was saved from a sinking yacht, and in gratitude left the RNLI £300 to station a lifeboat near the scene of her rescue. On 10 February 1861 this lifeboat went to the aid of the barque *Guyana* which had been driven ashore on the Carrig Rocks, some seven miles from Carnsore. Conditions were too bad for the boat to be launched from the fishing village itself; it had to be dragged along the top of the cliffs to the scene of the wreck. *The Life-Boat* journal describes the rescue:

Intelligence of the wreck having been conveyed to the life-boat station, the crew of the life-boat were
called up about three o'clock in the morning, and the boat immediately started on her mission of mercy.
Owing, however, to the dreadful state of the roads from heavy rains, and the circuitous route of many

miles that the boat had to travel, it was nearly nine o'clock before she reached the scene of the disaster, notwithstanding that no less than seven horses were employed to draw her. The life-boat had then to be taken off her carriage, and lowered down a steep cliff eighty feet in height. This was successfully accomplished, and the boat was then launched through a high surf, and proceeded to the wreck. On arriving near the vessel, however, the force of the wind, tide and sea was so great it was found impossible to reach her; the boat was therefore anchored for a while to rest the crew. Another attempt was then made, and the whole crew of the *Guyana*, numbering nineteen, were got safely into her, and conveyed to the shore, which was reached after more than five hours' severe exposure and exertion.

A few years later a rescue in Cornwall provided an even sterner test for a Peake lifeboat. On 6 December 1868, the barque *North Britain*, inward bound from Quebec with a cargo of timber, became embayed in Mount's Bay. There was a strong wind, a swirling mist and a heavy sea. It was Sunday, and in Penzance the church bells were ringing when a horse, white with lather, came galloping into the town centre, its rider shouting that a ship was in trouble. The Penzance lifeboat, the *Richard Lewis*, was launched, and hundreds – some reports say thousands – of people crowded the shoreline to watch.

The *North Britain* had gone aground about half a mile offshore, and was in danger of breaking up. Two local boats had tried to get to her but had failed, and her master, despairing of rescue, gave the order to lower one of his ship's boats. It was a mistake. The moment it hit the water, the boat was stove in, swamped and sunk. The master then, with great difficulty, managed to lower his bigger and heavier jolly boat; he and nine of the crew piled into her and, dwarfed by huge seas, made for the shore. An eye-witness describes what happened next: 'She was nobly manned and struggled hard, but in vain. Behind her is an immense breaker. "God save her" are the cries. But in less time than it takes to write, the wave whirls her round, turns her keel up, and ten precious human beings are struggling in the sea three hundred yards from the shore.' Some try to cling to the overturned boat, but huge waves loosen their grip and they are swept away. Some try to cling to oars, but the oars are sucked down by the undertow and splintered to matchwood. Some strike out for the shore. The people on the beach risk their lives to help them. They form a human chain, and, bracing themselves against breaking waves and undertow, wade out to sea. They manage to pull four barely conscious seamen to safety. The other six are drowned.

The onlookers' attention now reverts to the *North Britain*, the men still aboard her, and the lifeboat *Richard Lewis* which is at last approaching her. But this is to be no easy rescue. As the *Richard Lewis* tries to come alongside, she is flung into the air by an enormous wave and overturned. Some of her crew are tossed into the sea, others are trapped beneath the capsized lifeboat. Within seconds the *Richard Lewis* has self-righted; but her coxswain, with a huge gash from ear to temple, is unconscious, one of her crew is missing and three others badly injured. The lifeboat limps back to the shore, the injured are landed, and volunteers are called for to make another rescue effort. One of the original crew, William Higgans, says that he'll try again, and his

The Penzance lifeboat *Richard Lewis* attempting to help the barque *North Britain*, wrecked in Mount's Bay, December 1868. This service resulted in the loss of one lifeboat and seven lifeboatmen, and the award of five silver medals – including one to the French vice-consul in Penzance, a crew member of the *Richard Lewis*.

courage triggers off a surge of would-be rescuers. Another crew is formed, led this time by William Blackmore of the Penzance coastguards, and with the French vice-consul at one of the oars. They launch through heavy surf, fight their way to the *North Britain*, and manage to rescue the last of her crew only minutes before the barque breaks up.

An eye-witness gives us a moving if archaic postscript:

The crowds have dispersed, the broken fragments of the ship are strewed along the shore, night has settled on the scene . . . Mothers and daughters of England, when the wild storm howls around your secure and cheerful homes, pray for the sailor who, through many dangers and discomforts, ministers to your luxury and happiness; and forget not to include in your prayers the noble watchers of the tempest, our lifeboat crews, whose path of duty is a path of peril, and who, to save others, will even dare to die.

Less ubiquitous than the Beechings, but equally successful, were the Richardson tubulars.

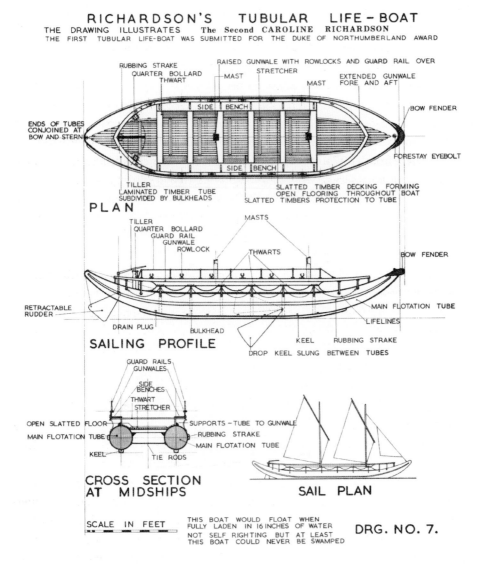

RICHARDSON'S TUBULAR LIFE-BOAT

THE DRAWING ILLUSTRATES   The Second CAROLINE RICHARDSON
THE FIRST TUBULAR LIFE-BOAT WAS SUBMITTED FOR THE DUKE OF NORTHUMBERLAND AWARD

RAISED GUNWALE WITH ROWLOCKS AND GUARD RAIL OVER

RUBBING STRAKE
QUARTER BOLLARD   STRETCHER
THWART   MAST   MAST   EXTENDED GUNWALE
FORE AND AFT

SIDE BENCH   BOW FENDER

ENDS OF TUBES
CONJOINED AT
BOW AND STERN

FORESTAY EYEBOLT

SIDE BENCH

TILLER
LAMINATED TIMBER TUBE   SLATTED TIMBER DECKING FORMING
SUBDIVIDED BY BULKHEADS   OPEN FLOORING THROUGHOUT BOAT
SLATTED TIMBERS PROTECTION TO TUBE

PLAN

TILLER
QUARTER BOLLARD   MASTS
GUARD RAIL
GUNWALE
ROWLOCK   THWARTS

BOW FENDER

RETRACTABLE
RUDDER   MAIN FLOTATION TUBE

LIFELINES

DRAIN PLUG   BULKHEAD   KEEL   RUBBING STRAKE

SAILING PROFILE   DROP KEEL SLUNG BETWEEN TUBES

GUARD RAILS
GUNWALES
SIDE
BENCHES
THWART
STRETCHER

OPEN SLATTED FLOOR   SUPPORTS – TUBE TO GUNWALE
MAIN FLOTATION TUBE   RUBBING STRAKE
MAIN FLOTATION TUBE
KEEL   TIE RODS

**CROSS SECTION
AT MIDSHIPS**   **SAIL PLAN**

SCALE IN FEET   THIS BOAT WOULD FLOAT WHEN
FULLY LADEN IN 16 INCHES OF WATER   **DRG. NO. 7.**
NOT SELF RIGHTING BUT AT LEAST
THIS BOAT COULD NEVER BE SWAMPED

Richardson's idiosyncratic tubular design had shortcomings; nonetheless his boats operated successfully in shallow west-coast estuaries for over fifty years and saved over a thousand lives.

Some years after the end of the Napoleonic Wars an officer of the Dragoon Guards, Henry Richardson, retired to Bala in North Wales. In 1851 he and his son submitted 'a tubular lifeboat' for the Northumberland award. The Committee did not think much of it; but if ever a design turned out to meet local needs, it was the Richardsons'. Their boat was thirty-three feet long, seven feet in the beam and weighed no more than one ton. It was called 'tubular' because its basic framework consisted of two parallel tubes of laminated wood, four feet apart at midships, but curving sharply together at stem and stern. The space between the tubes was divided into seven watertight compartments, and on top of these was a lightweight platform for the rowers. The Richardson boats had many shortcomings. They were unmanoeuvrable; they were unsafe in any sort of sea; they were not self-righting, and their crews were exposed to the elements and much of the time virtually awash. However, they had two great attributes. No matter how much water they shipped, their watertight compartments ensured they were never swamped. And they had an amazingly shallow draught – during a Lifeboat Day in Rhyl, a Richardson was floated on the children's paddling pool in no more than sixteen inches of water. These characteristics made them ideal for working in the shallow, sandbar-strewn estuaries of the Dee and the Mersey. The first Richardson, the *Morgan*, was stationed at Rhyl from 1856 until 1893, and a second tubular boat, the *Caroline Richardson II*, operated there from 1897 until, amazingly, 1939. No other class of lifeboat saw such long and continuous service. And in the eighty-three years during which they operated, the Richardsons saved thousands of lives. One coxswain alone, Hiram Linaker, in one spell of fifteen years (between 1862 and 1877) carried out thirty-seven rescues and saved ninety-six people.

Barry Cox describes a typical rescue:

19 October 1869: at 7 am the schooner *Elephant* ran aground on Taylor's Bank southwest of Formby. The New Brighton tubular lifeboat *Willie and Arthur* was towed out . . . to approach the wreck from windward. Coxswain Thomas went alongside and rescued one man; then another was seen, lashed high up in the rigging, unable to move. Although the wreck was breaking up rapidly, the Coxswain jumped on board and started to climb the rigging, when the foremast gave way and crashed over the side, drowning the man. The Coxswain narrowly escaped.

Another successful class of specialized lifeboat was the Norfolk and Suffolk.

In good weather the coast of East Anglia has a tranquil beauty, but in times of storm it is exceptionally dangerous. In little ports like Happisburgh you will find the mass graves of seamen who have been wrecked on this innocent-looking shore. Good harbours are scarce, the offshore waters are shallow and strewn far out to sea with bars of gravel and sand, and in the nineteenth century the North Sea was a busier thoroughfare than the Channel. More ships were wrecked off East Anglia than anywhere else in the British Isles. (Records show that lifeboats have been launched from Gorleston more often than from any other station, and that lifeboats from Caister have saved more lives.) The qualities needed by a boat in these exposed waters are very different from those needed in the sheltered Lancashire estuaries, and the Norfolk and Suffolks were a world apart from the Richardsons.

They were big, heavy sailing boats, at least forty feet long and eleven feet in the beam, flat-bottomed to enable them to be launched in shallow water, and with a huge spread of canvas to enable them to sail far out to sea to reach wrecks on sandbars that might be up to twenty miles offshore. Of all the boats in the Institution's rapidly expanding fleet, the Norfolk and Suffolks were probably the best sea boats: their great weight enabled them to smash through heavy seas; the water they shipped was drained away by their twenty-four relieving tubes and ten scuppers; and their twin drop-keels gave them stability when sailing. To quote Eric Fry: 'They were [basically] long-range sailing boats . . . with an extensive sail area; an exceptionally

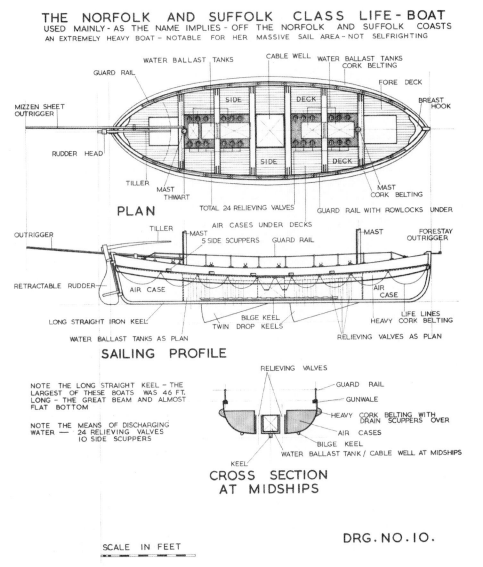

THE NORFOLK AND SUFFOLK CLASS LIFE-BOAT

USED MAINLY - AS THE NAME IMPLIES - OFF THE NORFOLK AND SUFFOLK COASTS
AN EXTREMELY HEAVY BOAT - NOTABLE FOR HER MASSIVE SAIL AREA - NOT SELFRIGHTING

WATER BALLAST TANKS   CABLE WELL   WATER BALLAST TANKS
CORK BELTING
GUARD RAIL
FORE DECK
SIDE   DECK
MIZZEN SHEET
OUTRIGGER
BREAST
HOOK
RUDDER HEAD
TILLER
MAST
THWART
SIDE   DECK
MAST
CORK BELTING

PLAN

TOTAL 24 RELIEVING VALVES   GUARD RAIL WITH ROWLOCKS UNDER

TILLER   AIR CASES UNDER DECKS
OUTRIGGER   5 SIDE SCUPPERS   GUARD RAIL
MAST   MAST
FORESTAY
OUTRIGGER

RETRACTABLE RUDDER
AIR CASE
AIR
CASE
LONG STRAIGHT IRON KEEL   BILGE KEEL   LIFE LINES
TWIN DROP KEELS   HEAVY CORK BELTING
WATER BALLAST TANKS AS PLAN   RELIEVING VALVES AS PLAN

SAILING PROFILE

NOTE THE LONG STRAIGHT KEEL - THE
LARGEST OF THESE BOATS WAS 46 FT.
LONG - THE GREAT BEAM AND ALMOST
FLAT BOTTOM

NOTE THE MEANS OF DISCHARGING
WATER — 24 RELIEVING VALVES
10 SIDE SCUPPERS

RELIEVING VALVES
GUARD RAIL
GUNWALE
HEAVY CORK BELTING WITH
DRAIN SCUPPERS OVER
AIR CASES
BILGE KEEL
WATER BALLAST TANK / CABLE WELL AT MIDSHIPS
KEEL

**CROSS SECTION
AT MIDSHIPS**

DRG. NO. 10.

SCALE IN FEET

The Norfolk and Suffolk class were big, heavy, almost flat-bottomed boats, ideal for working among the North Sea sandbars. They carried a massive spread of canvas.

high standard of seamanship was required to handle them in the storm conditions under which they frequently operated'.

In November 1872 the coast of East Anglia was hit by a severe gale, and the *Expedite*, on passage from the Baltic, was driven ashore on the Holme Sands, not far from Lowestoft. Conditions were so bad that for some time the Lowestoft lifeboat *Loetitia* could make little headway towards the casualty, but eventually she was towed into position by a steam tug. She found *Expedite* dismasted, pounded by heavy seas, breaking up and surrounded by flotsam – what was left of her cargo and her masts. *Loetitia* dropped anchor upwind of her, then veered slowly down on her quarter. Her coxswain waited for the right moment, then forced his way through the wreckage, came alongside and rescued the ten people on board. For this and 'in testimony of his (other) brave services in saving life from shipwreck', he was awarded a silver medal.

A few years later, in January 1880, the Bacton lifeboat *Recompense* launched in appalling conditions to go to the aid of a schooner aground on the shoals off the north coast of Norfolk. The lifeboat managed to manoeuvre alongside, but almost at once was swamped by a huge wave and capsized. Her second coxswain and one of her crew were trapped beneath the overturned boat and drowned. Further disaster was averted by the bravery of crewman William Cubitt, who dived under the boat and cut the rope which was jamming its rudder and preventing it being brought back to an even keel. When, after much difficulty, the *Recompense* was righted, she managed to take off all the crew of the schooner and bring them safely ashore. For his part in the rescue, William Cubitt was given a gold medal.

In the second half of the nineteenth century the Norfolk and Suffolks were probably the busiest lifeboats in the British Isles. In a single decade, between 1870 and 1880, their crews launched more than a thousand times, often saving lives in conditions in which less sturdy boats might not have survived. Later, the Norfolk and Suffolks' already fine record of service enjoyed a spectacular Indian summer during the First World War.

The last, but by no means the least, of the nineteenth-century lifeboats were the Watsons.

During the 1850s, '60s, '70s and '80s the majority of boats in the RNLI fleet were self-righting. However, in 1887 the Institution appointed George Lennox Watson as its consultant naval architectural adviser, and Watson held the then-heretical view that it was more important for a lifeboat to be easily launched and a good sea boat than to self-right. He designed a 'pulling and sailing lifeboat' which, to the surprise of the self-righting lobby, turned out to be an outstanding success. His boats were on average about thirty-eight feet long, nine feet in the beam and weighed less than five tons; they were fitted with water ballast tanks, and usually carried a jib and two sprit sails. During the 1890s some twenty were brought into service. Typical of their work were the rescues – three in one day – carried out by the *Maude Pickup* of Fleetwood.

A little before dawn on 16 June 1897 a ship was seen to be in difficulties at the approaches to Morecambe Bay. A severe gale from the west-south-west was churning up huge seas, and the *Maude Pickup* had to be towed out of harbour by a tug. The casualty was a Norwegian barque, the *Svalen*, and only three of her crew were aboard, the others having gone ashore the previous evening, before the storm blew up. The three were rescued 'with considerable difficulty', and the lifeboat headed back for Fleetwood. Almost at once, she spotted another barque, the *Louisa*, aground on the Pilling Sands. This proved an even more difficult rescue, for the *Louisa* was breaking up and sinking; however, her crew of nine, together with a pilot, were safely transferred to the lifeboat. By this time the *Maude Pickup* had been at sea for more than four hours in atrocious conditions; her crew were cold and exhausted, but

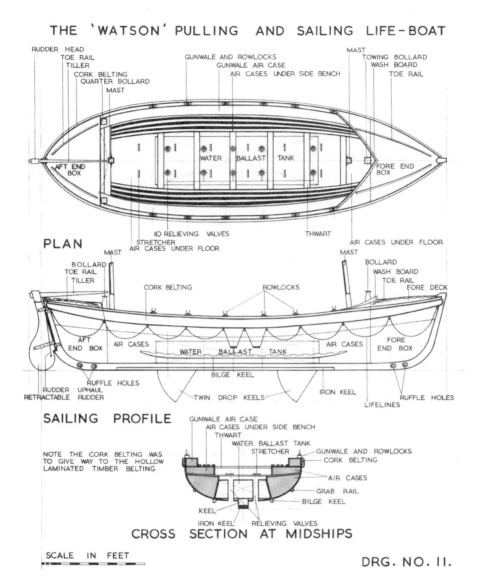

THE 'WATSON' PULLING AND SAILING LIFE-BOAT

PLAN

SAILING PROFILE

NOTE THE CORK BELTING WAS TO GIVE WAY TO THE HOLLOW LAMINATED TIMBER BELTING

CROSS SECTION AT MIDSHIPS

SCALE IN FEET

DRG. NO. 11.

Designed by George Lennox Watson, these 'sailing and pulling' lifeboats were the work-horses of the RNLI in the late 19th and early 20th century.

there was still more for them to do, for they now spotted a third vessel, the s.s. *Zillah* of Liverpool, also aground on the Pilling Sands. Only the top of the *Zillah*'s foremast and the top of her funnel were above water. Two of her crew were clinging to the funnel and three to the mast; they were being repeatedly submerged by huge seas which threatened any moment to sweep them away. These men, too, were saved. After six and a half hours the *Maude Pickup* returned to Fleetwood with eighteen survivors, 'amidst tremendous cheering from the huge crowd which had gathered to see their lifeboat return to harbour'.

The Institution decided not to award medals for these rescues, although they did give the coxswain, David Leadbetter, a pair of binoculars. However, a Birmingham businessman was so impressed by the work of the lifeboatmen that he had special bronze medals struck at his own expense and presented to them. These were the forerunners of the Institution's own bronze medals, which have been awarded officially since 1917.

More Watson boats were built in the first decade of the twentieth century, and some were to remain in service until the late 1930s. Their longevity was due to two facts. They were excellent sea boats and popular with the crews who manned them; and they were versatile and could be readily adapted to meet special requirements. And at the turn of the century versatility was needed. For the Institution was about to make not one leap in the dark but two. Not only were its self-righting lifeboats being replaced by boats that were easy to launch and pre-eminently seaworthy, but lifeboats powered by sail were being replaced by boats powered by either steam or petrol engines. In the case of steam engines, a whole new lineage of lifeboats needed to be built. In the case of petrol engines, existing boats could often be adapted to house the new source of propulsion.

Medals and Awards

At the founding meeting of the Shipwreck Institution on 4 March 1824, it was agreed that 'Medallions or Pecuniary awards be given to those who rescue lives in cases of shipwreck'.

The first medals, of gold or silver, were designed by William Wyon of the Royal Mint. The obverse bore the head of King George IV, the Institution's first patron. The reverse bore the representation of a lifeboat from which three seamen were rescuing a fourth, together with the inscription: 'Let not the deep swallow me up.' These remained unchanged, except for the head of Queen Victoria replacing that of George IV in 1862, until the first year of the twentieth century, when a new design was introduced. The obverse still bore the head of the sovereign, Edward VII, but the reverse depicted 'the figure of Hope

1824–1862

ABOVE The obverse of the first medals with the head of George IV, the first patron, who granted the Institution the use of the prefix 'royal'.

1862–1903

ABOVE The head of Queen Victoria replaced that of George IV on the obverse only in 1862, shortly after the granting of a royal charter in 1860. Designed by Leonard Charles Wyon, son of William Wyon.

1824–1903
1912–to date

LEFT The reverse of the first medals, designed by William Wyon of the Royal Mint.

assisting a Coxswain-Superintendent to buckle on his lifebelt, with a manned lifeboat in the background'. These medals remained in use only until 1912, when George V's head was placed on the obverse, and the reverse went back to the original design. In 1936 there was yet another change, when King George VI decreed that his effigy should appear only on medals for which he had given his sanction.

award have undergone a fundamental change. Today, a lifeboatman's gold medal is regarded as the equivalent of a serviceman's VC. Only one has been awarded in the last fifteen years – to Hewitt Clark of Lerwick.

The most decorated lifeboatman of all time was Henry Blogg of Cromer who, over a period of twenty-four years, won three gold medals and four silver.

1903–1912
FAR LEFT The obverse of the medals used during the reign of Edward VII.
LEFT The reverse of the Edward VII medals designed by G.W. de Saulles.

1937–to date
BELOW The obverse of the medals in use since 1937 showing the head of the founder, Sir William Hillary. Designed by Alan G. Wyon, a distant relative of William Wyon.

The obverse was therefore altered to bear the head of the RNLI's founder, Sir William Hillary. These designs have remained unchanged ever since. Bronze medals (of the same design) were introduced in 1917. Generally speaking, the recipient's name is engraved on the rim of the medal, together with the date of the award. Second and subsequent awards are recognized by the issue of a clasp. The medal ribbon is close to Garter blue.

To date (as of 1 January 2001) the Institution has awarded 2442 medals: 119 gold, 1556 silver, and 797 bronze.

Initially, gold medals were distributed lavishly. In its first ten years the Institution awarded no fewer than fifty-three, often 'with the view of exciting others to follow the example of the parties herein referred to ... [rather] than from any particular risk incurred'. However, over the years the criteria for the

Steam boats

and motor sailers

The hydraulic and propeller-driven steam boats

North Stack and South Stack jut out like horns from the west coast of Anglesey. Even in fine weather the waves cream white over the base of these rocky outcrops with a muted roar. In time of storm the waves are tossed over them steeple-high, and their thunder can be heard the length of Holyhead Bay. This is not a good place to be wrecked in.

It is the night of 21 February 1908, and a hurricane is raging in the Irish Sea. The wind is eighty knots, gusting to 100, and the waves are enormous. In the early morning the steamer *Bencroy*, which has run for shelter into Holyhead harbour, is driven against the breakwater. The lifeboat *Duke of Northumberland* goes to her aid.

The *Duke* is an innovatory and avant-garde monster of a lifeboat, fifty feet long, fourteen feet in the beam, and steel-built (it is said, with 72,000 rivets). She has fifteen watertight compartments, a twelve-stroke engine and a powerful centrifugal pump. This pump sucks in water at the rate of a ton per second, then blasts it out through nozzles in the lifeboat's hull, propelling her this way or that. She weighs over thirty tons, and her crew of eleven includes two engineers and two 'firemen'. She soon copes with the *Bencroy*. Two of her crew are hoisted aboard, a hawser is passed from ship to ship, and the *Bencroy* is towed to a safe place in Holyhead harbour.

Then comes a more daunting challenge. Out in the Irish Sea, a ship with her engines disabled is reported drifting towards the Stacks. The ship in distress is the s.s. *Harold*, a Liverpool freighter carrying china clay from Teignmouth to Runcorn. She is first sighted by another freighter, the *Sound Fisher*, about five miles offshore, being swirled helplessly towards the coast of Anglesey. The *Sound Fisher* tries to take her in tow, but in the

Coxswain William Owen struggles to keep his steam lifeboat the *Duke of Northumberland* alongside the freighter *Harold*, embayed off the coast of Anglesey in a hurricane. For this successful rescue the whole crew of the *Duke of Northumberland* were awarded medals.

The innovative *Duke of Northumberland*, first of the Institution's steam lifeboats. Powerful, seaworthy vessels, they needed to be berthed in a deepwater anchorage, being too heavy to beach-launch; they also needed time to get up steam.

huge seas and bludgeoning wind is unable to pass her a line. As the *Harold* nears the shore, she tries again and again to drop anchor. At last, a bare hundred yards from the Stacks, her anchor holds – at least for the time being, and with the aid of an ebb tide. Her crew try to launch their ship's boat, but it is dashed against the side of the hull and stove in. So all the nine men on board can do is huddle together on the bridge, just about the one part of the *Harold* not swept by huge seas, and hope that by some miracle they will be rescued.

And the miracle is about to happen. For out through the entrance of Holyhead harbour comes the *Duke of Northumberland*. No other type of lifeboat could have made headway against the seventy-knot wind and twenty-foot waves, but the *Duke of Northumberland*'s steam engine and water jets enable her to inch seaward in conditions in which no sailing ship could have survived. However, for her engineers and firemen, battened down in the stoke-hold, there is a price to pay. In stifling heat, short of oxygen, and flung from bulkhead to bulkhead by 'the insufferable motion of the lifeboat', they are hard put to it to remain conscious as they struggle to maintain sufficient power to keep the *Duke* under control. It takes them two hours to reach the *Harold*; and when at last they get to her, they find the seas are too heavy for them to come alongside. They also drop anchor.

So they lie at a little distance from one another, listening to the cacophony of the hurricane, watching the waves bursting white over the nearby rocks, and wondering how long their anchors will hold. Every now and then the coxswain tries to manoeuvre alongside, but each time huge seas either hurl the *Duke* off course or threaten what would be a fatal collision. They hope that if they are patient the hurricane may blow itself out, but there is no sign of it lessening. However, at dead low tide the waves tend for a few moments to slacken. The coxswain seizes his chance. He inches closer to the *Harold*. A line is thrown to her. And it is caught and held. Rescuers and rescued are in contact.

The coxswain now needs all his expertise to hold the two vessels close together while a breeches-buoy is rigged between them. At last, hawsers and sling are in place, and the crew of the freighter, one at a time, are swung perilously from ship to ship, now suspended high above the troughs of the waves, now dragged half-drowning through their crests. Seven men are transferred to the lifeboat. Then, just when they think they are safe, out of the darkness and blotting out the horizon, looms an enormous wave. It picks up the thirty-ton *Duke of Northumberland* as though she were straw and hurls her straight at the *Harold*. It looks like the end for both rescuers and rescued. But just as the *Duke* is about to smash into the side of the freighter the wave passes, and the lifeboat comes to rest parallel to and close beside the ship she is trying to rescue. Between them is about nine inches of water. With great presence of mind the coxswain holds his position, cries 'Jump!' and the last two crewmen come plummeting into the lifeboat.

The *Duke of Northumberland* has saved the crew of the *Harold*, but she is not yet safe herself. For it is now pitch dark, the wind is still force eleven, and huge seas are still rolling out of the west like ranges of snow-capped hills. The lifeboat, with the waves bearing down on her quarter and threatening any moment to overturn her, has a difficult return passage to Holyhead. But at last the crew of the *Harold* are landed safely. A few hours later their ship drags her anchor and is swept ashore and battered to pieces between the Stacks.

For this rescue all the crew of the *Duke of Northumberland* were given medals: gold to the coxswain, William Owen, and silver to the others. No one could begrudge them their awards. Yet it might be argued that the real hero of the rescue was the lifeboat.

Hydraulic steam boats were never a major component of the RNLI fleet. Only three were built: the *Duke of Northumberland*, the *City of Glasgow*, and the *Queen*. These three, however, did sterling work. They remained in service for more than forty years, saved 578 lives, and have the distinction of being the first RNLI lifeboats to be mechanically powered.

Their design was fifty years in gestation. At the very first technical committee meeting of the Shipwreck Institution, back in 1824, one member had proposed building 'iron' boats, while William Hillary had advocated building steam boats. Such ideas were too avant-garde (and too expensive) for the committee. But it is worth noting that Hillary's proposed design was, in most of its essentials, the one that was commissioned nearly sixty years later. He wrote one of his many pamphlets on the subject, 'A Plan for the Construction of a Steam Life-boat', pointing out the enormous advantages of steam, 'in that it would enable a vessel to proceed directly to windward, which is beyond the capacity of sail... Perhaps,' he went on, 'the boat could be at least 40 foot long, having valves or small ports to clear her of water... I would suggest she might be fitted with forcing pumps or engines to throw water by her own steam power'. As an ideas man Hillary was way ahead of his time. Yet his proposed steam boat would have needed years of testing, and would have been inordinately expensive, both to build and to maintain. If the Institution had heeded him, they would probably have been bankrupt before they had rescued anyone.

For a couple of decades there was little more talk of steam boats, but in 1851 several designs for lifeboats powered by steam engines were submitted for the Duke of Northumberland's award. These were looked at carefully. For this was an age when steam-driven railway engines were breaking new ground all over the world, and there was a feeling that steam-driven ships would soon be doing the same; surely, it was thought, it should not be beyond human ingenuity to design a workable steam-powered lifeboat? However, for many years the technical problems appeared to be insurmountable, the basic difficulty being that it proved almost impossible to keep the engine-room fires going while the lifeboat was being flung about by heavy seas to the point of capsizing – and indeed at times was capsizing, then self-righting. In the 1870s a report by the RNLI committee of management confessed that it 'did not feel able to expect that steam life-boats will ever come into general use'.

But George Lennox Watson thought differently. Watson was the most progressive ship designer of his day. Among other achievements, he designed the royal yacht *Britannia* and a succession of contenders for the America's Cup. Following his appointment as consultant naval architect to the RNLI in 1887, he orchestrated two fundamental changes to the Institution's fleet: the gradual replacement of the old Wouldhave-style self-righters by lifeboats which were, above all, good sea boats; and the gradual introduction of steam and petrol engines, first to complement sails and eventually to supersede them.

In the summer of 1887 he persuaded the Institution 'to offer a gold and silver medal for drawings or models of a mechanically propelled Life-boat, best adapted to meet the conditions under which life-boats are called upon to perform their work'. None of the entries submitted was thought good enough to merit a medal, but the following year the firm of J. and F. Green of Blackwall put forward the highly innovative proposal of a boat powered by steam-driven jet propulsion. Within a surprisingly short time the Institution's first steam lifeboat had progressed from draftsman's drawings to seagoing vessel. Launched in 1890 and christened the *Duke of Northumberland*, many people feared she would prove an expensive white elephant – to quote the *The Life-Boat*: 'Being so new a departure in Life-boat building, it was necessary to put her through very exhaustive trials'. She passed these with flying colours, and was sent to Harwich. A few months later the journal reported: 'She has been thoroughly tried in bad weather and heavy seas, and has proved a complete success... being remarkably handy in a seaway'. After a spell of duty on the east

The steam lifeboat *City of Glasgow*, virtually a sister ship of the *Duke of Northumberland*. Although these boats did sterling service, they were expensive to build and maintain, and were eventually replaced by petrol-driven lifeboats.

coast, the *Duke* was sent to Holyhead, where she remained – except for a short spell at New Brighton – until 1922, answering over a hundred calls and saving 295 lives. Her most dramatic service was her rescue of the crew of the *Harold*, a feat that no other type of lifeboat could, at the time, have achieved.

Of the other two hydraulic steam lifeboats, the *City of Glasgow* was also designed and built by J. and F. Green. She was slightly larger than the *Duke* – fifty-three feet long and sixteen feet in the beam – and incorporated a number of modifications, some but not all of which improved her performance. Launched in 1894, she too was sent to Harwich, where she remained until 1901. In these seven years she saved eighty-seven lives. The *Queen* was the largest of the steam hydraulic boats: fifty-five feet long, sixteen feet in the beam, and weighing thirty-one tons. She could carry either three and a half tons of coal or two tons of oil, the latter being sprayed into her furnace by compressed air, a job requiring considerable skill. Launched in 1897, she was sent to New Brighton, where she remained until 1923. In these twenty-six years she saved 196 lives.

Although these hydraulic steam boats were successful, they were nevertheless a dead-end in the evolution of the lifeboat, being superseded almost as soon as they were launched by boats with petrol-driven engines. For they had many shortcomings. They were too heavy to be beach launched, and had therefore to be kept permanently at anchor in a sheltered deep-water harbour. Before they could set out on a rescue, they had to get up steam; this took a good twenty minutes. And when they had got up steam, they were comparatively slow. In their trials it was claimed they

Horses help to beach-launch the *James Stevens* in Harlyn Bay, *circa* 1905.

could make nine knots, but in working conditions this was reduced to seven. They were costly to build, at about £5000 apiece (three times as much as the average Watson); costly to operate, because of the coal or oil that they burned; and costly to maintain, because their engines needed to be frequently serviced by skilled engineers, and their fuel bought and bunkered. Also, there was something intrinsically hazardous in working in a battened-down stoke-hold in the sort of conditions in which lifeboats often had to operate. In fact there was only one major accident in a steam lifeboat's engine room, and this took place during routine servicing in harbour. However, during rescue operations, conditions for the engineers and stokers were hot, suffocating, claustrophobic, and, to say the least, unpleasant; and in the event of an accident those in the engine room had little hope of survival. The hydraulic steam boats were a bit like the Neanderthals: in their day successful, but with no future.

At the same time as the Institution was experimenting with steam lifeboats driven by water jets, it was also experimenting with steam lifeboats driven by propellers.

Three of these were commissioned: the *City of Glasgow II*, stationed at Harwich; the *James Stevens No. 3*, stationed at no fewer than six stations (Grimsby, Gorleston, Angle, Totland Bay, Dover and Holyhead); and the ill-fated *James Stevens No. 4*, stationed at Padstow. They were all built by J. Samuel White and Company of Cowes; and although the boats themselves were not a great success, the Institution was delighted with White's high standard of craftsmanship.

From that day to this, many RNLI boats have been built on the Isle of Wight. In the late nineteenth and early twentieth centuries they were built entirely by hand, and generations of the island's shipwrights took justifiable pride in their work for the Institution, designing, sawing, planing, chiselling, dovetailing and polishing some of the toughest woods in the world (oak, mahogany, teak and red cedar) to create boats that were not only wonderfully seaworthy but works of art.

For all their shortcomings, the three propeller-driven steam boats came into this latter category; and as well as being meticulously constructed, they pioneered a major innovation. One of the disadvantages of a steam- or petrol-driven boat was that it had a number of exterior protuberances, such as propeller shafts and screws, which could easily be damaged. Trying to protect these while beach launching, manoeuvring in shallow water, or approaching wrecks that were surrounded by flotsam and jetsam was a nightmare. The three steam boats got round this problem by having their propellers set well forward from the stern and housed in a wooden tunnel. The effectiveness of this design can be judged both by its longevity (it was still being used by lifeboats such as the Barnetts right up to the end of the Second World War) and by the fact that no steam boat ever reported a serious accident as a result of damage to its propellers. There were, however, serious accidents for other reasons.

In good weather Padstow is idyllic: a quiet, sheltered estuary, with fine beaches and a plethora of people 'messing about in boats'. But in time of storm it can be a death-trap: a lee shore with huge waves rolling into it unchecked from the Atlantic. At such times the Doom Bar across the harbour entrance lives up to its name, and there is truth in the local saying: 'From Padstow Point to Lundy Light is a watery grave by day or by night'.

On 11 April 1900 the Padstow steam lifeboat, the *James Stevens No. 4* was called out to help a vessel that was in difficulties a couple of miles offshore. There was a near-gale blowing, but certainly not a full one. The seas were heavy, but by no means mountainous. The *James Stevens* had been stationed at Padstow for almost exactly a year; she had already saved nine lives, and had proved herself a good, reliable sea boat. So what happened next was totally unexpected. As was often the case when a shipwreck was in the offing, a fair number of people had turned out to watch from the top of the cliffs. At first everything seemed to be going according to plan. However, as the steam boat neared the casualty, a huge wave came bearing down on her port quarter. It broke just as it struck her. In an instant the *James Stevens No. 4* capsized. She was not a self-righter. She was swept ashore, bottom up, and became a total wreck. Eight of her crew, including the four trapped in the engine room, were drowned.

Steam lifeboats had always had their critics, and this disaster, coming so soon after the *James Stevens* had arrived in Padstow, confirmed sceptics in their view that this class of lifeboat had little future. No more were built, although it has to be said that the two remaining steam boats operated well, remaining in service for many years and saving eighty-six lives. It was their misfortune that they were conceived at much the same time as boats powered by petrol-driven engines. And it soon became apparent that as far as lifeboats were concerned the future lay not with steam but with petrol.

The petrol-driven motor sailers

It is the evening of 19 October 1922, and the 2000-ton *Hopelyn*, carrying coal from Newcastle to London, has run aground on North Scroby Sands off the mouth of the Yare. There is a strong gale blowing from the north-east, with winds of almost sixty knots whipping up the sort of huge seas that are particularly dangerous in shallow water.

Hopelyn fires her distress rockets. These are spotted by coastguards, and efforts are made to launch the Caister and Gorleston lifeboats. However, conditions are so bad that after an hour the Caister pulling and sailing lifeboat has to report 'unable to get away'. Meanwhile, the Gorleston Norfolk and Suffolk lifeboat *Kentwell* is having similar problems; she is launched successfully, but can make no headway against the gale-force winds and mountainous seas. Eventually, she is towed out of harbour by a steam tug, just as a radio message reports 'wreck breaking up'.

It is midnight before *Kentwell* arrives at the North Scroby Sands. The night is dark, with ten-tenths cloud blotting out the moon and stars. With visibility further reduced by sheets of spray being driven horizontally off the crests of the waves, the lifeboat can only wait for daylight.

It is not a hopeful scenario that dawn eventually reveals. *Hopelyn* has broken her back. Both her bow and her stern are impacted into the Sands and are totally submerged. Only the central part of the ship is above water, and this is being repeatedly swept by huge waves. There is no sign of life. The lifeboat does her best to approach the wreck, but sails and oars alone don't give her sufficient control to come alongside. Eventually, after ten hours at sea under appalling conditions, *Kentwell* comes to the conclusion there can be no survivors. She returns to Gorleston.

A few minutes after she enters harbour, it is reported that a flag has been seen waving from the wreck.

Kentwell is again towed out by a steam tug, which this time remains with her when she gets to the wreck. The lifeboat drops anchor only a couple of hundred yards from what is left of the *Hopelyn*; but once again not all her coxswain's courage and skill can bring the lifeboat alongside. For the wind is still gusting to fifty knots, and huge seas are breaking steeple-high over the Sands, which are now littered not only with the remains of a previous wreck but with debris from the disintegrating *Hopelyn*. By this time Commander Carver, Inspector of Life-boats for the Eastern District, has

The Norfolk and Suffolk-class sail-cum-motor lifeboat *Agnes Cross* of Lowestoft. She succeeded in rescuing the crew of the *Hopelyn* when all efforts by sail-only lifeboats had failed.

arrived on the scene. Realizing the Caister and Gorleston boats lack the power and control that are needed to get alongside the casualty, he telephones Lowestoft to ask for the help of their motor lifeboat, the *Agnes Cross*. Within a couple of hours the *Agnes Cross* has picked up Commander Carver and is on her way to the wreck.

Darkness is falling as they near the Sands, and in the last glimmer of daylight they come across the *Kentwell* limping back towards Gorleston. In a brave but unsuccessful effort to get alongside, the lifeboat has been flung violently on to the Sands; her mizzen outrigger has been damaged and her gunwale stove in. By the time Carver has satisfied himself that the Gorleston lifeboat is in no immediate danger it is dark, too dark to attempt a rescue, and the *Agnes Cross* also heads back for the safety of harbour.

Carver himself takes up the story:

> We left Gorleston again at 4.30 a.m. on the Saturday morning. NE gale with squalls, rough sea, very heavy on the Sands. We arrived at the scene of the wreck at daylight, and found only the bridge, funnel and fiddley casing above water. The fore and after decks were completely submerged, and the hull of the vessel was split open . . . with jagged edges of plates projecting, leaving barely the length of the Life-boat in which to come alongside. We dropped anchor astern and to windward of the wreck, and veered down. While we were doing this, the Life-boat was struck by a terrific sea, and almost thrown onto the afterdeck. Had it not been for the powerful Motor fitted in this Boat, I do not consider we could have got alongside.

By this time *Hopelyn* had been aground for more than a day and a half, with her crew confined to their wave-swept bridge. Miraculously, none had been seriously injured. And the second the *Agnes Cross* came alongside, all twenty-four of them came leaping or slithering down ropes into the lifeboat, the whole rescue being completed 'in about 30 seconds'.

However, they were not yet safe. The *Agnes Cross*'s cable had fouled on a sunken part of the wreck, tethering rescuers to rescued. There was no hope, in the terrific seas, of clearing the cable. It had to be cut. And in the moment of cutting it, the lifeboat was caught broadside on and completely buried by a larger than usual wave. For a moment the *Agnes Cross* teetered on the brink of capsizing. Then she righted herself, with water streaming out of her, and, by another near miracle, with none of her occupants washed overboard. A couple of hours later the lifeboat was approaching the safety of harbour; and a couple of hours after that the crew of twenty-four and one small black kitten were relaxing in the warmth of the Sailors' Home in Yarmouth.

For this difficult operation, extending over two days and involving lifeboats from two stations, an unprecedented twenty-seven medals were awarded (two gold, two silver and twenty-three bronze). But perhaps more important than the medals was the message: the days of pulling and sailing lifeboats were numbered; the future lay with lifeboats powered by petrol-driven engines.

It has been said with some truth that 'the advent of the internal combustion engine was the greatest single factor in the evolution of the lifeboat', and in the early 1900s experiments got under way to install these initially temperamental engines into a number of carefully chosen boats.

There were many potential advantages to mechanization. The old pulling and sailing boats had only been able to operate close to the place from which they had been launched, for in the sort of weather lifeboats were called out in it was often impossible for them to make headway against the wind. Boats powered by engines, on the other hand, could progress against the wind; they therefore had a far wider and more flexible operating range. The old pulling and sailing boats had been difficult to manoeuvre; in particular, they had had to approach a casualty downwind, and coming alongside had often been, to say the least, hazardous. As the rescue from the *Hopelyn* proved, motor boats, with their increased manoeuvrability, could save lives when pulling and sailing boats were impotent.

And in the long term there was another benefit from mechanization. Although lifeboat sails were kept as simple as possible, they took up a fair amount of space in a lifeboat; also, considerable expertise was needed to operate them. When eventually engines replaced sails, this created more room; also the lifeboat crew no longer needed to be expert sailors (using the word to mean people who could work sails). Landsmen as well as seamen could become crew members, and this enabled more

LEFT James Rennie Barnett. RIGHT George Lennox Watson. Forward-thinking naval architects who masterminded the RNLI's transition from sail to petrol-driven engines.

people to become involved in the work of the Institution – although, of course, to join a lifeboat crew one still needed the traditional qualities of endurance, devotion to duty and, above all, courage.

When it came to installing petrol-driven engines into lifeboats the technical problems were horrendous. The engine needed to be housed in a casing that was waterproof, even if the lifeboat capsized, but was not airtight, because a supply of air was needed for the carburettor. It had to start instantly and unfailingly under any conditions; it had to continue to run smoothly even when the lifeboat was upended in heavy seas with its screws threshing nothing but air. The lubricating system needed to be self-perpetuating, and the risk of fire had to be minimized. There were also problems with the propellers, which were liable to be damaged while launching or while working in shallow or wreckage-strewn waters.

George Lennox Watson masterminded the first experiments with petrol-driven engines. When he died at a comparatively early age in 1904, his successor, James

Rennie Barnett, continued his pioneering work. One of the earliest petrol-driven lifeboats with which Barnett experimented was the *J. McConnel Hussey*, a thirty-eight-foot self-righter stationed at Folkestone. She was fitted with a two-stroke Fay and Bowen engine, which gave her a speed of six knots, with a petrol consumption of one and a half gallons per hour. After successful trials in the Channel, the *McConnel Hussey* was sent to Tynemouth in May 1905. Here, however, she was viewed not only with suspicion but with hostility.

Seafarers tend to be conservative – when one has worked out a way of surviving the hazards of the sea, it goes against the grain to try something new. The Tynemouth lifeboat crews had a particularly proud history of doing their own thing in their own way under private ownership, and they now resented being told to act as guinea pigs to test an innovation in which they had little faith. They refused to man the *Hussey*.

Here was tinder for a conflagration. However, the situation was defused by an army officer, Captain H. E. Burton, who undertook not only to look after the controversial engine but to raise a volunteer crew to man the new-fangled boat. So for several years Tynemouth had two rival lifeboats. Eventually, however, the good work done by the *Hussey* won the respect of those who had at first been sceptical of her usefulness, one incident in particular providing evidence of the superiority of boats driven by engines over those powered by sail.

Early one morning in January 1913 the s.s. *Dunelm* was driven ashore near Blyth, about a dozen miles north of the Tyne. There was a full gale blowing from the northeast, and twenty-foot waves and a fifty-knot wind seemed to rule out the possibility of using a lifeboat. A line-throwing mortar was therefore set up on the beach, and at low tide a rope was landed across the *Dunelm*, a breeches-buoy was rigged up, and several of the crew were hauled to safety. However, as the weather worsened and the tide rose, using the breeches-buoy became first hazardous, then impossible. An attempt was made to reach the *Dunelm* using a small, locally launched boat; but it was almost immediately swamped, one man was swept away and drowned, and the would-be rescuers found themselves stranded on the wreck. Meanwhile, news of the disaster had reached Tynemouth. The Tynemouth sailing lifeboat was unable to help, finding it impossible to make headway against a combination of huge seas and a gale-force head wind. The motor lifeboat, on the other hand, manned by Captain Burton and his volunteer crew, fought their way through to the scene of the wreck in little more than an hour. The fact that they arrived only to find that the last man aboard the *Dunelm* had been rescued a few minutes earlier is irrelevant. A petrol-driven lifeboat had succeeded in reaching a casualty where a sailing lifeboat had failed. In the words of the Chief Inspector of Lifeboats, 'This was a case which demonstrated the immense value of a motor boat'.

In spite of a number of such incidents, the transformation from sails to engines proved a protracted business, largely because it was many years before the engines achieved the degree of reliability that was required. As late as 1911, a directive from the Institution made it clear that 'the motor is [still] an auxiliary to the sails, which latter are the principal motive power'. And the mishaps that befell a northbound flotilla of motor boats are evidence that although petrol-driven engines had enormous potential they also still had serious shortcomings.

In April 1909 three lifeboats headed north out of the Thames estuary. The flotilla consisted of a large Watson class sailing boat bound for Thurso (on the north coast of Scotland), a slightly smaller Watson boat powered by a forty horsepower engine bound for Stronsay (in the Orkneys), and a self-righting lifeboat powered by a thirty horsepower engine bound for Stromness (also in the Orkneys). The expedition was seen as a test for the new engine-powered boats, and the Institution's Motor Surveyor, Mr Small, and a number of skilled mechanics were included in the crews.

The flotilla left the London docks in the early hours of 15 April, with the Stromness boat in the lead and the Thurso boat in the rear. After an uneventful run of seventy-three miles they reached Harwich, where, we are told, they were given 'a very cordial reception'. Next morning the weather was bad: a strong south-westerly wind and heavy seas. Nevertheless the three boats set out, again in the same order, and reached Gorleston after a voyage of sixty miles at an average speed of seven and a half knots. So far the petrol engines had behaved impeccably. But this was not to last. The official report tells us that on the third day, 'owing to some little trouble with one of the motors, two stops had to be made'. This delay caused them to miss the flood tide going into the Humber, and they did not reach Grimsby until close on midnight. By this time the crews had been on duty for twenty hours, and the mechanics and their engines were not popular. During the next ten days a fair number of stops had to be made on account of the temperamental engines. And there seems to be a discrepancy between the events that actually happened and the way they are described in the journal. The engines seem, to say the least, to have been prone to breakdown. Off Scarborough 'one of the motors gave a little trouble'. Off Tynemouth 'troubles again befell them, as one of the motors refused to start, and three days elapsed before all was right again'. Off Aberdeen the flotilla had to be helped by a tug that 'plucked' them into harbour. And in the Pentland Firth the Stronsay boat had to return to the mainland and be 'put partially to rights before being towed to her destination'. Yet the journal continually claims that 'the boats behaved wonderfully'!

Why, one asks, were they given such a favourable write-up? The truth seems to be that the voyage of the motor boats encapsulated what has been an ever present problem for the Institution: what is the most desirable type of lifeboat? Those at headquarters have, over the years, tended to favour boats that are state of the art as regards performance and innovative equipment, while the crews who man the boats have tended to favour traditional designs that have been tried and tested. It would seem that the men in charge of the northbound flotilla, Commander Harold Rowney and his side-kick Mr Smith, were champions of the new petrol engines and that they leaned over backwards to give them a favourable report. And perhaps their economy with the truth helped, in a small way, to bring about a change that was both desirable and inevitable.

ABOVE Charles Macara. After witnessing the loss of two lifeboats and twenty-seven lifeboatmen on service to the *Mexico*, he and his wife Marion devoted their lives to fundraising for the RNLI.

OPPOSITE TOP The St Anne's lifeboat *Nora Royds*, a replacement for the *Laura Janet* (OPPOSITE BOTTOM) which was lost while trying to help the *Mexico*, aground near the mouth of the Ribble, 9 December 1886.

There may have been some doubt about the performance of the boats, but there was no doubt whatsoever about the warmth of the welcome accorded to their crews: 'a very cordial reception' at Scarborough, 'much kindness' at Dundee, and 'many courtesies' at Aberdeen. Wherever they landed, they were fêted as heroes. For the early 1900s were a golden age for the Institution. Its fleet, which in 1850 had consisted of 'perhaps not a dozen really efficient boats', now totalled 289 vessels which were well maintained and met local requirements. Its annual income had increased from £354 to over £100,000, while its work was being appreciated not only by seafarers but by an enthusiastic public, many of whom had never set eyes on the sea in their lives.

This change in the public perception of the RNLI was due in large part to a man who, like Richard Lewis, is one of the Institution's unsung heroes, the Scottish-born 'king of cotton', Charles Macara. Macara was the archetypal Scot who left home in his youth and through hard work and ability rose to pre-eminence in foreign fields. He made his fortune in Lancashire's 'dark satanic mills', and became president of the Master Cotton Spinners' Federation and chairman of the committee of the International Cotton Federation; he then built himself a magnificent home in what was then the unfashionable fishing village of St Anne's-on-Sea. Here he soon became friendly with the local lifeboatmen, and on more than one occasion put to sea with them in their thirty-four-foot self-righter, the *Laura Janet*.

It was lucky for him that he wasn't at sea with them on 9 December 1886. For that night the Institution suffered what were perhaps the most tragic losses in its history.

It was early evening when the barque *Mexico* of Hamburg went aground in a violent gale off the mouth of the Ribble. Her distress flares were spotted by the coastguards at Southport, and in spite of the terrible conditions it was agreed to attempt a rescue.

The Southport lifeboat, the *Eliza Fernley*, was hauled by horses three and a half miles across the sands to a point upwind of the *Mexico*. Here she was launched into what were said to be 'the most violent seas in living memory'. It took her three hours to reach a position from which she could drop anchor and hope to veer down on the barque; but just as she was about to try to come alongside, she was struck by an enormous wave and capsized. Some of her crew were killed instantly. Others tried desperately to cling to the overturned boat, but all except two were swept away and drowned. In the small hours of the morning the *Eliza Fernley* was washed ashore not far from Southport, and the two men still clinging to her, wracked by cramp and hypothermia, were hauled to safety.

Meanwhile the St Anne's crew had also been alerted. They too had difficulty launching their self-righting lifeboat, the *Laura Janet*, for huge seas were pounding the shore, making the sands tremble as though in the throes of an earthquake. It was ten thirty before they got under way. At first they used only their oars; but when they were about 500 yards from the shore, it looked to those watching anxiously from the beach as though they were trying to hoist sail. What happened next will never be known. The onlookers saw two red lights appear for a moment then disappear. Later that night the *Laura Janet* drifted ashore, bottom-up, with three dead men dangling head-down from her thwarts. Next morning the bodies of the other members of the crew were washed up on the sands. Not one of those aboard the St Anne's lifeboat survived.

The Lytham lifeboat, the *Charles Biggs* was launched at much the same time as the *Laura Janet*. She too was a self-righter, and had arrived in the Ribble estuary only a couple of weeks earlier, so this was her first rescue. Her crew took her across the mouth of the river under oars alone, then they hoisted sail. But in the gale-force wind and mountainous seas, sails were a doubtful asset. The *Charles Biggs* shipped so much water that on four occasions she came close to foundering. However, by one a.m. she had struggled to within a few hundred yards of the wreck. By now the *Mexico* was in danger of breaking up. She was on her beam ends; she had lost both her foremast and mainmast, and her crew had lashed themselves to what was left of the mizzen rigging. As the lifeboat veered down on her, she was struck by a larger than usual wave which flung her almost vertically into the air and broke four of her oars. In spite of this, her coxswain, Thomas Clarkson, managed to manoeuvre

ABOVE The Southport lifeboat *Eliza Fernley*, one of the boats lost on service to the *Mexico*, arguably the most tragic disaster ever suffered by the RNLI.

OPPOSITE A contemporary artist's view of the capsizing of the *Eliza Fernley*.

alongside, and the crew of the *Mexico* were cut from the rigging and half-carried, half-lowered into the lifeboat. All twelve were suffering terribly from cold and were in the last stages of exhaustion. But they were alive. And as light came seeping into a cloud-filled sky, they were brought to the safety of the shore.

But at what a price! In the space of a few hours two lifeboats and twenty-seven lifeboatmen had been lost.

The *Mexico* tragedy triggered off the usual questions. Were the lifeboats as safe as they should have been? Would it not be better if the Institution came under the aegis of the government? Were the families of those who had died going to be properly looked after?

These questions, and especially the last one, preoccupied Charles Macara. From his home overlooking the estuary of the Ribble he had watched the *Mexico* rescue operation unfold with the inevitability of a Greek tragedy. Next morning he had gone down to the sands and helped to drag ashore the bodies of the men who had been his

friends. In the afternoon he had helped to lay them out in the churchyards of Lytham and St Anne's. And he found himself wondering if the average member of the public had the slightest idea of the risks and sacrifices lifeboatmen and their families were called on to make. He thought the answer was almost certainly no. This, he told himself, was not as it should be: what was needed was for someone to do a PR job on the Institution. His friends persuaded him that no one was likely to do this better than himself, with the result that Charles and his wife Marion spent the better part of the rest of their lives helping to publicize, promote and finance the work of the RNLI.

The *Mexico* débâcle had resulted in sixteen wives being widowed, and fifty children under the age of fifteen being orphaned. A public appeal was launched to provide for them, and money fairly poured in, including £250 from the Kaiser and £1400 from the *Mexico*'s home port of Hamburg. However, this did not satisfy Macara, who felt – as Hillary had felt after the loss of the *Racehorse* some sixty years earlier – that money was being given not as a right but as a one-off and maybe never to be repeated gift. 'To offer a widow and her family a grant of £100, as had hitherto been the custom of the Institution when the bread-winner had given his life voluntarily, was utterly inadequate,' he wrote. 'Every lifeboatman ought to have the satisfaction of knowing that, if he never returns, those dependent on him should not suffer pecuniary loss through his self-sacrifice.' He put this to the Institution, but was told that the much needed money simply was not available. And when he delved into the state of the RNLI finances Macara found that this was indeed so. In spite of the foundations laid by Richard Lewis, the Institution's income still depended on an unacceptably small section of the public, and little effort was being made to broaden the base of its funding.

Macara was a patient man. It was almost five years before he felt ready to launch his campaign. Then, in the summer of 1891 the bandwagon started to roll, being given a kick-start by the press, and in particular the press of the north of England. The *Sheffield Daily Telegraph* and the *Yorkshire Post* opened subscription funds for the RNLI. The editor of the *Post* wrote a stirring leading article, 'Man the Life-boat': 'When', he asked, 'will the shillings and half-crowns of the gentlemen of England who live at home at ease . . . be forthcoming with half the readiness with which these gallant [lifeboat] men tender their lives?' Within a fortnight £10,000 had been subscribed.

Encouraged by this initial success, Macara decided to launch what has been described, perhaps with some licence, as 'the world's first ever street collection for charity'. On 1 October 1891, Manchester hosted the first Lifeboat Day. There were three bands, a column of wondrously decorated floats, and two lifeboats pulled by horses. More than 30,000 people turned out to watch, lining the streets and waving from windows and the upper decks of trams. Marion Macara and her friends followed the procession with collecting buckets and purses tied to the ends of poles, which were thrust up to the windows. More than £5000 was taken, about £600 of it in coppers.

This was a red-letter day, with the people of Manchester acting as pathfinders and inaugurating both a new style of fundraising and a new role in the Institution for women. It was not long before the towns of the industrial heartland were vying with

OPPOSITE
Survivors from
the *Mexico*,
finally brought
ashore by the
Lytham lifeboat
Charles Biggs
(inset).

Lifeboat Days, with the boats being hauled through the streets of inland cities, were once a major source of RNLI income.

one another to hold Lifeboat Days. Sheffield, Birmingham, Salford, Bolton and Stockport were among the earliest, and by the end of the decade the idea was being taken up as far north as Dundee and as far south as Southampton. The resulting street collections not only more than doubled the Institution's annual income (from £42,000 in 1890 to £101,000 in 1900), but from that day to this they have been a recurring reminder to the public of the importance, and the cost, of saving life at sea.

Equally important were the opportunities now given for the first time to women. Prior to 1891 few women had been involved with lifeboat work apart from those who had helped with beach launching or with overland hauling, and, of course, the families of the crews.

Throughout the nineteenth century and for the first couple of decades of the twentieth century, beach launching was the most common method of getting a lifeboat into the water. These launchings were usually community efforts, with local farmers loaning their horses, and the men and women who lived near the lifeboat station forming a team to haul the boat to its launch site. Contemporary paintings and early photographs confirm that nearly always a large proportion of the helpers were women; indeed in places such as Runswick women formed a team of their own. Overland hauling, a frequent necessity in the days of sail, was another job in which women were often

The first 'Lifeboat Saturday' in Manchester, organised by Charles and Marion Macara.

involved. Probably the most famous overland haul, in which women played a leading role, was made from Lynmouth (Devon) in the winter of 1898/9.

On the evening of Thursday, 12 January, a full gale from the west-north-west was making the coast of Exmoor a death-trap for sailing ships. A little after seven p.m. a message was picked up in Lynmouth that a vessel was in distress in Porlock Bay, about ten miles to the east. It would have been almost impossible, in such terrible conditions, for

Lifeboat Day in Salisbury, July 1907.

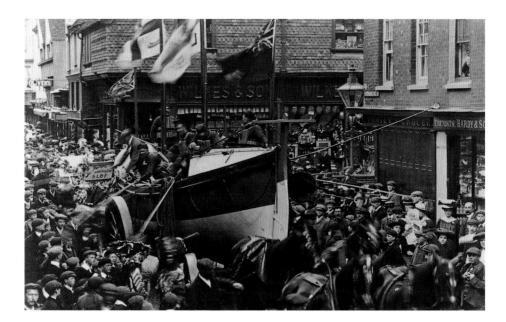

the Lynmouth lifeboat to have fought her way out of harbour, and quite impossible for her to have reached Porlock Bay in the face of the fifty-knot head wind. With telegraph lines brought down in the gale, there was no way of calling on another lifeboat for help. So the men and women of Lynmouth reckoned there was only one thing for it: they would have to haul their lifeboat east along the coast until they came to the next possible launch site, Porlock Bay itself. This involved a climb of nearly 1400 feet up Countisbury Hill, which had a gradient of more than one in five, a journey of some nine miles along narrow moorland lanes, then a descent down the even steeper Porlock Hill.

Farmers from Lynton provided eighteen horses, and the rescue teams assembled: one group of men and women with flares, lanterns, picks and spades to widen the road; and another with the ten-ton lifeboat, the five-ton carriage, and a cart piled high with wooden skids, the idea of these last being to put them under the lifeboat so that she could be hauled forward in places too narrow for the carriage to pass through. No one seems to have counted the exact number of helpers, but a fair guess would be fifty or sixty.

They set out at eight p.m. It took them more than an hour to reach the top of Countisbury Hill, for the horses were unused to hauling such a heavy load, and a wheel was wrenched off the carriage when it was halfway up. Once on top, they

Women's Work

In the old days, women's work for the RNLI was restricted to helping with launching and fundraising. (Above) The Boulmer lifeboat and some of its women launchers and (right) 'every woman to the rope'.

The part played by women in the work of the RNLI has altered enormously over the years. At first, their role was more passive than active: supporting their menfolk. It can sometimes be easier to face danger oneself than to know that a person one loves is facing it. Anxiety always has been and always will be an unwelcome bedfellow for the mothers, wives, daughters, sisters and lovers of lifeboatmen. These women have no memorial; but the debt that both the Institution and the public owes them is incalculable.

Women also used to help with launching and recovering lifeboats. The majority of early lifeboats had to be launched from the beach, and in small fishing villages it was often the women who did the launching. In Newbiggin there was a saying: 'Every man to the boat, every woman to the rope.' Margaret

Armstrong (*née* Brown) of Cresswell is said never to have missed taking part in a launch for fifty years. For more than seventy years women of the Tart family helped to launch and recover the Dungeness lifeboat, hauling it over hundreds of feet of greased timbers. 'It was never a woman's job,' the Dungeness coxswain admitted. 'It was too hard. But there was no one else to do it.'

Women have also played a major role in fundraising. In 1891 Marion Macara formed a Ladies' Committee to help organize the first street collection

Today, women play a much more 'hands on' role. They can do *any* job for the Institution – seen here is one of the many female crew members.

for the RNLI in Manchester. Within a decade, Ladies' Committees were at work in more than fifty towns, and RNLI income had doubled. In 1921 the Ladies' Lifeboat Guild was formed. Its members organized events such as flag days, coffee mornings and tea dances. Some women devoted almost their whole lives to fundraising: Bella Mattison, wife of a Cullercoats fisherman, raised hundreds of thousands of pounds and was known throughout the north of England as 'Bella the Lifeboat Lady'. To quote the Mumbles coxswain: 'A rescue starts not when the maroons are fired, but when the lady sells her flag or arranges her coffee morning'.

Today women play a more hands-on role. They can do *any* job for the Institution. There are women administrators, fundraisers, press officers, medical advisers, instructors and tractor drivers – also, of course, women crew members.

The first woman to become an accredited crew member was Elizabeth Hostvedt, an eighteen-year-old Norwegian student training at the Atlantic College in Wales. That was in 1969. Today some 300 women are crew members, most but not all of them serving on inshore inflatables. It is generally felt that lifeboat stations are happier, better balanced and more up to date places now they are no longer exclusively male territory. To quote *The Lifeboat* journal: 'A good team is made up of different types of people, both men and women, who can work well together'.

found themselves in about the most exposed part of Exmoor. It was dark. The wind was bludgeoning. And rain was scything near-horizontal over the moor. The women were hard put to it to keep their oil-burning lanterns alight. After about a mile, they came to their first serious obstacle. The road became so narrow that the carriage couldn't get through. The lifeboat was offloaded, and the rescue party split into two. One group began to place skids under and in front of the boat, haul her forward a few feet, then pick up the skids and place them in front again, so that inch by reluctant inch she was half-levered, half-rolled through the mud. Meanwhile the other group took the carriage over the open fields and moorland, now forcing their way through hedges, now enlarging gateways, now dismantling loose stone walls, until they came at last to a place where the road widened, and carriage and boat could again move forward together. By now it was past midnight, and the rescuers were cold, sodden and exhausted. But few gave up. Men and women alike took turns at tending the lanterns, widening the road, and manoeuvring the carriage round difficult corners, until in the small hours they came to Porlock Hill.

Porlock Hill has a gradient of one in four. Not in living memory had anything as heavy and cumbersome as a lifeboat on its carriage been taken down it. Drag ropes were attached to the carriage. Safety chains were attached to the wheels. Lifeboat and carriage were bonded by treble lashings. And the perilous descent got under way. If things had got out of control, that would certainly have been the end of the lifeboat and probably of some of her crew. But with the help of more men and women from

In January 1899 the Lynmouth lifeboat was dragged many miles across Exmoor to go to the aid of a vessel in Porlock Bay. The picture shows a 1999 re-enactment of this famous overland haul.

Porlock, the descent was completed without mishap. Then in the village itself they came to an obstacle that seemed insurmountable. The street was so narrow that at a bend the lifeboat couldn't be squeezed through between the buildings. An old lady living in one of the cottages came out to see what was happening. And when the urgency of getting the lifeboat past was explained to her, she told them to knock down the outside wall of her home.

Dawn was breaking as, after ten and a half hours of hauling, the lifeboat at last reached the beach at Porlock. The crew didn't pause to eat or rest. They launched immediately through heavy surf; and a couple of hours later, thanks to the men and women of Lynmouth and Porlock, the water-logged casualty, the *Forest Hall*, was towed to safety.

There is one other way in which women have been involved in lifeboat work. Without their encouragement and support, few men would have been willing to crew the boats.

It can sometimes be harder to wait for a loved one who is risking his or her life than to put one's own life at risk; and it would be impossible to place too high a value on the debt the public owes to the mothers, daughters, sisters, wives and lovers of generations of lifeboatmen. These unknown and unsung women have not only had to suffer vicariously all the exhaustion, pain and danger endured by their men, they have sometimes had to pay a terrible price for their loyalty. It is said that for fifty years Mrs Margaret Armstrong never missed giving a helping hand at the launch of the Cresswell lifeboat, for she knew the importance of a quick get-away; in separate incidents involving the lifeboat, her father, her four brothers and her son had all been drowned.

A totally different role for women became possible after the events of 1891.

Charles Macara's Lifeboat Days and street collections gave the task of raising money for the RNLI a new impetus in a new direction. Charles's wife Marion was a dedicated aficionado of this new way of raising money; 'Great as was my enthusiasm,' Macara wrote, 'it did not exceed hers'. It was due largely to Marion Macara that Ladies' Auxiliary Committees were set up in Manchester and Salford to organize fundraising events, and it was not long before similar committees were at work in more than fifty towns all over the British Isles. These women fundraisers were precursors of the Institution's hundreds of thousands of supporters whose efforts today play an essential role in making the work of our lifeboats possible.

With its finances on a sound footing, and its 290 or so lifeboats efficient, seaworthy and in the process of being converted from sail to petrol engines, the Institution was in good heart in the early years of the twentieth century. But the golden age was not to last. In 1914 the lamps began to go out all over Europe.

Lifeboat Day in London, 1932. A picture showing the old style of model lifeboat collecting boxes.

The World Wars

The First World War

N o flashing beacons, no guiding marker buoys, not even a sliver of light where in a fisherman's cottage a curtain has been left undrawn. For it is October 1914, blackout is in force, and the east coast of England lies dark as a forest on a moonless night and bludgeoned by an east-north-easterly gale. It would have been difficult in peacetime to pilot a course that night through the North Sea's shallows and sandbars. In wartime it proves too much for the *Rohilla*. Without navigational aids and with visibility less than fifty yards, she gets too close to the shore and piles up on the reefs that jut out from Saltwick Nab, a little to the south-east of Whitby.

In one of the most difficult services ever carried out, lifeboats from five stations struggled for two and a half days to rescue over 200 survivors from the hospital ship *Rohilla*, October 1914.

Once a 7000-ton passenger liner on the run to India, the *Rohilla* has just been converted to a hospital ship. She is bound for Dunkirk where, it is hoped, she will embark wounded from the Western Front. There are 229 aboard her, nearly all of them crew or medical staff. Among the latter are five nurses, one of whom, Mary Roberts, knows all about the perils of the sea. She was a survivor from the *Titanic*, which had sunk a couple of years earlier with the loss of more than 1500 lives.

Within seconds of striking the rocks the *Rohilla* breaks in half, and those unlucky enough to be in her stern section, some sixty people, are swept away and drowned. For although the ship has gone aground only a quarter of a mile from the shore, the reefs off Saltwick Nab were, that night, a place of death: a maelstrom of white water in which no swimmer, and it would seem no boat, could live. The survivors huddle together on and around the bridge, and hope against hope for rescue.

At daybreak they are spotted by the people of Whitby, and one of the Institution's most difficult and hazardous operations gets under way.

There are two lifeboats at Whitby. With the wind still a full gale and, if anything, increasing, and huge waves piling up across the entrance to the harbour, there is no hope of launching the boats direct. However, Thomas Langlands, coxswain of the *John Fielden*, reckons they might be able to haul their lifeboat along the shore and launch her close to the reef. It seems a mission near-impossible. But with ropes, pulleys and some hundred helpers, the lifeboat is manhandled along the rocky foreshore and over an eight-foot sea wall, until she reaches a possible launch site. But at a cost. The *John Fielden* has been damaged: in two places actually stove in. However, she manages to launch. Her crew strain at their oars; and at times almost swamped by the weight of the water they take on board, and at other times crunching against the half-submerged rocks, they manage to come alongside the *Rohilla*. Seventeen survivors, including the five nurses, scramble aboard. The return journey is, to say the least, hazardous; and rather than risk another beach launch, Langlands offloads his survivors in the surf. They are dragged over the rocks to safety, and the lifeboat goes back for more. But by now the *John Fielden* is in a bad way. She manages once again to come alongside the *Rohilla* and take off another eighteen, but is flung against the side of the hospital ship and badly holed. She limps back, near-foundering, and her coxswain has no option but to let the waves drive her on to the rocky foreshore. The *John Fielden* is too badly damaged to help the hundred-odd men still stranded onboard the hospital ship.

But other rescuers are on their way. Next to arrive is the lifeboat from nearby

The Whitby lifeboat *John Fielden* and its coxswain Thomas Langlands played a major role in the *Rohilla* rescue, a long and difficult service for which three gold and five silver medals were awarded.

Upgang, the *William Riley*. She too has made a remarkable journey, being manoeuvred through the narrow streets of Whitby, dragged across the waterlogged fields, and finally lowered down a thirty-foot cliff. However, the weather has been worsening all this time; it will soon be dark, and the Upgang coxswain has little option but to make that most difficult of all decisions for a lifeboatman, the decision not to launch. His crew sleep fitfully, listening to the cacophony of the storm and thinking of the men still aboard the *Rohilla*. Conditions next morning are no better, but at dead low tide they attempt a rescue. They manage to launch, but can make little headway against the huge seas and an adverse current. For all their strength, fine oarsmanship and courage they can't get near the *Rohilla*.

Meanwhile, telephone calls have alerted stations as far south as Scarborough and as far north as Teesmouth. The Scarborough lifeboat is towed out to sea by a steam tug. By the time she arrives off Saltwick Nab it is dark; she stands by all night in conditions described as 'hellish', but to no avail for next morning the huge seas, bludgeoning wind and scouring current prevent her, too, from reaching the wreck. Driven by oars alone, she has neither the power nor the manoeuvrability to effect a rescue. The Teesmouth lifeboat fares even worse; no sooner has she reached the open sea than she crashes into the trough of a huge wave, springs a leak, and has to be towed back to harbour.

Seeing the other boats have failed, the Upgang's *William Riley* makes yet another effort. By now the *Rohilla* has been aground for more than thirty-six hours; the storm shows no sign of abating, and there is real danger that the hospital ship will break up. The *William Riley* launches a little after nine a.m., again at dead low tide when, tradition has it, the waves momentarily slacken. But once more the rowers simply haven't the strength to make headway. They manage to get to within fifty yards of the wreck, only to be driven back. The sight of salvation so near and yet so far away is too much for some of the men aboard the *Rohilla*. More than fifty of them jump overboard in a desperate attempt either to reach the lifeboat or to swim ashore. Some are drowned but some, caught by the current, are swirled towards the land. The onlookers, by this time numbering more than a hundred, form a human chain; risking their lives, they wade into the surf and manage to haul a number of the swimmers to safety.

But there are still some forty or fifty men aboard the hospital ship, and with the weather showing no sign of improvement there seems little hope of saving them. Then, albeit belatedly, someone thinks of the motor lifeboat lying at anchor at Tynemouth, some forty-five miles to the north.

The petrol-driven *Henry Vernon* of Tynemouth. She succeeded in reaching the *Rohilla* after all efforts by sailing lifeboats had failed.

Within an hour of being asked to help, Tynemouth's *Henry Vernon* is at sea, heading into the twilight for Whitby. Soon it is dark. The waves are still high, there are no coastal lights or navigational aids, and the voyage calls for both skill and endurance. It is past midnight before the *Henry Vernon* drops anchor in Whitby harbour. Her crew have time for no more than a catnap. Then, by five a.m., they are on their way again, having taken aboard a senior Lifeboat Inspector from London, Commander Basil Hall, and a surprising quantity of oil.

An eye-witness records for the *Yorkshire Post* what happened next:

The light was just rising over the sea when I saw the boat creep out of harbour again ... Hastening to the top of the cliffs, I rejoined the crowd of watchers, who gazed with eager intensity as the lifeboat, looking fearfully small and frail, throbbed her way towards the wreck. Nearer and nearer she got; then, within 200 yards of the *Rohilla*, she turned away ... [apparently] unable to face the current and the curling seas. 'She'll never get there,' declared one of the watchers. But a burly fisherman remarked, 'Just wait; she knows what she's about.' Presently, she stopped dead and discharged over the boiling sea gallons and gallons of oil ... The effect was remarkable; within seconds, as the oil spread over the surface of the water

Near and yet so far. The wreck of the Rohilla, a newly converted hospital ship in the early days of the First World War. But some two hundred lives were saved over two and a half days in a rescue involving six lifeboats.

and was carried by the current towards the wreck, the waves appeared suddenly to be flattened down . . . The lifeboat turned about, raced at full speed outside the line of breakers then turned directly to the shore. The most dangerous moment came when she was inside the surf and broadside on to the waves; but guided with splendid skill and courage, she moved forward steadily, and a cheer of relief went out from the shore when she reached the lee of the wreck, immediately beneath the crowded bridge. The feelings of those on board as they saw salvation at hand can only be imagined. But there was not a moment to be lost, for already the effects of the oil were beginning to wear off . . . A rope was let down into the lifeboat, and immediately figures could be discerned scrambling down into the boat with a quickness and agility that seemed extraordinary in men one presumed to be exhausted almost to death. In less than a quarter of an hour more than forty men had been taken into the boat . . . Then two enormous waves were seen rolling up from the sea at tremendous speed. One after the other they swept over the bridge, and across each end of the remnants of the deck, into the lifeboat, enveloping it fore and aft. Each time the tough little craft disappeared for a moment beneath the spray, reappeared, tottered and righted herself gamely. Not a man was lost. Closer still she hugged the vessel's side till every man aboard had been hauled into the rescuing boat. The last man to leave was the captain, and as he slipped into the lifeboat the crew of the latter gave a rousing cheer that was echoed again and again by the people ashore.

The *Rohilla* rescue involved six lifeboats over a period of two and a half days; it resulted in the saving of some 200 lives, and the awarding of three gold and five silver medals. The official view was that it 'added another splendid page to the annals of heroism and humanity which make up the story of the Life-boat [Service]'. Certainly no one could doubt the courage and commitment of the lifeboat crews. However, a devil's advocate might argue that the *Rohilla* rescue also highlighted shortcomings in the Institution.

Why, one cannot help wondering, did it take so long to co-ordinate the various attempts at rescue? It was thirty-six hours before Commander Hall arrived from London to take charge of the operation. And why, in 1914, were motor lifeboats still regarded with such suspicion that thirty-six hours elapsed before the *Henry Vernon* was even considered?

Getting lifeboats to sea and co-ordinating their efforts at rescue is a complex business. On most occasions the first people to know about a casualty are the coastguards – in the old days, by sighting her; nowadays, by virtue of a Mayday call. The coastguards alert the honorary secretary of the nearest lifeboat station. The honorary secretary decides whether a launch is justified, and if in his opinion it is, he alerts the coxswain and crew. The coxswain then has the final say as to whether or not a lifeboat puts to sea. This rather cumbersome procedure works well enough today thanks to the introduction of what is arguably the most sophisticated paging system in the world. However, in the early twentieth century communication was a problem. Telephones were not yet wholly reliable, wartime restrictions had to be complied with, and those on land were unable to speak directly to those at sea – it was not until

Medals proudly worn: an RNLI coxwain displaying his medals awarded for his service during World War I.

1929 that radiotelephones were installed in lifeboats. With so many links in the chain of rescue, delays and misunderstandings were inevitable, and a better system of communication was a sine qua non of a better lifeboat service.

The failure to make immediate use of the *Henry Vernon* brings to light another problem: the tendency of many lifeboat personnel to prefer the old to the new. In the late nineteenth and early twentieth centuries Britannia really did rule the waves. The ships of the Royal Navy guarded the strategic nerve-centres of empire; the ships of the merchant navy plied the trade routes that were the arteries of empire; and the ships of the RNLI provided a service to seafarers unequalled anywhere in the world. It was perhaps inevitable that such a satisfactory state of affairs should lead to a touch of complacency and a reluctance to appreciate the need for change. As evidence of this, as late as 1934 lifeboats were still launching from horse-drawn carriages (from Wells in Norfolk); as late as 1948 sailing lifeboats were still in operational service (at New Quay in Cardiganshire); and as late as 1957 lifeboat crews were still saying that they preferred oar-driven lifeboats to those with engines (at Whitby in Yorkshire).

This tendency to cling to the old and well tried was accentuated by the restrictions imposed during two World Wars. The First World War was a difficult time for the Institution. Operations were hampered by the laying of minefields, the removal of navigational aids and the extinguishing of coastal lights. The RNLI's traditional allies, the coastguards, suffered an inevitable decline in efficiency when more than seventy per cent of their workforce joined the services. Many younger lifeboatmen also joined up, and by 1916 the average age of a lifeboat crew had increased to over fifty – indeed some crewmen were over seventy. The Institution's annual income declined, because fundraising other than for the forces was declared illegal. And perhaps most serious of all, the modernizing of the fleet suffered a major setback, for the badly needed petrol engines were diverted to the services, and the Institution's rebuilding programme ground to a virtual halt. In spite of these difficulties more lives were saved during the war years than ever before. The annual reports give details.

In 1914 lifeboats were launched 426 times. They saved fifty ships and 1112 lives. For this, three gold and thirteen silver medals were awarded. Twenty-four new lifeboats were reported to be under construction, but no more than five (of which only one was a motor boat) were actually built. The Institution's annual income fell by £11,000. There was one major disaster. The Fethard self-righting lifeboat *Helen Blake* capsized in heavy seas while going to the aid of a Norwegian schooner aground on a tiny island off the coast of County Wexford; nine of her crew were drowned. This was another service in which no one could question the gallantry of the crews. However, there was a delay of forty-eight hours before a Chief Inspector of Lifeboats arrived to co-ordinate the attempted rescues. The crew of the schooner and the survivors from the *Helen Blake* were therefore stranded on the island for three days, during which, we are told, 'all they had to eat were two small tins of preserved meat and a few limpets; their only drink was a small quantity of brandy and a half pint of wine which the Captain had. With no shelter, they were exposed to a biting wind and were drenched by rain and spray. One of the crew, a Portuguese, died from exposure.'

In 1915 lifeboats were launched 441 times. They saved sixty-one vessels and 832 lives. For this four silver medals were awarded. During the year twenty-one new boats were reported to be under construction, but only six (of which two were motor boats) were completed. The Institution's annual income rose slightly. Perhaps surprisingly, there were only two fatal accidents to lifeboatmen. On 17 February the Worthing lifeboat capsized; she at once self-righted, but one of her crew was swept away and drowned. A few months later, the Bridlington lifeboat was launching to go to the aid of a minesweeper when 'she was lifted off her carriage by a tremendous sea which also washed the horses off their feet. In the pitchy darkness and terrific gale, two of the horses sank into the shifting sands and were drowned, one of them dragging with it its rider, Robert Carr.'

In 1916 lifeboats were launched 385 times, and saved thirty-three ships and 1301 lives – at the time, the largest ever annual total. For this twenty-one silver medals were awarded. Thirteen lifeboats were said to be under construction, but only three (and none of them a motor boat) were completed. The Institution voiced 'grave concern' over the government restrictions that prevented the building of its motor lifeboats. It pointed out that even more lives could have been saved if these powerful boats had been available, and promised that 'no effort will be wanting . . . to ensure at least the completion of the very important Motor boats which have been so long under construction'. The Institution's annual income showed a marginal increase. There were two serious lifeboat disasters. Early in January the Port Eynon lifeboat capsized going to the aid of the s.s. *Dunvegan*; although she quickly self-righted, three of her crew were swept away and drowned. In the autumn the Salcombe lifeboat, the *William and Emma*, was returning to harbour after giving assistance to a ship in diffi-culties off Bolt Head. 'Just as [she] reached the terribly dangerous waters over the bar, she was struck on the quarter by a huge wave, and, before she could be got under control, a following wave lifted the stern in the air and turned the boat clean over. Thirteen of the crew of fifteen were drowned.' The bar at Salcombe is thought to be the inspiration for Tennyson's well known poem:

> Sunset and evening star
> > And one clear call for me.
> And may there be no moaning at the bar
> > When I put out to sea.

The Salcombe lifeboat *William and Emma* capsized in 1916 while crossing the bar at the mouth of Kingsbridge estuary. Of her fifteen-strong crew, thirteen were drowned.

In 1917 lifeboats were launched 364 times. They saved twenty-one ships and 1348 lives. One gold, ten silver and sixteen bronze medals were awarded. This was the first time bronze medals were given officially, the committee wanting 'to enable a brave and skilful Life-boatman [whose rescue work did not quite merit a silver] to be able to point to some tangible proof that he has taken part in a service of exceptional merit'. During the year the Institution's annual income showed a modest increase, from £146,000 to £150,000. More than a dozen lifeboats were said to be under construction, but only one was launched. By this time the Institution was seriously at odds with the government over the latter's continuing refusal to free men and materials to install engines into the half-built lifeboats. In its annual report the committee 'deplored the fact that these splendid [motor] boats, which could have been completed two-and-a-half years ago, are still lying incomplete [because] their engines have not been finished'. The committee pointed out that thousands of tons of shipping and hundreds of lives had been lost, 'all for the lack of a few fitters'. They therefore decided to take the calculated risk of authorizing the use of ordinary everyday motor boats at a number of selected stations. Such makeshift rescue boats would obviously be nothing like as safe as bona fide lifeboats, but in moderate weather they would at least have a chance of getting to casualties.

In 1918 lifeboats were launched 250 times. They saved twenty-six ships and 852 lives. For this six silver and six bronze medals were awarded. Annual income rose to £181,000, thanks mainly to the lifting of the ban on fundraising and the revival of Lifeboat Days. The saga of the motor boats dragged on. Twelve were said to be under construction, but only one was launched, and the committee again felt obliged to 'deplore the fact that the majority of these [motor boats] are still lying incomplete after four and a half years of war, owing to the fact that it was not possible to obtain the few fitters needed to complete the engines'. Reading between the lines, it would seem that there was, to say the least, a lack of co-operation between the Institution and the chiefs of staff. However, the makeshift motor boats managed to save seventy-seven lives, a figure which, the committee were quick to point out, would have been far higher had their purpose-built boats been available.

In spite of these difficulties, the Institution had a war record of which it could be proud. Its boats were launched 1702 times; they saved 173 ships and 5032 lives. This was achieved at a cost of four lifeboats lost and twenty-two seriously damaged; twenty-one lifeboatmen were drowned. Two typical wartime rescues were carried out by lifeboats from Lowestoft and Crail.

In September 1918, the sloop *Pomona* went aground off the coast of Suffolk, and the Lowestoft lifeboat *Kentwell* went to her aid. The weather was foul: a full gale from the north-east with waves twenty feet high. Within hours the *Pomona* had broken up, but not before her ship's company had been rescued by the *Kentwell* after five hours of service that would have taxed a crew who were young and fit. And the crew of the *Kentwell*, with due respect, were neither. Records tell us that four were over fifty, twelve were over sixty, and two were over seventy. To quote an eye-witness, it was 'a

most impressive sight to see these old men, greyhaired and bent . . . and afflicted with the attendant ills of old age, struggling in the darkness against the wind and the rain, without a moment's thought of the dangers they had to face'. All round the British Isles, throughout the war, this sort of rescue was being carried out by men who today would be classed as pensioners. In their 1918 report the Institution acknowledged the debt owed to these 'heroic veterans', who stepped into the breach when their younger colleagues joined the services.

The Lowestoft lifeboat *Kentwell*. In World War II, with a crew whose average age was over sixty, she carried out many successful rescues off the coast of East Anglia.

In December 1914 the destroyer HMS *Success* went aground on the Carr reef off the coast of Fife, and the Crail lifeboat went to her aid. Crail was typical of the many small stations that did sterling work in the late nineteenth and early twentieth centuries, but then had to be closed. It had opened in 1884 with the launching of the thirty-four-foot *George Patterson* – a ceremony attended, we are told, by over 2000 people, and 'enlivened by the Anstruther Volunteer Band, Freemasons in full regalia, and the ploughmen of the district' (horses still being used for the majority of beach launches). In 1910 the *George Patterson* was replaced by the *Edwin Kay*, a lifeboat of much the same size but with a drop keel and automatic ballast tanks, and it was the *Kay* that now went to help the destroyer.

The lifeboat launched a little after dawn on 27 December. The wind was forty to fifty knots, and huge waves were thundering over the Carr reef, 'an area where storm and sea often play havoc with ships seeking entrance to the Forth and Tay estuaries'. The *Kay*'s coxswain, Andrew Cunningham, handled his boat with great skill, but was unable to prevent her being holed on the underwater rocks at the approaches to the reef. Her crew were assessing the damage when the lifeboat was swamped by a huge wave, and Cunningham and one of his men were washed overboard. They were saved by the fact that they were wearing lifejackets and were attached to lifelines. The rest of the crew managed to haul them back on board, and with great aplomb they continued with the rescue. In spite of the high wind, the heavy seas, and the absence of coastal lights or marker buoys, Cunningham managed to find the *Success* and manoeuvre alongside her. Twenty of the destroyer's crew scrambled into the lifeboat and were put ashore at the foot of the cliffs at Kingsbarns. The *Kay* then made two more trips to the destroyer and took off a further thirty-four men. Cunningham was wondering if his holed and battered lifeboat would survive a fourth attempt at rescue when 'his dilemma was resolved by the appearance of the Saint Andrews lifeboat, which plucked the remaining 13 men from the destroyer and landed them safely'.

The Crail lifeboat carried out a further twelve rescues off the coast of Fife. Then in 1923 the station was closed. For some forty years a lifeboat had been part and parcel of everyday life in Crail and, as in many other towns and villages, an enormous rapport had grown up between boat and town. However, the postwar trend was to reduce the number of lifeboats in the Institution's fleet and increase their size. Soon, all round the British Isles, small sailing and pulling boats such as the *Edwin Kay* were being superseded by larger and more effective motor lifeboats. The latter could carry more survivors; they were more manoeuvrable; they were faster; and, above all, they had a far wider and more flexible operating range, being able to reach vessels in distress even when wind, wave, tide and current were against them.

The Table below shows how, between the beginning of the First World War and the end of the Second World War, the old sailing and pulling lifeboats were replaced at virtually every station by motor lifeboats.

RNLI fleet in First World War

1914 (As at 31.12.14)		1918 (As at 31.12.18)	
Sailing and pulling boats	245	Sailing and pulling boats	233
Steam lifeboats	4	Steam lifeboats	3
Motor lifeboats	17	Motor lifeboats	20
	266		256

RNLI fleet in Second World War

1939 (As at 31.12.39)		1945 (As at 31.12.45)	
Sailing and pulling boats	15	Sailing and pulling boats	3
Motor lifeboats	145	Motor lifeboats	151
	160		154

By the end of the Second World War the sight of grizzled oarsmen digging their blades deep into incoming rollers had been consigned to the past. But their image and their tradition of service lived on.

The Second World War

They are handed gas masks and tin helmets. Their lifeboat, the *Prudential* of Ramsgate, is loaded with cans of water for the troops, and they head into the night for Dunkirk. An eye-witness wrote:

> Even before it was fully dark we had picked up the glow of the flames and could see the shapes of other ships coming home already fully loaded . . . Then aircraft started dropping parachute flares. We saw them hanging all about us in the night, like young moons. The sound of the firing and the bombing was with us always, growing steadily louder as we got nearer . . . [We found] the place a shambles of old wrecks – British and French – and all kinds of odds and ends, and the beach black with men, illuminated by the fires. The din was infernal: the whistle of shells overhead, the scream of falling bombs . . . the angry hornet noise of dive bombers.

Charles Cundall 1940

The water is too shallow for *Prudential* to get close to the beaches. She has therefore to stand off, about a quarter of a mile from the shore. A string of flat-bottomed wherries is then used to take the cans of water ashore and to bring troops to the waiting lifeboat. Soon some 150 combat-weary men have been first helped into the lifeboat, then ferried offshore and transferred to a waiting destroyer. All that night and all next day the evacuation continues, with *Prudential* under frequent attack from the air, until this one lifeboat has rescued 2800 men. Then, out of the darkness – or so the story goes – a voice hails her: 'I can't see who you are. Are you a naval party?' 'No, sir,' *Prudential* replies, 'we're the crew of the Ramsgate lifeboat.' 'Thank you,' the voice calls back. 'And thank God for such men as you have proved yourselves to be. There's a party of fifty Highlanders coming next' – words that today sound so stilted, one is left with the unworthy suspicion that the story may be apocryphal. Be that as it may, after almost forty hours' continuous rescue work *Prudential* and her exhausted crew limp back to Ramsgate.

The Margate lifeboat, the *Lord Southborough*, plays an equally heroic role. She arrives off the beaches at Nieuport (a few miles east of Dunkirk) on the night of 30 May. She edges inshore as close as she can, so close that her keel is continually bumping along the sandy bottom. After a while she hears voices calling to her out of the darkness, and soon French soldiers come wading out to her. They are helped aboard. When the lifeboat is full, the soldiers are transferred to a waiting barge, and the barge is then towed out to a destroyer waiting about half a mile offshore. Hour after hour men are taken off the beaches, until the crew of the *Lord Southborough* have lost count of the number of journeys they make. 'It was', writes their coxswain, 'very heavy work dragging out soaked and exhausted men, but we kept at it until the weather worsened.' By evening, the wind has risen and fair-sized waves are pounding the shore. A whaler and a pinnace working alongside the lifeboat are swamped. As darkness falls, men are still streaming down to the beaches, but the *Lord Southborough* is the only rescue boat still afloat. Troops keep trying to wade out to her, but the waves knock them down and suck them under; many, in their heavy combat gear, are drowned. Unable to get closer inshore, the lifeboat has no option but to leave them. In the small hours of the morning

An artist's impression of the evacuation from Dunkirk. Reproduced in the *Illustrated London News*, 8 June 1940.

she heads for home. On the way she takes in tow a near-foundering naval whaler manned by seventeen exhausted seamen, sole survivors from a ship's company of 150 who have been helping people off the beaches for the last three days. After twenty-one hours at sea the *Lord Southborough* returns to Margate. The commander of the destroyer *Icarus*, who worked beside her that day off the beaches, writes: 'The magnificent behaviour of the crew of the Margate lifeboat, who, with no thought of rest, brought off load after load of soldiers under continuous shelling, bombing and aerial machine-gun fire, will be an inspiration to us all as long as we live'.

This is how we like to think of Dunkirk: brave men fashioning victory out of defeat. However, there is another way of looking at things: 337,000 Allied troops may have been rescued, but over 80,000 have to be left behind and are captured. Although Dunkirk proves less of a disaster than it might have been, it is nonetheless a defeat. And not all those who are asked to help with the evacuation turn out to be heroes.

At one fifteen p.m. on Thursday, 30 May, the Ministry of Shipping telephones the Lifeboat Institution and asks them to send as many lifeboats as possible as quickly as possible to Dover. The lifeboat crews don't have to be clairvoyant to realize they are going to be asked to help with an evacuation. Many come equipped with tin hats, towing ropes, provisions and extra fuel. But they, better than most, realize the magnitude of the task ahead. For the flat sandy beaches between Dunkirk and Nieuport are not a good place from which to evacuate an army. There is little cover; the inshore waters are shallow, and it is impossible for vessels with any sort of draught to haul up on the beaches.

While the Ramsgate and Margate boats go direct to France, another seventeen lifeboats, some from as far west as Poole and as far north as Lowestoft, assemble at Dover. One of the first to get there is the *Viscountess Wakefield* from Hythe. Her coxswain is told by the Navy that he should run his boat on to the Dunkirk beaches, load up with troops and bring them back to England. He rightly points out that this is asking the impossible, because the water is known to be too shallow for his heavy fifteen-ton lifeboat to reach the shore. This problem would almost certainly have been sorted out if the Hythe coxswain hadn't gone on to press for an assurance that if any lifeboatmen were killed during the evacuation their families would get pensions. And he insisted that this was put in writing.

The Navy, facing a crisis in which every minute counts and hundreds of thousands of lives are at stake, are not amused. They see the Hythe coxswain as a troublesome 'sea lawyer'; he and the coxswains from Walmer and Dungeness who support him are sent packing and their boats are appropriated. Worse is to come. In his book *Storm over the Waters*, Charles Vince puts the position very clearly: 'The harassed and overburdened Naval officers at Dover were organizing, in the heat and pressure of events, a complicated and perilous operation. They wanted boats. They wanted men. They wanted no more argument.' When the other lifeboats arrive at Dover, the Navy, afraid that their crews may be equally obstructive, commandeer them, and send them to the beaches manned by RN and RNVR crews.

Over the next few days these lifeboats and their stand-in crews save thousands of lives. They are shelled, bombed, strafed, rammed, capsized and grounded. Almost all are damaged, but only one is sunk. The *Viscountess Wakefield* is last seen aground on the sands at La Panne. As her coxswain prophesied, she is hopelessly stranded, unable to get afloat.

Two facts are beyond dispute. The lifeboats did magnificent work at Dunkirk. But if they had been manned by RNLI crews they would have achieved even more.

Many of the problems the RNLI had to face in the Second World War were similar to those they had faced in the First World War: a reduction of income; the loss of their younger crews; the removal in coastal waters of navigational lights and aids; restrictions in the use of telecommunications; and the danger from enemy aircraft, motor torpedoboats and mines. But one problem they were spared. In 1914 their fleet had been in urgent need of modernization, about to make the changeover from sail to petrol-driven engines; this vital work had had to be put on hold for the duration. In 1939 the fleet was in far better shape. It had been modernized. Some lifeboats, it is true, were about to make

The Eastbourne lifeboat *Jane Holland*. Badly damaged while evacuating troops from Dunkirk, she was later salvaged by the Royal Navy and returned to the RNLI.

the transition from petrol to diesel; but this was a relatively minor improvement and, generally speaking, lifeboats in the Second World War were strong enough and powerful enough to meet the demands made of them.

And how varied these demands were. Lifeboats not only went to the aid of ships that had been wrecked, mined, torpedoed or bombed. They towed to safety vessels loaded with explosives; they dealt with mines; they rescued aircrew (both British and German); they ferried food to remote islands where people had been cut off by storms, and to remote villages cut off by snow; they brought doctors to the injured and priests to the dying. All told, and exclusive of Dunkirk, they saved 6376 lives. Each year of the war saw a different type of service.

On 26 November 1939 an unusual rescue took place in the middle of a minefield. The Naval trawler *Blackburn Rovers* was on antisubmarine patrol off Dover when her propeller fouled drifting wire. Her crew let go their anchor, but in the high wind and heavy seas it failed to hold and the disabled trawler started to drift into a minefield.

Her call for help was answered by the Dover lifeboat *Sir William Hillary*, which put to sea a little after ten a.m. Aboard her was the assistant harbourmaster, Richard Walker, who had with him a chart showing the positions of minefields. When, in worsening weather, the lifeboat found the *Blackburn Rovers*, the trawler was already on the edge of a minefield and drifting farther into it. Aboard the trawler was top secret equipment, including experimental Asdic; and rather than risk her being disabled by a mine and possibly captured, it was decided to transfer her papers and sensitive equipment to the lifeboat, then scuttle her. The service that followed would have been difficult in any case, for the trawler was rolling violently, with huge seas breaking over her, and the lifeboat coxswain, Colin Bryant, needed all his skill to hold the two vessels close together. An added danger was that while the transfer was taking place, lifeboat and trawler drifted ever deeper into the minefield and were likely any moment to be blown to kingdom come. It would have been easy to have done a rush job and run for safety. But the *Sir William Hillary* spent more than an hour alongside the trawler, and did not leave her until every member of the crew and every piece of even remotely sensitive equipment had been taken off. Only then did the lifeboat edge cautiously out of the minefield and set course for home. By now the weather had deteriorated still further. Although the *Sir William Hillary* reduced speed, she was almost swamped by mountainous waves, and it took her three hours to cover the fifteen or so miles to Dover. For this rescue her coxswain Colin Bryant was awarded a silver medal; bronze medals were awarded to Richard Walker and three of the crew.

In 1940 the skies over the English Channel were the backdrop for the Battle of Britain. Hundreds of aircrew, both RAF and Luftwaffe, ended up in the sea, and lifeboats often played a major role in saving their lives. A typical rescue took place on the morning of 3 September. The official report reads:

> About 10.15 a.m. a Telephone message was received by the [Margate] Coxswain from the Coastguard Station saying a Parachutist was down in the sea 7 miles N.E. Reculver. The lifeboat was at once launched and proceeded to the position given. A very extensive search was made, visibility being bad, and at 11.45 a.m. the airman was found 3½ miles NNW of Reculver. He was very badly burned (most of his clothes having caught fire), and on the point of collapse. He was at once taken aboard, and with the help of the Hon. Sec. bandaged and made comfortable. Owing to his state the Hon. Sec. administered Brandy, with wonderful results . . . After a journey at full speed the Lifeboat arrived at the Stone Pier at 1 p.m, and the Airman [was] handed over to the Doctor and officials.

All this is confirmed by the pilot himself, who later wrote:

> I remember as in a dream hearing somebody shout: it seemed so far away and quite unconnected with me . . . Then willing arms were dragging me over the side; my parachute was taken off; a brandy flask was pushed between my swollen lips; a voice said, 'O.K., Joe, it's one of ours and still kicking'; and I was safe. I was neither relieved nor angry; I was past caring. It was to the Margate lifeboat that I owed my rescue. Watchers on the coast had seen me come down, and for three hours they had been searching for me. They were just giving up and turning back for land when one of them saw my parachute. They were then fifteen miles east of Margate.

What gives this overtly routine rescue a touch of piquancy is that the name of the rescued airman was Pilot Officer Richard Hillary, whose posthumously published *The Last Enemy* is one of the classic books of the Second World War. It was suggested at the time, and has been claimed as fact ever since, that Pilot Officer Hillary was a descendant of the RNLI founder Sir William Hillary. This is a good story, given substance by the fact that the two men seem to have been uncommonly alike: both had a touch of arrogance and almost unbelievable courage. However, if Richard had been a direct descendant of Sir William he would have inherited his

ABOVE Spitfire pilot Richard Hillary. After being shot down in flames over the English Channel, he was rescued by the Margate lifeboat.

RIGHT The dramatic rescue of a Second World War pilot.

title, and it would seem that all Sir William's indirect descendants died without issue. There is also the not unimportant fact that Richard Hillary's father disclaimed any family connection. (A letter dated 9 April 1965 to the RNLI's public relations officer reads: 'Pilot Officer Hillary's father told me yesterday, when I saw him for a chat, that as far as he knew there was no connection between his family and the founder'.) So although the story is a good and often repeated one, it may be apocryphal.

A rescue in the North Sea in 1941 highlights another aspect of lifeboat work, taking damaged vessels in tow. During the night of 27 March the Glasgow-built s.s. *Somali* was damaged by enemy action and set on fire. Her crew were rescued, a sal-

vage tug took her in tow, and the Boulmer and North Sunderland lifeboats stood by. A little before midday it was decided to transfer the tow. Three men were therefore put aboard the still burning *Somali* (one was subsequently taken off). The transfer was about to get under way, and the Boulmer lifeboat the *Clarissa Langdon* was approaching the *Somali* with a hawser, when there was a terrific explosion, 'and the whole blazing forepart of the steamer blew up'. We are told that although the *Clarissa Langdon* was seventy yards away, the force of the explosion 'lifted the boat clean out of the sea . . . It knocked the crew flat on their faces, and whirled away their caps. It broke windows in a village five miles away.' In the moment of silence that followed the explosion burning fragments of wood and metal showered down on the lifeboat, injuring the bowman. Although the coxswain knew there might at any moment be another explosion, he drove the lifeboat through the fumes, smoke and floating debris, and brought her alongside. The two men, one of them injured, threw a rope over the stern, slid down it and plummeted into the sea. The *Clarissa Langdon* picked them up. She was about to make a quick getaway, when her propeller fouled in the floating wreckage and she shuddered to a halt, still alongside the blazing *Somali*. It was as well the North Sunderland lifeboat saw what had happened, came in at full speed and towed her colleague to safety. For this rescue the Boulmer coxswain James Campbell was awarded a bronze medal.

A series of rescues off the east coast of Scotland in 1942 provides evidence that not all wartime services stemmed from enemy action. The elemental forces of wind and wave still took their toll of shipping.

In the small hours of Friday, 23 January, in worsening conditions, two Whitby steamers, the *Runswick* and the *Saltwick*, collided at the approaches to Peterhead Bay. The Peterhead lifeboat, the *Julia Park Barry of Glasgow*, went to their aid and escorted them into the comparative safety of the bay. Here they were joined by a third merchant-

The Peterhead lifeboat, *Julia Park Barry of Glasgow* in high seas and a snowstorm, goes to the aid of the *Fidra*, *Runswick* and *Saltwick*.

man, the s.s. *Fidra*; she too was seeking shelter from what was already a gale and was soon to become a hurricane. The crew of the lifeboat had only a few hours' rest before they were called out again. The *Runswick* had dragged her anchors and been driven ashore. In spite of the darkness and the squalls of snow, Coxswain John McLean found the grounded vessel and managed to manoeuvre alongside her. Lines were passed from ship to ship and, 'in very difficult conditions', the crew of forty-four were taken off and landed safely ashore. Again the crew of the lifeboat had only a short rest before they were called out for the third time. The wind by now was blowing directly into the bay and gusting to over 100 miles per hour; huge seas had demolished part of the harbour breakwater, and *Saltwick* and *Fidra* had been driven on to the rocky foreshore. Edward Wake-Walker in his *Gold Medal Rescues* tells us what happened next:

> The *Fidra*... was about to break up in the mountainous seas. She lay head on to the weather, providing no lee for the lifeboat. Coxswain McLean risked all as he turned head to sea and ran alongside the casualty. Only because of his extraordinary seamanship was he able to keep the boat there for 50 minutes while 26 men chose their moment to leap to safety. They were scarcely ashore when the plight of the men on the *Saltwick* became [equally] desperate. Their ship was now lying over on her starboard side on the beach, with seas breaking right over her. This time the coxswain's only approach to the casualty was between her and the shore. First a wave deposited the lifeboat upon some rocks, then another nearly washed every lifeboatman overboard. But he made it to the sheltered side of the wreck in spite of a severely damaged boat, and 36 survivors were helped on board.

They were brought safely ashore, by which time the lifeboat crew had been standing by for fifty-four hours. They had put to sea three times, twice in pitch darkness and heavy snow. They were soaked to the skin, numb with cold, and so physically exhausted they had to be helped out of their lifeboat. They had saved 106 lives. For these outstanding rescues the coxswain John McLean was awarded a gold medal; the mechanic David Wiseman was awarded a silver and the rest of the Peterhead crew a bronze.

In 1943, two rescues by the St David's *Swyn-y-Mor* indicate what a variety of tasks lifeboats were called on to perform.

On the night of 28 February a man was reported to have been trapped by the rising tide at the foot of the cliffs near Llanunnas, Solva. It was pitch dark, and wartime restrictions precluded the use of lights. The St David's Watson class motor lifeboat *Swyn-y-Mor* launched a little after ten thirty, and an hour later arrived at the bottom of the 200-foot cliffs. The offshore waters near Solva are shallow and strewn with rocks. The *Swyn-y-Mor* therefore dropped anchor some 500 yards out to sea, and the second coxswain and one of the crew rowed ashore in their boarding boat. They spotted the man on a narrow ledge about forty feet up, unable to move either up or down. It looked impossible to reach him from below. However, one of the crew, Gwillym Davies, who was something of a rock climber, volunteered to scale the cliffs farther along the coast and try to get to the man from above. By this time the coastguards had also been alerted, and when Davies got to the top of the cliffs he found them searching for the trapped man. The coastguards had with them their life-saving apparatus, and

In a ninety miles per hour hurricane, coxswain William Gammon takes the Mumbles lifeboat, *Edward, Prince of Wales* over Port Talbot bar to rescue the crew of the Canadian frigate *Chebogue*, 11 October 1944.

this was used to lower Davies down the near-vertical face of the cliffs. He reached the man, helped him into the lifelines, and they were lowered together to the shore. From there they were picked up, uninjured, and taken to safety by the lifeboat.

A couple of months later the *Swyn-y-Mor* was called out on a very different type of service. Two tank landing craft were caught by an unexpected storm off St Ann's Head, close to the south-west tip of Pembrokeshire. Aboard them were eighty seamen and marines. Tugs from Milford Haven went to their aid and tried to take the unwieldy vessels in tow, but in the gale-force winds and heavy seas the tow ropes parted, and first one tank landing craft and then the other capsized and sank. It was ten p.m. before the St David's lifeboat was alerted. She launched immediately and set out into the darkness through waters known to have been heavily mined. To quote the official report:

> It was one in the morning before she reached the scene. She knew she was there by the strong smell of oil from the sunk craft and the smoother seas. She heard a shout, and in the beam of a searchlight turned on from a naval vessel, saw a man swimming towards her. He was covered with oil, and as the lifeboatmen lifted him aboard he collapsed. He was the last alive. The lifeboat cruised about all night, but found no more. As dawn was breaking, she saw a floating mine, right in front of her and only a few yards away. She managed to steer clear of it just in time . . . and returned to station at 8.30 a.m.

Of the eighty men aboard the tank landing craft, seventy-two had drowned – an incident that underlines the fact that not all lifeboat services are successful, especially when there is a delay in calling for help.

A rescue off Swansea in 1944 was not only dramatic in itself, but epitomized the work of lifeboats in the Second World War.

The drama began in mid Atlantic, when the Canadian frigate *Chebogue* was torpedoed by a U-boat. Part of her stern was blown away, and she suffered heavy casualties. However, she remained afloat, and was taken in tow by a succession of vessels and helped back to the British Isles. On 11 October she limped into Swansea Bay and dropped anchor only a couple of hundred yards from the shore. Her crew must have thought their troubles were over. But they were wrong. For that evening the weather took a dramatic turn for the worse. Within a couple of hours the wind increased from a forty-knot gale to a seventy-knot hurricane, and the luckless *Chebogue* dragged her anchors and was swept across the bay and driven stern-first on to Port Talbot bar. The local lifeboat, stationed at the Mumbles, was alerted. When her crew heard where the frigate had gone aground, nobody had much to say. Port Talbot bar in time of storm was known to be a place of death. In 1883 and again in 1903 Mumbles lifeboats had capsized there, and many lifeboatmen had been drowned; one of the crew now about to try to help the *Chebogue* was a survivor from the 1903 disaster. However, waiting for better weather was not an option the coxswain, William Gammon, considered. He ordered an immediate launch, and the *Edward Prince of Wales* headed seaward into darkness, driving squalls of sleet and hail, and enormous seas.

As they approached the bar, they saw that the *Chebogue* was impacted on to the rocks, with huge waves sweeping over her, and her plunging bow and anchor chains making it, to say the least, extremely hazardous to come alongside. Faintly, above the roar of the storm, they heard the frigate commander's cry: 'Can you take off all my men?' 'Yes,' Gammon shouted back. 'If they keep their heads.' Realizing there was only one hope of saving them, he drove the *Edward Prince of Wales* at full speed over the bar, circled the *Chebogue*, then ran down the seaward side of her. As he drew level with her forecastle, where the men were gathered, he tried for a moment to hold the lifeboat steady to give the crew the chance to leap into her. But what a perilous leap it was! Timing was literally a matter of life or death, and not everyone landed safely. One man broke a leg, another landed flush on top of the coxswain, another plummeted into the sea and was hauled aboard only seconds before the two vessels crashed together. For the lifeboat to have come alongside once was a fine piece of seamanship. Gammon did it again and again and again, with a handful of men on each occasion jumping into the lifeboat before it was swirled away. Not until the operation had been repeated twelve times were all forty-two of the frigate's crew transferred to the lifeboat. The return journey, with an overloaded boat and huge following seas, called for patience and skill, but in the small hours of the morning the Canadians were safely landed. Within fifteen minutes the *Edward Prince of Wales* was called out to another casualty.

For a crew in their physical prime the events of that night would have been a challenge. And the crew of the Mumbles lifeboat were some way past their prime. Their average age was over fifty-five; two were over sixty and two over seventy. One would have liked to think that with the end of the war these men might have enjoyed a happy retirement. But for many of them this was not the case. Only a couple of years later, on her way to help the s.s. *Samtampa* not far from Port Talbot bar, the Mumbles lifeboat was wrecked. There were no survivors.

Many lifeboatmen went through horrific experiences in the Second World War; a fair number were killed, and a great deal of damage was done to lifeboats and lifeboat stations. Yet the Second World War was in many ways an easier time for the Institution than the First World War had been. In the 1914–18 war there had been a sharp divide between services and civilians; everything had gone to the former, and the latter, including the RNLI, had been considered of little importance. In the 1939–45 war there was no such divide; civilians suffered too; there was a greater awareness of the meaning of war, a greater feeling of everyone being in it together, and a greater understanding of the valuable role that lifeboats were playing in helping to win the war. Between 1914 and 1918 the size and effectiveness of the RNLI fleet diminished. Between 1939 and 1945 it increased.

From

petrol to diesel

t is Monday, 10 February 1936, and the gale that has been lashing the coast of County Cork for twenty-four hours has increased to a hurricane. Huge waves are pounding the shore, tossing spray over the top of the lighthouse that stands at the approaches to the harbour. The lighthouse is 196 feet high. Slates are being torn off the roofs of houses, and people rash enough to venture into the open are knocked off their feet. Not within living memory have the people of Ballycotton known such terrible conditions.

The lifeboat crew have spent most of the night trying to secure the boats in Ballycotton harbour. It is dangerous work, 'with huge seas surging over the breakwater, and stones a ton in weight being torn from the quay and flung about like sugar lumps'. Early on Tuesday morning the local lifeboat secretary, Robert Mahony, gets the message he has been dreading. A vessel is in distress. The Daunt Rock lightship, usually anchored some dozen miles off the tip of Ballycotton Bay, has been torn from her moorings and is drifting ashore.

The crew of the Ballycotton lifeboat, *Mary Stanford*, coxswain Patrick Sliney, hail the Daunt Rock lightship. The lightship has been torn from her moorings in a hurricane, but her crew are reluctant to be taken off, knowing that an abandoned lightship will be a danger to shipping.

Robert Mahony tells us what happened next:

I gave the coxswain the message, and he made no reply. Seas were breaking over the lifeboat house. I did not believe it was possible for the coxswain even to get aboard the lifeboat. I was afraid to order him out. He left me and went down to the harbour. I followed a little later. To my amazement the lifeboat was already at the harbour mouth, heading out between the piers. The coxswain had not waited for orders. His crew were already at the harbour. He had not fired the maroons, for he did not want to alarm the village. Without a word they had slipped away . . . As I watched the lifeboat, I thought every minute she must turn back. One moment a sea crashed on her, the next she was standing on her head. But she went on. People watching her left the quay to go to the church to pray.

The coxswain takes his boat, the Barnett class *Mary Stanford*, through the sound between the two little islands off the west horn of

Ballycotton Bay. The seas are terrifying. Huge waves continually sweep over the lifeboat, knocking the crew off their feet and bludgeoning them near-insensible. After each wave has passed, the coxswain, Patrick Sliney, counts his men. Visibility, in the sleet and spray, is not good, often no more than fifty yards, and after searching in vain for the lightship for some two hours, Sliney decides to put in to the nearby port of Queenstown to see if anyone there has an exact position for her. The coastguards at Queenstown are able to help; and a little before midday the lifeboat, with new information, resumes her search. Almost at once she locates the lightship. The luckless vessel has drifted to the south-east of the Daunt Rock, but has managed to drop anchor about a half a mile from shore. One might have thought that a rescue would now be set in motion. But in fact, the work of the Ballycotton lifeboat has barely begun.

The crew of the lightship know that if their vessel is left abandoned and out of position, she will be a serious danger to shipping. They are reluctant to leave her. However, they are very much afraid that in the hurricane-force winds and heavy seas their anchors may not hold and they are likely to be swept to destruction on the nearby shore. So they ask the lifeboat to stand by.

And stand by the *Mary Stanford* does. Almost continuously. For seventy-two hours.

On the first day of her vigil she has company. The destroyer HMS *Tenedos* is also keeping an eye on the casualty, and both rescue vessels do their best to take the lightship in tow. But in the huge seas and violent winds every towline parts, and as darkness falls even attempting a tow becomes out of the question. The destroyer captain offers to stand by for the night, so that the *Mary Stanford* can return to Queenstown to refuel, pick up new towlines and drogues, and give her crew the chance of a change of clothes and something to eat. That night Sliney and his men catnap aboard the lifeboat in harbour, ready, if needed, to put to sea immediately. Dawn sees them heading again for the lightship.

On the second day of their service they keep watch alone. For the destroyer has to leave soon after daybreak, and although a vessel belonging to the Commission of Irish Lights is expected, she fails to materialize. The wind by now has moderated a little. Not so the sea. Huge waves are still surging out of the south-west, each threatening to engulf the lifeboat and dislodge the lightship's anchors. But *Mary Stanford* remains close to the casualty all that day, leaving her only occasionally to warn approaching vessels that her lights are out of position. The weather forecast that evening is bad. And the lightship asks Sliney if he will continue to stand by throughout the night. It is a cri de coeur few coxswains would refuse.

However, by dawn on the third day, the crew of the *Mary Stanford* are near the end of their tether. They have been at sea, in terrible conditions, for more than twenty-five hours. Sliney has injured his wrist and is in constant pain. His son William is racked by constant seasickness. Every member of the crew is suffering seriously from saltwater burns and hypothermia. And they are low on petrol. There is, however, one bit of good news. The Irish lightship *Isolda* has at last arrived, and Sliney leaves her keeping watch on the casualty while he heads back a second time to Queenstown.

After sixty-three hours at sea the Ballycotton lifeboat
Mary Stanford takes off the crew of the endangered lightship:
a long and difficult service for which the Ballycotton crew were
awarded one gold, two silver and four bronze medals.

When the lifeboat gets there, she suffers an unexpected setback: the eighty gallons of petrol needed to refuel her are not available. It is late afternoon before her tanks are full and she is heading yet again for the lightship.

She is almost too late. For the weather has been worsening all that day. The seas are still enormous, and the wind has now backed to the south-east and again increased to a hurricane. The lightship has had one of the red lanterns that indicate she is out of position swept clean away; she has dragged her anchors, and is now wallowing out of control in heavy seas less than sixty yards from the Daunt Rock.

The *Isolda* has been trying all afternoon either to take her in tow or to take off the crew, but conditions are too bad. Sliney is asked to do what he can.

The coxswain realizes he has little hope of coming alongside the lightship on her starboard (leeward) side because of her anchor cable. He must therefore run in at full speed on her port side (next to the rocks), check, go full astern, and hope that in the split second the two vessels are close together and roughly parallel her crew will jump.

He hails them, and tells them what he wants them to do. He discharges oil in the hope of calming the sea, but in the high wind and strong tide the effect is minimal. He manoeuvres astern of the lightship, then drives in at full speed alongside her, checks, and one man leaps to safety. He circles and comes in a second time, but at the last moment the two vessels swing apart and no one is able to jump. On the third run in five men jump. Then comes near-disaster. On the next run in, the two vessels are flung together; the stern of the lightship crashes down on the *Mary Stanford*, breaking her deckrail and staving in her deck. Her crew leap for their lives; by a miracle no one is hurt. Sliney comes in again and yet again, but no one jumps. There are still two men aboard the lightship. They can be seen clinging to the rails, apparently transfixed with fear and unable to let go. The coxswain tells two of his crew to stand in the bow of the lifeboat and try to grab the men as they come alongside. It is a risk. All four are all too likely to be swept overboard and drowned. But the risk turns out to be worthwhile. The two lightshipmen are snatched to safety, although both are injured in the process. The *Mary Stanford* then heads for Ballycotton. We are told by Robert Mahony that such was the stress everyone had been under that 'shortly after the rescue, one of the men from the lightship became hysterical, and two lifeboatmen had to hold him down to prevent anyone being hurt or knocked overboard'.

By the time they land, the Ballycotton crew have been on call for seventy-six hours, on service for sixty-three hours, and at sea for forty-nine hours; twice they have been without food for nearly twenty-four hours. No wonder they are so cold, cramped and physically exhausted they have to be lifted out of their lifeboat.

If ever men deserved their gold, silver and bronze medals it was the crew of the Ballycotton lifeboat. Yet once again a devil's advocate might argue that the Daunt Rock rescue brought to light deficiencies in the service provided. It highlighted the need for better radio communication between ship and shore; also, and more importantly, it highlighted the relatively short time that a petrol-driven lifeboat was able to remain at sea without refuelling.

The *Mary Stanford* was a comparatively new boat – a Barnett class fifty-one-footer. Yet she had a range of less than a hundred miles, and an endurance of not much more than twenty-four hours. The reason for this was that her petrol-driven engines used a great quantity of fuel. This same problem of excessive fuel consumption had initially bedevilled the commercial development of buses. However, in the late 1920s it had been discovered that buses fitted with diesel engines were able to run twice as long and twice as far, and therefore a great deal more cheaply, than those fitted with petrol engines. It was not long before the Institution took note of this and began to experiment with diesel engines in lifeboats.

In the autumn of 1932 a massive six-cylinder diesel engine, weighing nearly a ton and designed by the Ferry Engine Company, was fitted into the Watson class lifeboat *S.G.E.* stationed at Yarmouth (Isle of Wight). At much the same time, a CE4 petrol engine of exactly the same horsepower was fitted into a similar Watson class lifeboat stationed at Portpatrick (Dumfries and Galloway). The performance of these two vessels was monitored and compared. It was found that the Portpatrick boat could run for only fifty-seven miles, using sixty-four pints of petrol per hour; whereas the Yarmouth boat could run for 118 miles, using only twenty-nine pints of diesel per hour.

There was no denying the evidence. Diesel was more economic than petrol. Nor was their frugal fuel consumption the only plus point for diesel engines. Diesel is less volatile than petrol and less inflammable; the risk of fire is therefore reduced. And even more importantly, by switching to a type of engine that was being used commercially the Institution was able to save money and simplify maintenance. The old petrol-driven engines of that period had been beautifully constructed and housed; they were works of art. Yet from their manufacturers' point of view they were one-off creations, with too small and specialized a market to be commercially successful. They were therefore inordinately expensive; and if anything went wrong or wore out, obtaining spare parts was a nightmare.

By the time the Second World War had ended, forward-thinking members of the Institution were convinced that the lifeboats of the future would be powered by diesels. They therefore set in motion a series of experiments to discover (a) if it would be possible to replace the existing petrol-driven engines with diesels; and (b) assuming it was possible, what sort of diesel engine would be best. The lifeboat chosen for these experiments was the forty-one-foot Watson class *Matthew Simpson*, stationed at Port Erin in the Isle of Man.

The very first diesels fitted into lifeboats had been big six-cylinder cell-type engines, not dissimilar to those used in buses. However, it was soon found that smaller, lighter engines were equally effective. Among those tested were the Perkins P4s (developing forty-three horsepower at 2000 rpm), the Admiralty Coventry two-strokes (developing fifty-two horsepower at 2000 rpm), and the Parson-Ford Porteagles (developing fifty-two horsepower at 2000 rpm). All were satisfactory. Then in 1952 a pair of standard Gardner diesels was installed. These performed equally well, and since Gardners were in widespread use commercially, the Institution decided to go for them. Commander Gould, the RNLI's superintendent engineer wrote:

> It was apparent that there would be advantages in adopting an engine which was in daily use in the commercial world, and was made in a wide range of horse-power and cylinders, all with standard parts easily obtainable . . . In 1954 a lifeboat fitted with Gardner diesel engines was sent to Coverack. Since then all 42, 47 and 52-foot boats have been fitted with Gardner engines, which have proved extremely satisfactory in all conditions . . . The policy of fitting these commercial diesel engines has been an outstanding success, and will result in marked financial saving in running and upkeep.

As lifeboat after lifeboat went into the yards to have its engines replaced, the opportunity was taken to carry out other modifications and improvements. The pitch of the propellers was made coarser. Propeller shafts of stainless steel were replaced by Monel (a hard-wearing, non-corroding alloy). Stern exhausts were superseded by water-cooled side exhausts. And fundamental changes were made to the way in which, and the position from which, the boats were controlled.

Lifeboats have always, by tradition, been controlled by the coxswain. In the earliest boats the position of the coxswain was determined by the length of his sweep-oar, which acted as a rudder. The advent of built-in rudders and the development of wheel steering enabled the coxswain's position to be moved slightly forward, but it was not until reliable engines replaced sails that the coxswain and his wheel could be put in their best place, a little forward of amidships. Towards the end of the Second World War the Institution's long-serving naval architect James Rennie Barnett designed a lifeboat in which the coxswain and his wheel were protected by a simple cockpit, and incorporated into this cockpit was a novel system of single lever control.

The essence of single lever control is that the man at the wheel can not only manoeuvre the boat, but also control its engines and hence its speed. This system was easy to install, and, Gould tells us, 'once coxswains have handled it they like it very much indeed' – a claim substantiated when in 1954 the Coverack lifeboat *William Taylor of Oldham* put the new equipment to the test.

Before any innovative type of lifeboat goes into production it is RNLI policy to ensure that its prototype is subjected to the most rigorous sea trials. In 1909 a flotilla of boats fitted with the new petrol-driven engines had sailed from the Thames estuary to the Orkneys. Now, in 1954, a Watson class boat fitted with the new diesel engines and single lever control was required to sail, with minimal stopovers and at near-maximum speed, round virtually the whole of the British Isles. In 1909 the petrol-driven boats had been bedevilled by problems. It was a different story for the *William Taylor*, which now set out from Osborne's yards in Littlehampton where she had been built.

The idea was for her to be manned by different crews at different stations, so as to give as many experienced lifeboatmen as possible the chance to handle and assess her. On her first day out from Littlehampton, her crew reported that 'the quiet smooth running of the Gardner diesels gave a feeling of great power'. On her second day she ran into a gale off Beachy Head, but 'responded in exhilarating fashion, always leaving the helmsman with a feeling of complete control'. On her third day the weather was still bad, but when the Dungeness crew came aboard they were dressed not in oilskins but in their Sunday best, because, they said, 'We don't expect to get wet in a fine new boat like this!' Nor did they. As *William Taylor* rounded the Goodwins and headed up the east coast, the bad weather and the good reports continued. We are told that while on passage from Whitby to Berwick, 'plunging into a big head sea, she received a severe testing, which she came through splendidly'. Passing Inverness after only seven days, she cut through the Caledonian Canal, then ran down the west coast of Scotland, across the Irish Sea, round Land's End, and

OPPOSITE

The Watson-class *William Taylor of Oldham*. In 1954 she successfully tested the RNLI's proposed new diesel engines and a new system of single lever control; the latter enabled the helmsman not only to manoeuvre the lifeboat but also to control its engines and hence its speed.

after a passage of less than a fortnight reached what was to be her permanent station at Coverack. The Chief Inspector of Lifeboats wrote:

> This trial was an outstanding success. The lifeboat completed 1,500 miles in 181 steaming hours, at an average speed of 8.3 knots, despite very heavy weather . . . Some 19 deputations from lifeboat crews were given an opportunity of going afloat in her. All, without exception, expressed themselves entirely satisfied both with her engines and the new equipment . . . What better record could her designers and builders wish?

The message came through loud and clear. And it was acted on. In 1951 there were eleven diesel-powered lifeboats in the RNLI fleet. By 1961 there were 122.

A rescue that may not have been particularly dramatic, but that demonstrates very well the value of the new engines, took place in the early 1950s.

On the evening of 17 January the weather off the west coast of Scotland was, to say the least, difficult: nine-tenths cloud, a full gale, and a heavy swell rolling down through the Minches. The 6600-ton m.v. *Tapti* lost her bearings and ran aground between the islands of Tiree and Coll in the Hebrides. She radioed for help, but gave her position incorrectly, believing she had gone ashore off the coast of Mull.

The first lifeboat to go to her aid was the *Lloyd's* from Barra. Not surprisingly, since she was looking in the wrong place, she failed to find her. A little before midnight the

Mallaig lifeboat *Sir Arthur Rose* joined in the search, and in the small hours of the morning she was given the *Tapti*'s correct position by Oban radio. We are told by 'The Lifeboat' journal that 'the Mallaig lifeboat journeyed over forty-five miles of rough, gale-swept sea, in continual showers of sleet, until about six o'clock in the morning she sighted the *Tapti*'. The motor vessel was lying stern to the shore in rock-strewn waters, listing dangerously.

A Barnett-class lifeboat. Barnetts were good seaworthy boats, able to take over a hundred survivors. However, prior to the introduction of airbags in the 1970s, they were not self-righting.

The Mallaig coxswain, Ian Watt, did his best to come alongside. But it was still dark, there was a heavy swell, and the lifeboat could edge forward only a few feet at a time, using her lead-line to gauge the depth of the water. Watt did manage to get to within thirty yards of the *Tapti*; but the lifeboat was in constant danger of being swept on to the rocks, and the coxswain very sensibly decided to wait for daylight before trying to take off the crew. He signalled his intentions to the *Tapti* by Morse, and backed away, stern first because there wasn't room among the rocks for the lifeboat to turn round.

The hours passed slowly. As the light strengthened and the tide fell, the *Tapti* shifted uneasily. Her list increased: to forty degrees, fifty degrees, sixty degrees. Watt realized she was in danger of keeling over, and he could wait no longer. To windward of the stranded vessel the waves were enormous, cascading like avalanches of milk over her bow. To leeward the waters were calmer, but dark with reefs of jagged, half-submerged rocks. Watt edged cautiously towards the casualty, until he was close under her lee bow. One of her ship's boats, half-lowered, hung from its davits, and this provided a modicum of shelter. A rope was flung down from the *Tapti*'s forecastle. The *Sir Arthur Rose* made fast to it. Watt did his best to hold steady, so that the crew, one by one, could swarm down the rope and come tumbling into the lifeboat. It was a perilous manoeuvre, with the surge and backwash of the swell now sending the lifeboat crashing against the hull of the motor vessel, now sending her swirling towards the nearby rocks. But, to quote the Institution's report, 'By fine seamanship and judgement ... the rescue was successfully carried out'. In the course of the next couple of hours, all sixty-two of the *Tapti*'s crew, one at a time, were transferred to the lifeboat.

The *Sir Arthur Rose* was a comparatively large lifeboat – a forty-six-foot Watson – but with more than seventy men crammed aboard her she was seriously overloaded. The weather was still spectacularly bad: the sky a mosaic of fragments of blue and rolling banks of jet-black cumulus, brilliant sunshine alternating with squalls of sleet, the waves huge and the wind frenetic.

By now the *Lloyd's* from Barra had also located the casualty and was standing by. However, conditions were too bad to risk transferring men from one lifeboat to the other. Too bad also to risk returning to Mallaig. It was decided to make for Tobermory on the island of Mull. It took the two lifeboats, labouring through heavy seas and gale-force winds, twelve hours to cover the thirty-odd miles to the safety of Tobermory harbour.

One of the few things the crew of the *Sir Arthur Rose* hadn't had to worry about during this service of twenty-three and a half hours was running out of fuel. They knew that their diesel engines would enable them to remain at sea for however long it took them to complete the rescue.

The transition from petrol to diesel caused few headaches, but the postwar years did see the re-emergence of two longstanding problems for the RNLI. What was the best type of lifeboat: a boat that was pre-eminently seaworthy, or a boat that was self-righting? And should the RNLI remain a charity or be brought under the aegis of the government?

The first of these issues led to controversy and indeed acrimony in the 1970s. Some twenty years after the end of the war, the majority of the RNLI fleet were Watson or Barnett class diesels: splendid sea boats, but not self-righting. A succession of tragic disasters, within a comparatively short time, made people ask if the Institution had been right to phase out its self-righters. For accidents at Fraserburgh, Arbroath, Scarborough, Broughty Ferry, Seaham and Longhope led to the loss of six lifeboats and no fewer than thirty-six lifeboatmen.

In 1953 the Fraserburgh lifeboat *John and Charles Kennedy* went to help local fishing boats that were trapped outside the harbour on a lee shore. The *John and Charles Kennedy* was a tried and tested boat with an experienced crew; she had already saved 199 lives, and her coxswain Andrew Ritchie had been serving in lifeboats for twenty years. The wind was not much more than a stiff breeze that afternoon, but a heavy swell was rolling across the harbour entrance, and it seems that as the lifeboat was returning a huge wave suddenly reared up astern of her, broke over her starboard quarter and capsized her. She did not self-right. Six out of her crew of seven were drowned.

Later that year, the Arbroath lifeboat *Robert Lindsay* was called out 'in atrocious conditions' after coastguards had reported distress flares to the south. The lifeboat searched for several hours, but could find no sign of a vessel in difficulties. Returning that night to Arbroath, her coxswain David Bruce very sensibly decided to wait until it was half-light before trying to enter harbour using his drogue. However, 'the entrance was a boiling cauldron as the gale blew against the tide and backwash off the piers threw the seas into a wild confusion. As the lifeboat approached, suddenly her lights reversed, the red going over the green, then both disappeared. She had been hit by a huge cross sea and was capsized.' Once again, the lifeboat did not self-right, and six out of her crew of seven were drowned.

In 1954 the *E.C.J.R.* of Scarborough was also escorting local fishing boats to safety when she met the same fate as the *John and Charles Kennedy*. In a severe mid-winter gale she towed one fishing boat into harbour and escorted the others to

ABOVE LEFT
The *E.C.J.R.* in happier times. Overwhelmed as she approached her home harbour of Scarborough, she capsized. Although she self-righted, three of her crew were drowned.

The Watson class lifeboat *The Robert* was funded from an anonymous donation following the loss of *Mona* and her crew. She served at Broughty Ferry from 1960 until 1975.

Whitby. She was then recalled. However, as she was approaching the entrance to Scarborough harbour, she was overwhelmed by a huge wave and capsized. She self-righted; but not quickly enough, and three of her crew were drowned.

In 1959 the Broughty Ferry lifeboat *Mona* was launched, to go to the aid of the North Carr lightship, which had broken away from her moorings and was drifting ashore in a severe south-easterly gale. No one will ever know exactly what happened; but in the small hours of the morning *Mona* suddenly stopped transmitting, and at first light she was found drifting bottom-up in the Firth of Tay. She had not self-righted, and her crew of eight had been drowned. (It was at the subsequent procurator-fiscal's inquiry that a passage was quoted from the Bible which, for many people, encapsulates the ethos of lifeboat crews: 'Greater love hath no man than this, that a man lay down his life for his friends'.)

In 1962 the Seaham (County Durham) lifeboat rescued five men from a fishing coble; but returning in a sixty-knot gale, she capsized. According to the inquiry: 'She was hit by successive waves when broadside to wind and tide in the confused water at the entrance to the harbour. These conditions were further aggravated by backwash and undertow from the breakwaters.' She did not self-right, and all five of her crew and all but one of the fishermen they had rescued, were drowned.

In 1969 the Longhope lifeboat *TGB* went to help a Liberian tanker out of fuel and out of control in the Pentland Firth. The Pentland Firth, between the north coast of Scotland and the Orkneys, is not a good place for a ship to be out of control in. Waves in this narrow seaway can be gargantuan, tides and currents can run at up to nine

The lifeboat *TGB*, lost with all her crew in the Pentland Firth in 1969, a tragedy that 'took someone out of virtually every house in the little Orkney village of Longhope'.

knots, and winds gust frequently to over 100 miles per hour. Longhope is a tiny village on the island of Hoy (the most westerly of the Orkneys). Its lifeboat crew at that time were a close-knit family. Both the coxswain Dan Kirkpatrick and the mechanic Robert Johnston had two sons with them in the boat. When they launched in flurries of snow on the evening of 17 March everyone knew the risk they were taking, and as they struggled out of harbour against a flood tide and heavy seas, anxious signals were exchanged between lighthouse keepers and coastguards. At nine twenty-eight p.m., in worsening weather, the *TGB* acknowledged a message from Wick radio, giving her the position of the freighter. After that there was silence. The lifeboat was never heard from again. Next day, after a search by ships, aircraft and helicopters, she was found floating hull-up off the island of South Ronaldsay. No one will ever know exactly what happened, but the odds are that she was overturned by a giant wave. Dan Kirkpatrick, as he stood at the wheel, was probably killed by the impact of the sea; his crew, trapped inside the lifeboat when it capsized, were probably drowned. For the *TGB* was not a self-righter.

It would be hard to overstate the heartache to which this disaster gave rise. Margaret Kirkpatrick and Maggie Johnston both lost a husband and two sons; and in one tragic moment seven women in the village were made widows and eight children fatherless. As the Inspector of Lifeboats for Scotland, Brian Miles, put it when he went to comfort the families: 'I looked down the hill, and it struck me like a physical blow. We had taken someone out of virtually every house.' But perhaps the last word on the Longhope tragedy should be left with one of the bereaved women. When told that the Liberian freighter had gone ashore on the cliffs of South Ronaldsay, but that by a near-miracle coastguards had managed to rescue her crew, she said simply: 'My husband would have been very pleased to know that'.

OPPOSITE
The Fraserburgh lifeboat *Duchess of Kent*. All but one of her crew were drowned when she capsized on service to the Danish trawler *Opel*.

Next year there was yet another disaster – one that placed the whole future of the Institution in jeopardy. On 21 January, the Danish trawler *Opel* was on her way to the Fladden fishing grounds off the east coast of Scotland, when she reported that her engine room was flooding and her pumps had failed. Lifeboats at Wick, Peterhead and Fraserburgh were alerted, and when a Mayday signal was transmitted, the Fraserburgh lifeboat was launched. The weather was not good – winds of fifty miles per hour and waves of more than fifteen feet – and it took the lifeboat, the Watson class *Duchess of Kent*, over four hours to reach the casualty. When she got there, she found to her surprise that three Russian vessels, the factory ship *Victor Kingisepp* and two trawlers, were already standing by, and that one of the trawlers had taken *Opel* in tow. There had obviously been a breakdown in radio communication between the various rescuers, possibly stemming from the exigency of the Cold War; and the fact that the Fraserburgh lifeboat was not actually needed made what happened next all the more tragic.

The *Duchess of Kent* was approaching the towing vessel to try to read her name, when she was struck by an enormous freak wave, tossed bow over stern, and capsized. (A photograph taken by one of the crew of the *Victor Kingisepp* shows her

being thrown almost vertically into the air, and almost clean out of the water.) One man, Jackson Buchan, was flung clear and managed to clamber back on to the hull. The others were trapped inside the lifeboat and drowned. The *Victor Kingisepp* came alongside the lifeboat, and her crew made frantic efforts, 'at great personal risk', to right her; but in the gale-force wind and huge seas they were unsuccessful. So they took her in tow.

Photograph taken from the Russian factory ship *Victor Kingisepp*, showing the spray-covered *Duchess of Kent* the moment before she capsized.

Next day Brian Miles found himself on another distressing mission. A helicopter flew him aboard the Russian factory ship to ask for the return of the lifeboat and the bodies of her crew. At first the Russians were unsympathetic. Their minds were on salvage and salvage money, whereas all Brian Miles was interested in was getting the bodies back to Fraserburgh. For several hours there was an impasse. But at last, either because of Brian's negotiating skills or because of a directive from Moscow, the atmosphere thawed, and permission was granted. The Buckie lifeboat, which had been standing by, came alongside, the bodies were laid on her deck, the *Duchess of Kent* was taken in tow, and the sad procession set course for the coast of Scotland. As they drew away from the factory ship, not a word was spoken; but the whole of the Russian crew were lined up on deck, silently waving.

These last two disasters coming so close together, and following half a dozen previous ones, were more than people could accept. There was a spate of criticism. Why, the RNLI were asked, were they not providing safer (i.e. self-righting) lifeboats for their crews? And if, as seemed to be the implication, they were not doing their job properly, why were they not brought under the control of the government?

These two issues, which have surfaced at regular intervals throughout the RNLI's history, have always been addressed in the same way – by an official court of inquiry – and with the same verdict: that no one was likely to provide better lifeboats or do a better job than the Institution itself under its existing regimen.

Whether a self-righting lifeboat is preferable to a non-self-righting one had been a matter of dispute ever since the days of Wouldhave and Lukin. Wouldhave's boat and its successors owed their ability to self-right to high end-boxes at their bow and stern and a comparatively narrow hull. The resulting boats certainly righted themselves if they capsized, but they were unstable in bad conditions. In heavy seas they were described as 'lively', which is a polite way of saying they pitched and rolled excessively. This did not give their crews a great deal of confidence. In spite of this, Secretary Lewis was a firm advocate of the self-righting principle, and he produced statistics – very convincing on paper – to show that more lives were lost in 'ordinary' boats than in those that self-righted. So throughout the second half of the nineteenth century, in spite of the reservations of their crews, the Wouldhave style boats were in vogue. Almost all new lifeboats that were built were self-righters.

Then the pendulum swung, perhaps excessively, in the opposite direction. The naval architects George Lennox Watson and James Rennie Barnett were well aware of the fact that most lifeboatmen favoured boats that were, above all, good sea boats. They therefore abandoned Wouldhave's principles and concentrated on building boats that were basically big, heavy, broad beamed and seaworthy. These proved so popular with their crews that throughout the first half of the twentieth century virtually no self-righters came out of the builders' yards.

In 1900 there were 237 lifeboats in service, of which 184 were self-righters. In 1960 there were 152 lifeboats in service, of which only five were self-righters. However, the spate of postwar accidents led to a growing conviction that there was a lot to be said for going back to Wouldhave's principles. It clearly was not practicable to scrap virtually the whole of the existing fleet, and it would be many years before new self-righting lifeboats could be built in large numbers. It was therefore decided to try to modify the ageing Watsons and Barnetts to give them the capacity to self-right.

This was easier said than done. However, RNLI designers, with the co-operation of technicians from the British Hovercraft Corporation, eventually came up with an idea that was simple in theory but took time to perfect in practice. If you hold an inflated balloon under water, the buoyancy of the trapped air will force the balloon to the surface. So if you tie a balloon to one side of a lifeboat and the lifeboat capsizes, the balloon should, in theory, act as a buoyancy chamber and come to the surface bringing the lifeboat with it. Substitute an airbag for a balloon, stow one on top of the after cabin, install a device that will make the airbag automatically inflate if the boat rolls to more than, say, 100 degrees, and you should have a self-righting lifeboat.

This theory was put to the test in the early hours of 18 November 1979. The weather that night in the Hebrides was the worst in living memory. Winds were gusting to 118 miles per hour; waves of thirty feet were interspersed with the occasional fifty-footer; the sea was white with sheets of driving spindrift; and the Danish coaster *Lone Dania* was in trouble. Roughly midway between the Skerryvore lighthouse and the island of Tiree, her cargo of marble chips shifted and she took on a dangerous list. A little after midnight she transmitted a Mayday.

Two lifeboats went to her aid: the modern, self-righting Thames class *Helmut Schroder of Dunlossit* from Islay; and the older Barnett class *R. A. Colby Cubbin No. 3*, fitted with an airbag, from Barra. The *Helmut Schroder* set out from Islay at full speed, seventeen knots, but this soon had to be reduced to eight knots in the huge seas and poor visibility. Even at this slower speed, the lifeboat took a terrible beating. She crashed some twenty-five feet into the trough of a wave, landing with such force that one of her crew broke his ankle. A few minutes later, she was hit by an enormous cross-sea. She broached to in its trough, and the next wave broke clean on top of her, turning her upside-down. Being a self-righter, she spun through 360 degrees, her crew commenting afterwards on the 'smooth almost gentle motion', as the lifeboat hung for three or four seconds completely upside-down, then resurfaced the right way up. If the *Helmut Schroder* had not been a self-righter, her crew would have been drowned.

The *R. A. Colby Cubbin No. 3*, meanwhile, had a longer and even more eventful passage. It took her nearly three hours to get within range of the Skerryvore lighthouse. Her coxswain, John Macneil, was just checking his position by its beam, when the lifeboat dug her bow diagonally into a huge wave and started to roll broadside on. Looking back, Macneil saw a great thirty-foot wave towering over them. Before he had time to cry warning, it burst flush on top of them, not only submerging the lifeboat but turning her upside-down. The *R. A. Colby Cubbin*, a non-self-righter, had only one hope: her airbag. As she rolled past 120 degrees, the mercury capsize switch activated, releasing compressed gas from a bottle and inflating the bag. And the airbag rose to the surface, dragging the lifeboat through a complete 360 degree circle and turning her right way up. She was so badly damaged that it took her twelve hours to limp back to Barra. As Ray and Susannah Kipling point out in their *Strong To Save*:

> Ten years earlier both lifeboat crews would probably have died, trapped beneath their upturned boats. They escaped – shocked and cold, but with only minor cuts and bruises. RNLI teams were sent to investigate the capsizes, Brian Miles going to Barra. 'As we flew in' [he wrote] 'I saw the lifeboat lying alongside the pier, looking very battered. I remember thinking "the last time I was in this situation there were no crew left – now they are all alive." It really brought home to me what self-righting meant.

Today all but the smallest rescue boats have the ability to self-right. This reduces the risk of disaster, but is no guarantee against it – a point made clear by the man who was arguably the greatest lifeboatman of all time, coxswain Henry Blogg of

The Barra Island lifeboat *R A Colby Cubbin No 3*. She capsized in a hurricane off the Hebrides, but her airbag enabled her to self-right.

Cromer. 'I have been a seaman all my life,' he is reputed to have told his biographer, 'and forty-five years of it have been spent as a lifeboatman. From that experience, I'd say, it is impossible to guarantee any boat against disaster. It does not matter what type of boat it is, you cannot insure against accidents. It all depends on the force of the storm and the judgement of the crew.' This is something lifeboat crews are aware of every time they launch.

The other issue raised by these postwar accidents was the status of the RNLI. Should it remain a charity, or should it be brought under government control?

The justification for any charity that provides a public service is that it should be successful. It is therefore hardly surprising that demands for the RNLI to be brought under state control should have corresponded with what were perceived to be the lows in its success rate. These were (a) in the late 1840s and early 1850s, when its boats fell into disrepair through lack of funds; (b) at the turn of the nineteenth and twentieth centuries, when its fundraisers faced charges of corruption; and (c) in the 1970s when a succession of disasters led people to question the competence of the Institution's boat designers.

On the first occasion, the Institution was obliged to accept a degree of state aid and therefore state control. And it is perhaps significant that this did not work, largely because it was found that bureaucratic landlubbers hampered the work of RNLI committees; there was an increase in paperwork and a decrease in efficiency. So as soon as the Institution got its finances in order the government subsidy was rescinded, and was never asked for again, the feeling being that 'no Government Department could ever do the work of the RNLI, [or] evoke that generous sympathy with heroism which has characterised the work of the Institution . . . and that saving life at sea is an innately hazardous operation for which men volunteer – they cannot be employed for, or directed to, such work'.

On the second occasion, the RNLI was accused not only of inefficiency and the concealment and misappropriation of funds, but also of manslaughter. It was suggested that the Institution was 'behind other nations in the service it provided', and that the Queen should withdraw her patronage. These allegations were looked into by a parliamentary committee of inquiry in 1897. This inquiry summarized its findings in a weighty, thousand-page report which included interviews and statistics. Its conclusions were unequivocal. The evidence brought against the Institution was found to be flawed and in some cases malicious. The charges of inefficiency and corruption were dismissed. The inquiry concluded, 'Your Committee see no ground for recommending that the life-boat Service be taken over by the State, so long as it is maintained efficiently and successfully by private benevolence'.

On the third occasion, in 1970, the Institution came under fire because of a widespread feeling, brought to a head by the Fraserburgh disaster, that its lifeboats were not all they should be. As usual, the root trouble was financial. Towards the end of the 1960s RNLI income stagnated, or in some years actually declined, and this at a time when the Institution needed money urgently to finance the converting of its fleet to boats that had the capacity to self-right. This unhappy state of affairs was brought to the attention of the public by the media; and it was due largely to media pressure that a public inquiry was set up, not only to look into the Fraserburgh tragedy, but to examine just about every facet of the RNLI and its work.

Few people would doubt the impartiality of such a court, and again its findings were unequivocal: '*The Duchess of Kent* [the Fraserburgh lifeboat] was well equipped and in a seaworthy condition when she sailed on her last mission . . . No blame for the disaster can be attributed to her coxswain and crew or to the R.N.L.I. The Court emphasizes that life-boat rescue operations always are, and always will be, extremely hazardous'. Once again it had been confirmed that the Institution was the best organization to do a difficult and at times heartbreaking job; and, as *The Life-Boat* put it: 'It is questionable whether any other national organisation with such a wide range of duties as the RNLI would have come out from such an examination so well, in spite of the impression which may have been created by a number of newspaper headlines'.

Two challenges had been met successfully. A third was in the offing. For there was about to be a fundamental change in the type of work that lifeboats were called on to do.

'Bring

em back alive!'

About ten o'clock on the morning of 6 February 1972, Patrick Pile saw a small fibreglass dinghy, with four or five people aboard, heading out of Southwold harbour. The weather was not good: low cloud, squalls of rain and a twenty-five-knot wind. Heavy seas were breaking over the shoals outside the harbour. It looked to Patrick like a recipe for disaster.

He ran to his car and drove to the lifeboat house, picking up en route another member of the Southwold inshore lifeboat crew, Martin Helmer. As they were getting ready to launch their D class inflatable, a car came racing down the road from the harbour entrance. The driver wound down his window: 'They've turned over!' he shouted.

Patrick and Martin realized that a few seconds' delay might make the difference between life and death. They didn't put on their protective clothing. They launched right away.

As soon as they had cleared the mouth of the harbour they spotted the capsized dinghy, about 300 yards from Walberswick beach, and beside it a figure in the water, floating face-down. A D class inflatable is small, light, and built for use in inshore waters; in any sort of sea it is difficult to manage. The seas that morning were confused and choppy. Patrick had a difficult job manoeuvring alongside the man in the water, and Martin an even more difficult job hauling him aboard. He was in his teens, unconscious, blue in the face, and not breathing. They thought he was probably dead; but Patrick, who was qualified in first aid, struck him several times in the stomach to induce vomiting. Before they had a chance to try to resuscitate him, they spotted two more people in the water. The first they got to was a young man also in his teens; he too was face-down, apparently being kept afloat by air trapped in his anorak. As they struggled to haul him aboard, the lifeboat swung broadside-on to the waves and shipped a fair amount of water. This man was also

In the 1960s and 1970s lifeboats were called out with increasing frequency to help holiday makers in difficulties in inshore waters. This has led to the development of RNLI beach rescue teams – seen here taking part in exercises at Poole in Dorset.

unconscious, blue-black in the face, and not breathing. The lifeboat then went to the third casualty: a young boy who was semi-conscious as they hauled him aboard but unable to speak. Patrick felt sure there had been more than three people in the dinghy. And sure enough, as the lifeboat circled, they sighted yet another body. This was an older man, subsequently found to be the father of two of the teenage boys. Although he weighed more than eighteen stone, the lifeboatmen managed, with great difficulty, to drag him aboard, only to find he was beyond hope of resuscitation.

Patrick now had a problem. He had four people onboard: one dead, two apparently dead, and one looking as though he might die at any moment. The four of them were lying in the bottom of the boat with water sluicing all over them, while to add to his difficulties his overloaded inflatable was answering her controls sluggishly and seemed to be in some danger of capsizing. Patrick had the choice of making the hazardous and comparatively long return to Southwold (where help would be immediately at hand), or the safer and much shorter run to Walberswick beach (where there was likely to be a delay in getting ambulance or doctor).

A look at the state of the men they had rescued convinced him their only hope was the beach. He headed fast for land. They grounded about a dozen yards offshore, and two local fishermen helped carry the inert bodies through the surf and up the beach. As they started artificial respiration, their inflatable capsized and was swirled away by the waves.

It seemed at first that there was little hope for the two young men who had stopped breathing. However, to quote the journal, 'The lifeboatmen drove themselves to do all in their power to restore life before they themselves collapsed.' Without their protective clothing both Patrick and Martin were now cold, exhausted and suffering from hypothermia. They hadn't even enough breath to try mouth-to-mouth resuscitation, but attempted the Holger-Neilsen method. This involved pressing their hands on the victims' backs and rocking them to and fro. And after about half an hour of pummelling, interspersed with cardiac massage, one of the teenagers started breathing normally and the other intermittently.

The lifeboatmen concentrated on the latter. They tore off the door from a nearby shed, made a makeshift stretcher, and carried the man to the shelter of the sanddunes. Here they worked on him for more than half an hour. Every time he stopped breathing, they managed to get him started again. At last an ambulance arrived, and the survivors were given oxygen and rushed to hospital. Meanwhile an RAF helicopter had been searching the area for other survivors, but without success.

Out of the five people who had been aboard the dinghy, two were drowned: the father of the teenagers, and a man whose body was subsequently washed ashore. Three came out of their ordeal alive, almost certainly owing their survival to the fact that Patrick and Martin had put their own lives at risk by not taking time to put on protective clothing before they launched.

The crunch line to this cautionary tale is the first sentence of the penultimate paragraph of the RNLI report: 'None of those rescued was wearing a lifejacket'.

Those who live in the higher reaches of the Alps have a saying that might be roughly translated as: 'People who visit the mountains only occasionally don't know them well enough to be afraid of them'. For 'mountains' you could substitute 'sea'.

We are so used nowadays to travelling all over the British Isles, and indeed all over much of the world, that it is difficult for us to appreciate that only fifty years ago many British families had never seen the sea; or if they had seen it, their knowledge of it was limited to a single overcrowded beach in summer. We may think of ourselves as a nation of seafarers, but until quite recently the sea, for most Britishers, was an alien environment. And, like those occasional visitors to the high Alps, what people did not understand they did not have the sense to fear.

During the late 1950s and early 1960s the average person in Britain enjoyed an increase not only in wealth but also in leisure time. In the words of the then Prime Minister, Harold Macmillan, we had 'never had it so good', and a large number of people used their new-found wealth and leisure to indulge in sea-associated activities: cliff walking; swimming; surfing and windsurfing; diving and snorkelling; and putting to sea in a multiplicity of craft, ranging from nine-foot dinghies to ninety-foot yachts, not to mention Li-los, canoes and motor boats. Many of these people, unfamiliar with the ways of the sea, got into difficulties and put at risk not only their own lives but the lives of those who went to help them.

The RNLI suddenly found itself facing a new challenge. Instead of being asked to rescue a relatively small number of fishermen and merchant seamen who had been wrecked during the storms of winter, they were being asked to rescue a much larger number of holidaymakers who had got themselves into trouble during the halcyon months of summer. The Table below shows how radically the workload had not only increased but shifted. This new type of rescue work called for a new type of lifeboat.

Monthly lifeboat launches in the late nineteenth and twentieth centuries

Lifeboat launches during 1885		Lifeboat launches during 1985	
January	27	January	114
February	12	February	107
March	25	March	163
April	12	April	336
May	6	May	390
June	3	June	397
July	1	July	668
August	13	August	817
September	14	September	368
October	30	October	218
November	29	November	146
December	15	December	141
Total launches	187	Total launches	3865
(26% summer, 74% winter)		(77% summer, 23% winter)	

The Lifesaving Jacket

Lifeboats sometimes capsize. Crews are sometimes washed overboard. Crews also often have to enter the water to rescue casualties. For all these eventualities a lifejacket can be a lifesaver.

In 1851, Captain Ross Ward, subsequently an Inspector of Lifeboats, proposed that all lifeboatmen

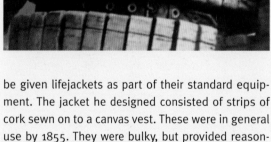

In 1972, the innovative Beaufort jacket came into service. It consisted of a single inflation bag filled with foam. The Beauforts were extremely buoyant but excessively bulky. The RNLI therefore asked the independent research and development team Crewsaver to design a lifejacket that met the following requirements:

LEFT A cork lifejacket – these were the original lifejackets used by lifeboatmen, and consisted of strips of cork sewn on to a canvas vest.

BELOW In 1904 the kapok lifejacket was introduced – kapok is three times as buoyant as cork, and these lifejackets remained in use for almost seventy years.

be given lifejackets as part of their standard equipment. The jacket he designed consisted of strips of cork sewn on to a canvas vest. These were in general use by 1855. They were bulky, but provided reasonable buoyancy and were popular with the crews.

In 1904, the kapok lifejacket was introduced. Kapok, a fibre of the silk-cotton tree, does not absorb water and is three times as buoyant as cork. However, there were design problems, and the first kapok jackets were so cumbersome that some lifeboatmen said they would rather drown than wear them! Modifications were made, and kapok remained in vogue for almost seventy years.

- It must give confidence.
- The crews must be willing to wear it at all times.
- It must be comfortable and not interfere with the function of whatever protective clothing is worn.
- It must be quick and simple to put on.
- It must have minimal bulk so the wearer is not restricted when moving about the lifeboat.
- It must be simple to use.
- It must be of strong construction.
- It must adequately support the crew member in the water, when he or she is wearing any type of RNLI protective clothing.

- It must enable the wearer to enter the water without thought for his or her own safety, and provide sufficient buoyancy to support him or her adequately.
- It must be provided with a light, whistle and 'buddy' line.

After four years' research, Crewsaver evolved a compact jacket with two stoles superimposed one on top of the other. The first stole is inflated automatically by a needle which pierces a canister of carbon dioxide within five seconds of entering water. The second stole can be inflated manually if more buoyancy is needed. ALBs, as the jackets are known, are liked by the crews who wear them, and are now in use in all offshore lifeboats.

Crewsaver also designed a lifejacket-cum-harness for inshore lifeboatmen and women (whose rescue work often involves their entering the water); also a close-fitting jacket for tractor drivers (who may need to escape from their cabs via a narrow hatch). A different type of 'Compact' lifejacket is stored in all lifeboats for the use of survivors.

ABOVE AND RIGHT Crewsaver lifejackets, which were developed for the RNLI and remain very popular with crews today.

TOP RIGHT The Beaufort lifejacket was introduced in 1972. Although it was extremely buoyant, it was also excessively bulky.

Throughout the first half of the twentieth century the tendency had been for lifeboats to get larger and more sophisticated. In the early 1900s a typical boat was a thirty-five-foot self-righter; in the mid 1920s it was a fifty-one-foot Barnett; the late 1950s saw the design of the seventy-foot Clyde. These big, expensive and comparatively slow-to-launch boats were clearly not what was needed for working close inshore – say, rescuing a swimmer or someone out of control on a Li-lo. What was needed for this new type of casualty was a smaller and more manoeuvrable craft that could be launched at a moment's notice and could operate in shallow or rocky water.

It was, however, some time before the Institution was convinced that it should add such boats to its fleet. One reason for this hesitation was that the RNLI had been founded 'for the preservation of life from the hazards of shipwreck', and in the 1960s some members of the Institution's hierarchy felt that since beach casualties were not shipwreck casualties, they should therefore be the responsibility not of the RNLI but of local councils. There was also the point that the outboard motors that would be needed for inshore lifeboats were 'unreliable in the service conditions to be expected in lifesaving work'.

In spite of these doubts, in 1959 the Institution's naval architect Richard Oakley suggested to a colleague that he should look into the possibility of making inflatables and their engines more reliable. A boat was bought for trials, and a delegation was sent to France where the Société des Hospitaliers Bretons was also experimenting with inflatables. The French were enthusiastic about the performance of their boats, and made the point that Professor Bombard had recently made an important fact-finding voyage across the Atlantic in one. The result was that when the delegation got back to England, a group of enthusiasts set to work to improve the seaworthiness of inflatables and to lobby the RNLI to include them in their fleet. Among the most active of these pioneers were Captain Fuller (warden of the Aberdovey Outward Bound Sea School), Alfred Schermuly (owner of the rocket company that supplied pyrotechnics to the Royal Navy and the merchant marine), and the RNLI inspectors David Stogdon and Tony Wicksteed. A lot of people owe their lives to these little-known men.

We take it for granted nowadays that inflatables are an integral part of the lifeboat service; these lightweight craft not only now outnumber 'ordinary' lifeboats, they make more launches per year and save more lives. In the early 1960s, however, it was by no means certain that the RNLI management committee would take them on board. The turning point probably came in 1962 when an inflatable piloted by the Walmer coxswain did an unofficial test run, circling a Polish fishing fleet in the Channel in heavy seas and a full gale, and returning safe and undamaged. Another key moment occurred later that year, when Tony Wicksteed presented a paper on inflatables to the Institution's operations committee. In the discussion that followed, one of the committee's most influential members, the Hon. V. M. Wyndham-Quinn gave the new-fangled craft his blessing. 'Gentlemen,' he said, 'I have been out in one of these animated Carley floats, and Wicksteed has convinced me'. The 'inshore rescue boat', as it was then called, had been taken into the fold, and it and its derivatives were there to stay.

There were, however, a host of teething problems, and the earliest boats to go into service, known as the D class, could be used only in daylight and moderate weather. The main problems were the unreliability of their engines, and the tendency of their sponsons (inflatable tubes) to deflate. As generations of gardeners know to their cost, small petrol-driven engines have a tendency not to start when they are most needed. This is not a good trait for an engine used in a lifeboat. Careful tuning and frequent servicing led to some increase in reliability, but the Institution still had to issue a standing order that all its outboard engines were to be replaced once a year.

Deflation was an equally intransigent problem. The early inflatables were made of a nylon-type fabric coated with neoprene. This was tough but porous; air seeped out

D class inflatable (*circa* 1967)

Length	16 feet
Beam	6 feet 4 inches
Weight	700 lb
Engine	single 40 hp outboard
Speed	21 knots
Endurance	3 hours (at maximum speed)
Crew	2 or 3

of the sponsons, and crews complained that their boats often had to be pumped up before they could be launched. Again this was not a desirable trait for a lifeboat the express purpose of which was to get to a casualty quickly. The Institution's first thought was to fit inner air tubes into the sponsons; this, however, turned out to be a job of mammoth proportions, and the problem was eventually solved by adding a sealer, hypalon, to the fabric. Another difficulty was that in any sort of sea the early inflatables gave their crew an unacceptably rough ride, slamming into and bouncing over the waves with such violence that the crew were sometimes injured.

Because these D class boats were continually being modified, their size and performance differed slightly from year to year. The table on page 149 shows the approximate statistics for an inflatable in service during the mid to late 1960s. Such a boat would originally have cost about £1200 to build and £1600 per year to maintain.

By 1969, some 108 of these D class inflatables were in service, and between them they had launched 1210 times and saved 541 lives. This was a fair record. However, it became increasingly clear that a larger boat was needed, one that could operate in worse weather and at night. The result was the evolution of the Atlantic 21, a powerful and sophisticated craft that was to attract worldwide attention and become the mainstay of the inshore fleet.

One of the smaller and more fragile-looking entries for the 1969 Round Britain Power Boat Race was the *Psychedelic Surfer*, a twenty-one-foot inflatable with a plywood hull. The *Surfer* was based on a design by Rear-Admiral Desmond Hoare, warden of Atlantic College in South Wales. Its sides and bow were enclosed within a continuous inflated buoyancy tube of neoprene rubber, divided into airtight compartments. Its stern consisted of a heavy transom, which supported its two fifty horsepower outboard motors. When fully loaded, its waterline lay below the inflated tube, and the water that was inevitably shipped escaped via the open stern. In spite of bad weather, the *Psychedelic Surfer* rounded Britain undamaged, and finished in the top twenty in the race.

A year later the Institution decided to add this type of improved inflatable to its fleet, and the first hulls, tubes, transoms and engines were sent to the RNLI base at Cowes for assembly. Cowes shipyards have an association with the RNLI dating back to 1913, when pulling and sailing wooden lifeboats were built in the yards of S. E. Saunders. An adjacent yard, the Minerva, was used in those days for storage and for the repair of lifeboats; and in 1963 this yard was revamped as the RNLI Cowes Base, later to become the Inshore Lifeboat Centre. Throughout the 1960s D class inflatables were sent here for servicing; and when in 1970 the D class was superseded by the Atlantic 21 class, the latter were not only serviced at the base but assembled there. This was skilled work. The hulls of glass-reinforced plastic, the sponsons and the engines all arrived from different manufacturers. To these basic components were added fuel tanks, rollbars, self-righting airbags, and a plethora of ancillary equipment such as radios, fire extinguishers, anchors, and tool and first aid kits, while the engines themselves were inversion-proofed (so that they would restart

TOP Inshore Lifeboat Workshop. LEFT Cowes storeyard, 1928.
RIGHT Inshore Lifeboat Centre. Cowes shipyards have an association
with the RNLI dating back to 1913. Today the yards have been
converted into an Inshore Lifeboat Centre, where the Institution's
inflatables are assembled and maintained. The Centre claims that no
station is ever left without its inshore lifeboat for more than 24 hours.

instantly after a capsize). The resulting craft had to measure up to the RNLI's tradi-
tionally high standards; and in addition to all this the base was expected to carry out
an annual refit on every inflatable in the fleet, and make repairs to boats whenever
they were needed (these being done, if possible, by sending a builder or fitter to do the
job on site). Today the Inshore Lifeboat Centre can claim that no lifeboat station is
ever without its inflatable for more than twenty-four hours.

We often praise lifeboat crews. The men who built the lifeboats seldom get acco-
lades. Yet without the expertise of these dedicated shipwrights, most of whom regard
their work as something more than a nine to five job, many rescues would fail and
fewer lives would be saved. Mariners throughout history have hardly ever made a
worthwhile voyage without a decent ship.

Atlantic 21s first came into operation in 1972. In their first twenty years of service they launched over 15,000 times and saved nearly 5000 lives. They were also
bought by several other countries who were members of the International Lifeboat
Federation. The table below shows the key statistics for a typical Atlantic 21. Such a
boat would originally have cost about £22,500 to build. Atlantic 21s have now been
replaced by Atlantic 75s and 85s: slightly longer, heavier and faster. The 85's top
speed of 35 knots makes it the fastest lifeboat in the fleet.

Atlantic 21 inflatable (circa 1980)

Length	22 feet 9 inches
Beam	8 feet
Weight	2750 lb
Engine	two 70 hp outboards
Speed	32 knots
Endurance	3 hours (at maximum speed)
Crew	3

The first of the inshore lifeboats to go into service, a D class, was sent to Aberystwyth in May 1963. Over the next twenty-five years the 'rubber ducks', as they were originally called, launched more than 24,000 times and saved some 11,000 lives. And what a variety of jobs they have been asked to do! They have rescued bathers, divers, cliff walkers, pier walkers and people trapped by the tide. They have saved people in difficulty with Li-los, surfboards and sailboards; they have saved people from rafts, dinghies, pinnaces, motor boats, power boats and yachts. They have saved not only innumerable cats and dogs, but such diverse creatures as canaries, cattle, deer, dolphins, goats, geese, horses and seals. They have worked not only inshore but inland, rescuing people from flood tides, swollen rivers, icy lakes and choked canals. They have been sent on rescue missions to distant countries such as East Pakistan and Mozambique. They have brought the traditional concern and courage of lifeboat crews to the cognizance of a whole new generation of sea-lovers and holidaymakers.

A look at some of the jobs they have done shows just how versatile they are. On 3 June 1963 the first ever rescue by an inshore lifeboat (ILB) was carried out near Aberystwyth. It was nothing very exciting: just three people and their dog who had got themselves cut off by the tide and were lifted to safety. A year later Aberystwyth's 'proper' or offshore lifeboat was withdrawn from service. This led to a public outcry. People were unhappy at being left with only a 'rubber duck' to turn to in an emergency. However, Aberystwyth's D class inflatable proved equal to her task. In her seventeen years of service she carried out 140 rescues and saved the lives of 155 people and four dogs.

On 29 September 1969 the first ever medals to be awarded to an ILB crew were won by Robert Stewart and Andrew Scott of Amble (Northumberland). This was a rescue that involved co-operation between an offshore and an inshore lifeboat. A little before sunset, an RAF pinnace, trying to enter Amble harbour, capsized in heavy swell. Amble's D class inflatable launched within four minutes of the capsize, and, as her crew approached the overturned pinnace, they spotted two men clinging to a nearby buoy. We are told that 'without regard to their own safety the ILB crew

Robert Stewart (left) and Andrew Scott (right) of Amble, Northumberland. The first inshore lifeboat crew to be awarded medals.

Overseas Rescue Operations

Normally RNLI crews do not work abroad. However, when there has been a major water-related catastrophe in another part of the world, volunteers are sometimes authorized to take inshore inflatables to help in areas devastated by floods. This happened in 1970 in Bangladesh, and in 2000 in Mozambique.

On 21 November 1970, twenty D class lifeboats and fifty-seven personnel were airlifted from Stansted to Dacca, following an appeal by the Red Cross. The delta of the Ganges and Brahmaputra had been hit by successive cyclones, and a combination of high tides and monsoon rains had inundated thousands of square miles of low-lying land. This is a densely populated area. It was known that many people had been drowned, and that many more were facing starvation and disease.

On arrival, the lifeboats were loaded on to the m.v. *Bilkis*, 'an antiquated river launch', and taken inland through a maze of channels. 'We soon found evidence of disaster,' wrote the expedition leader David

Stogdon. 'Bodies of men, cows, women, goats and children were piled up close to the shore. We landed and met survivors. They were all men.' During the next eight days the team operated in demanding conditions. Strong currents and scouring tides tested the lifeboats' capabilities to the full; back-up was problematical, and there were times when 'looters had to be repelled by violence'. The boats worked in pairs. Each morning they were lowered over the side of the *Bilkis* and loaded with blankets and food; a Red Cross organizer and a doctor would be taken aboard, and the inflatables would set out to find the various distribution centres set up beside the river. It was hard, frustrating work, often hazardous, occasionally harrowing. But the team kept at it, until *Bilkis*'s hold had been cleared and their own food and fuel exhausted. Then, when it was felt that the need for immediate relief had been superseded by the need for long-term rehabilitation, the team and their lifeboats returned to England.

The lessons learned in 1970 in Bangladesh proved

RNLI crews and inshore lifeboats are sometimes sent abroad to help in areas devastated by floods. (Right) In 1970 to Bangladesh and (Left) in 2000 to Mozambique.

invaluable in 2000 in Mozambique. In March seven D class inflatables and eight volunteers led by Ian Canavan were airlifted to Beira, near the mouth of the Buzi River in Mozambique. Nearly a thousand miles of East Africa's low-lying coastal plain, between the Zambezi and the Limpopo, had been inundated by the worst floods in living memory. In the south, several towns with a population of over 100,000 had been totally submerged, and South African helicopters were rescuing people at the rate of 2000 a day. In the north, whole areas had been written off as hopeless, because there was no access to them by road, and the floods were too widespread for helicopters to land. In what was dubbed a 'mission impossible', the RNLI team were asked to try to take their inflatables some eighty miles up a swollen river which was flowing at ten knots and had burst its banks and split into a confusion of uncharted channels. 'You haven't a chance in hell of achieving anything,' a local told Ian Canavan; but the pessimist was made to eat his words.

The D class inflatables, and their crews, had a hard time. With the air temperature at 130°F and water temperature at 100°F, the engines constantly overheated and stalled. One lifeboat exploded; when they put ashore it was so hot that the soles of the crew's boots melted. Yet against all the odds they made it to the upper reaches of the Buzi. Here they found 'over 10,000 people desperately short of food and in poor health... it was very thought provoking'. Their lifeboats lacked the carrying capacity to have brought much food or medical aid, but they landed the little they had. They also landed two relief workers they had brought with them – a woman doctor and a logistician from Médecins du Monde – who made on-the-spot assessments of what was needed, so that the rescue teams on their way from France could bring the right aid to the right place. The inflatables then returned to Beira, their mission impossible having become a mission successfully accomplished.

took their boat into water breaking heavily . . . and hauled the two men aboard'. They were searching for other survivors when Amble's offshore lifeboat, the *Millie Walton*, arrived on the scene, and began desperate efforts to right the pinnace, since it was thought men were trapped beneath her. The inflatable, meanwhile, returned to harbour to land the two survivors who were in 'a very distressed condition', and to pick up skin-divers to help with righting the pinnace. While the inflatable was away, two more survivors were picked up, one by the *Millie Walton* and one by a helicopter.

When the ILB returned to the capsized pinnace, tapping could be heard from inside her hull, and the skin-divers, both experienced men, struggled until they were weak with hypothermia and exhaustion either to right the boat or get underneath her. But

Blue Peter has sponsored the building of many lifeboats – 'a gift from a community of the air to a community of the sea'. *Blue Peter* presenters Peter Purves, Lesley Judd and John Noakes, with the crew of North Berwick's lifeboat *Blue Peter III*, December 1973.

the heavy swell made it impossible. It was therefore decided to try to tow the pinnace into the calmer waters of Amble harbour, and the two lifeboats, together with another would-be rescuer, the seine boat *Ocean Vanguard*, worked together to get the necessary cables in place. However, with a scouring ebb tide and a huge swell, the tow proved far more difficult than expected. The mast of the upside-down pinnace fouled on the bar at the harbour entrance. The towlines parted. The tapping grew fainter.

What happened next shows that *any* rescue can go tragically wrong. The weather that evening could hardly be described as bad: fair visibility, a light wind, and the sea no more than moderate. The problem was the heavy and continuous swell breaking over shoal-water near the entrance to the harbour. In the confused seas, the lifeboats couldn't drag the casualty clear and the divers couldn't right her. Eventually she was washed ashore behind the south pier. Divers then waded out to her and managed to cut open her hull. Miraculously, one man inside was still alive. The others had drowned. No rescuers could have done more than the two-man crew of Amble's inflatable. They had been on service for three hours, much of the time in white water around the bar. They earned their bronze medals.

A totally different sort of rescue took place near St Agnes (Cornwall) on 17 July 1977.

A little before four thirty p.m., coastguards reported a surfer in difficulties off Porthtowan beach. It was not a good afternoon to have gone surfing. It was misty and raining, there was a twenty-knot wind, and huge waves were rolling in from the

Atlantic. Within minutes of being alerted, St Agnes's inflatable, *Blue Peter IV*, was launched and heading for Flat Rock Cove, into which the surfer was thought to have been swept. Flat Rock Cove has a narrow, rock-strewn entrance; its 150-foot cliffs are not only sheer but overhanging, and at high tide its sliver of shingle beach is under twelve feet of water.

The surfer who had got himself into trouble was, ironically, a lifesaver! Since there had been no bathers that afternoon on Porthtowan beach because of the weather, he had put on his wetsuit and taken his surfboard out to sea to practise. However, the waves had unexpectedly steepened and he had got into difficulties; a fierce current had carried him along the coast, and finally a huge wave had swept him, ricocheting from rock to rock, into Flat Rock Cove. Here he was left, bruised and dazed, on a strip of shingle that was growing smaller by the minute as the tide rose. He tried to climb the cliffs, but fell, breaking his wrist. He tried to swim out to sea, but great waves repeatedly flung him back. He had almost lost hope, when he heard a shout from the top of the cliffs: 'The lifeboat's coming!'

However, the lifeboat itself was in some difficulty. The offshore waters around Flat Rock Cove are shallow; waves that afternoon were breaking half a mile from land, and *Blue Peter IV* was being repeatedly swamped and near-capsized. At the approaches to the cove her helmsman, David Bliss, hove to in order to assess the situation. He realized that the overhanging cliffs precluded a rescue by helicopter, and that the rising tide precluded a rescue team getting down the cliffs to the surfer before he drowned. So the man's only hope was the lifeboat. To quote *The Life-Boat*:

> He [Bliss] knew that the surf would be worse as it funnelled into the cove, and there would be no turning back once approaching the entrance. He would have to keep going fast to keep control of the boat, and everything depended on the engine. If it failed, it was doubtful whether anyone would survive. But so skilful was his control of the lifeboat that he chose the right moment between waves and the right speed, and avoided all the rocks in his path. He beached close to the injured man, at the base of cliffs against which the waves were already washing 3 feet deep.

Blue Peter IV was turned head into sea, the surfer was given a lifejacket and helped into the boat, and the crew steeled themselves to attempt the even more hazardous passage out of the cove. Bliss asked his crewmen, Barry Garland and Roger Radcliffe, to spreadeagle themselves on the forward canopy so that their weight would hold the bow of the lifeboat down. As *Blue Peter IV* edged out of the cove, heavy seas again and again broke over her, so that the two men were totally submerged; but they managed to keep the lifeboat on a more or less even keel as she butted through successive twelve-foot waves. She was almost in the clear when a larger than usual wave flung her clean out of the water. Luckily, she landed right way up, her engine still running, and water cascading out of her self-bailers. Half an hour later Bliss ran *Blue Peter IV* ashore on Porthtowan beach, where an ambulance was waiting to take the surfer to hospital. You might say all's well that ends well; but the story could easily have had a not so happy ending.

An even more difficult rescue was carried out on Sunday 24 July 1983, by Largs's Atlantic 21 rigid inflatable, the *Independent Forester Liberty*.

A little after seven thirty in the evening, red flares were sighted off Great Cumbrae Island in the Firth of Clyde. Within nine minutes of the flares being spotted, the inflatable had been launched and was approaching the casualty, a capsized motor cruiser with only her bow above water. Several other vessels had already gone to her aid, and two survivors and one body had been recovered. However, it was thought that a young girl remained trapped inside the cabin of the overturned boat.

John Strachan, helmsman of the *Independent Forester Liberty*, realized there was little hope of righting the motor cruiser. So they had to get the girl out. Fortunately, the weather was fine, with good visibility, a light wind, and only a gentle swell; and one of the lifeboat crew, Arthur Hill, took off his lifejacket and swam to the capsized motor cruiser. He decided not to use a lifeline, in case it got tangled up and hampered the rescue. On his third attempt he managed to dive deep enough to get inside the hull. Here he found the girl, trapped in a tiny air pocket. She was wearing a lifejacket, fully conscious, and up to her neck in water. The air was stale and stank of fuel fumes. Arthur talked to the girl, who was naturally extremely frightened, but also commendably calm, and seemed more worried about her father than herself. He explained to her that he was going to try to push her down beneath the coaming, in the hope that she would surface outside the hull. However, on the first attempt he wasn't able to push her deep enough, and she surfaced not outside the hull but still inside it, barely conscious and completely disorientated.

Meanwhile John Strachan had twice dived down to see what was happening and try to help. He could hear Arthur talking to the girl, and trying desperately to keep her head above water; and he knew that if their next effort to free her failed, she was unlikely to survive. As Arthur struggled to push the girl down a second time, John managed to grab hold of her legs, pull her clear of the hull and bring her to the surface. A few seconds later Arthur also surfaced, dead white and near-unconscious from lack of oxygen. The two were hauled aboard, and the lifeboat headed back to Largs where an ambulance was waiting. The story has a sad postscript. The girl recovered, but the man who had drowned was her father.

On 1 December 1985, the Appledore inshore lifeboat put out to help what was in those days a comparatively new type of casualty, a windsurfer. It was midwinter. The wind was forty knots, gusting to fifty. There was six-tenths cloud and intermittent rain. The seas were twenty feet high, and it was bitterly cold. Soon after midday the Hartland coastguards spotted a man and his sailboard out of control and in imminent danger of being swept on to the Asp Rocks, where he would have had little hope of survival. The coastguards alerted the lifeboat station at Appledore.

Speed was clearly essential. So, although conditions for operating an inshore boat were marginal, it was decided to risk launching the Atlantic 21 rigid inflatable *Long Life I*. Even inside the harbour there was a nasty swell, and crossing the bar at the entrance was a test of seamanship; the wind was blowing against the tide, the seas were heavy and confused, and the helmsman, John Pavitt, needed all his skill to prevent the lifeboat capsizing. Nor were things a great deal easier in the open sea. Here the waves were a good twenty feet, and *Long Life I* became airborne almost every time she bounced off a crest. They soon spotted the man, only a few hundred yards from the rocks, with a helicopter hovering overhead. John gathered from his radio that the helicopter had tried to winch the man to safety, but he had been either unable or unwilling to get into the harness. So it was up to the lifeboat. Because the rocks were so near, John had little seaway in which to manoeuvre. Nevertheless, he managed to bring his lifeboat, head into wind, alongside the casualty, and the man was grabbed and hauled aboard, all mixed up with his harness and sailboard. He was incoherent, and suffering from exhaustion and hypothermia.

John would have liked him to be winched up by the helicopter, partly to get him to a doctor as fast as possible, and partly to spare him the danger of recrossing the bar. However, the difficult conditions and the man's weakness made a hoist too dangerous. So they headed back for Appledore. At the bar they found their offshore lifeboat *Louisa Anne Hawker*, waiting to stand by and assist. And her assistance was needed. For all this time the weather had been deteriorating; around the bar the waves were now so high and the spray so thick that all navigational aids were obscured, and John could see only the mast of the larger lifeboat as it led them in. Returning to harbour was even more difficult than leaving it. But after an exhausting and hazardous

RNLI inflatables have helped to rescue and evacuate
thousands of people and animals in areas
devastated by floods. (Top left and bottom right)
Uckfield. (Top right) Llandudno. (Bottom left) Lewes.

service, the windsurfer was landed safely. One hopes he realized that his foolishness had put at risk not only his own life but those of other people.

On 26 January 1990, a more lighthearted rescue – a comic opera scenario – took place at West Mersea. The inshore lifeboat rescued a taxi! Off much of the Essex coast the offshore waters are shallow; sandbars and mudflats are criss-crossed by winding channels, and the areas of higher ground are often linked by causeways. On one of these causeways, a little after midnight and in the pitch darkness of midwinter, a taxi broke down. The tide was rising, and the driver knew that at high water there would be more than a dozen feet of sea over the roof of his cab. He radioed for help. The crew of West Mersea's Atlantic 21 were local men who knew local waters; but their job was far from easy for, as a coastguard put it, 'To run aground at that state of the tide was easy, to stay afloat was almost impossible.' However, guided by the taxi's headlights shining eerily under the water, they located the 'casualty'. Her driver and passenger were helped into the lifeboat, unhurt but considerably shaken, for the roof of their cab was already under a foot of water. When West Mersea's honorary secretary made his report, under the heading 'Casualty's Port of Registry' he entered 'DVLC Swansea'.

Between 26 February and 1 March 1990, inshore lifeboats from Rhyl, Llandudno and Flint carried out another unusual service. Towards the end of February, a combination of high tides and hurricane-force onshore winds caused chaos in the low-lying coastal areas of north Wales. Sea walls collapsed, rivers burst their banks, and towns and villages had to be evacuated. The local inshore lifeboats were called into service. To quote the journal: 'The conditions which greeted their crews were difficult in the extreme. Water up to 6 ft deep, currents up to 5 knots, floating debris, and underwater obstructions ranging from collapsed walls to open manhole covers.' For several days the lifeboat crews worked virtually non-stop, snatching what little food and rest they could in between ferrying people to safety. It was not spectacular work – though live street lights under the water, open sewers, unstable walls and rivers in spate were not to be taken lightly – but it was certainly appreciated. After working virtually non-stop for four days, the lifeboat crews had lifted nearly 600 people to safety, not to mention countless farm animals and pets.

On 14 January 1991, a rescue took place even farther inland: in the middle of a Liverpool park.

In mid-January a cold spell in north-west England sent temperatures plummeting to −5°C. Ice formed on inland waterways. And while playing with his dog, thirteen-year-old Fred Allen fell through the ice that covered one of the lakes in Liverpool's Walton Hall Park. Both boy and dog managed to scramble on to a small island in the middle of the lake; but because of the broken ice, neither police, firemen nor ambulance crews could get to them. So a lifeboat was called for. West Kirby's D 322 inflatable was loaded on to her trailer and towed by Land Rover some fourteen miles to the 'casualty'. With police escort and flashing blue lights, her route took her through the Mersey Tunnel and the centre of Liverpool. However, when she got to the park there was a problem. Walton Hall Park was ringed by eight-foot iron railings, and at nine p.m. in midwinter none of the gates was open. So the 700-pound lifeboat had to be hoisted over the railings before she could be launched. Then, using their wellies as icebreakers, the crew smashed their way through the ice, and rescued both boy and dog. They were taken to hospital, not seriously hurt but suffering from hypothermia. As West Kirby's honorary secretary told the press next morning: 'We're not called an inshore lifeboat for nothing!'

A year later, Tiffany, Timothy, Chocolate Drop, Snuffles and Gem were the dramatis personae in an even more offbeat rescue.

When the Allandale Animal Sanctuary relocated from the isle of Inchkeith (in the Firth of Forth) to the mainland, five goats managed to avoid capture and remain on the island. Left to their own devices, the animals were thoroughly enjoying their freedom; but when it was found that illegal shooting parties were landing on Inchkeith, the trustees of the sanctuary became concerned for the goats' safety. A group of volunteers hired a small ferry, the *Spirit of Fife*, and set out on a rescue operation. After 'an exciting chase' three of the goats were rounded up. However, the other two leapt into the sea and swam to an offshore skein of rocks. As the tide rose, and waves began to sluice over the rocks, it was clear that the goats were in danger of drowning. It was another case for the lifeboat.

The rescue that followed was probably the least dangerous and most frustrating the crew of Queensferry's Atlantic 21 were ever called out on. The lifeboat came alongside the rocks, and the goats – with no little difficulty – were lassoed. One was persuaded aboard. The other resisted so stoutly that the crew were afraid it might be injured; it was therefore towed back to the island behind the inflatable on the end of a rope. Once ashore, the goats were handed over to their would-be rescuers. And promptly escaped! No more efforts were made to catch them. It was felt they had earned their freedom.

In October 1992, a rescue took place in Chichester harbour that looked both back to the past and forward to the future. It was an old-fashioned service, in that it involved saving people from a foundering vessel in appalling conditions; it was also

Cartoon from *Self Writer* (the RNLI in-house magazine).

BELOW

The ocean-going ketch *Donald Searle*, aground in Chichester harbour, 25 October, 1992.

a modern service, in that it involved not only inshore and offshore lifeboats but a helicopter.

Chichester harbour has been called 'a magnet for sailors'. In particular, it has been a magnet for the new breed of first-time sailing enthusiasts born of the affluence of the 1960s and '70s. However, with its reedbeds, mudflats and narrow channels, it is by no means as safe as it looks, and its inshore lifeboat station on Hayling Island is one of the busiest in the British Isles. In the late morning of Sunday, 26 October, the seventy-five-foot ketch *Donald Searle* was approaching the bar at the mouth of Chichester harbour in worsening weather. The *Donald Searle* was (to quote the helmsman of the Hayling Island inflatable) 'a huge boat, capable of sailing any-where in the world in any conditions', and it probably never occurred to her crew that approaching a flat estuary, within a few hundred yards of land, things could go seriously wrong. But the weather was bad and worsening, and as the *Donald Searle* was crossing the bar, first her engines failed, then her anchors. And suddenly the great boat was being battered by twenty-five-foot waves and in danger of being driven on to the mudflats. She sent out a Mayday.

Helicopters

Many lifeboat crews are now given special training in helicopter winching, which is now playing an increasingly important role in rescue work.

The first recorded sea rescue by a helicopter was off Long Island (USA) in 1938, when an experimental R-4 from a research establishment lifted off the crew of a sinking barge. During the Second World War, helicopters were used for search and rescue operations, and in 1948 the RNLI began trials to see how they could best be used to help save lives at sea.

It was agreed that it would be 'wasteful of money, material and hours' for the Institution to have its own helicopters, and that the way ahead lay in co-operation with the services. Postwar, the Navy and the RAF were operating an increasing number of helicopters from airfields all over the country, and both services agreed that their 'choppers' should work with the RNLI on emergency rescue operations.

On 27 November 1954, the South Goodwins light-ship capsized during a violent storm. Lifeboats from Dover, Ramsgate and Walmer went to her aid, but found no sign of life. However, an Albatross helicopter, flown by Captain Curtis E. Parkins of the United States Air Force, spotted and managed to winch up a solitary survivor. This was the first time a helicopter effected a rescue when lifeboats were present but had failed. It marked the dawn of an era of co-operation – co-operation that has become increasingly effective over the years.

A typical present-day lifeboat-cum-helicopter rescue took place in the winter of 1998/9, when the Dutch training ship *Eendracht* went aground off Newhaven. As the ship was listing heavily and being pounded by huge seas and gale-force winds, her skipper asked for the fifty-one people on board to be taken off. Newhaven's Arun class lifeboat managed

The RNLI has no helicopters. It relies on co-operation with the Royal Navy, the Royal Air Force, H M Coastguards and the Rescue Co-ordination Centre. Helicopters are on permanent stand-by.

to manoeuvre between ship and shore, and made three attempts to come alongside, but was crushed and damaged. Helicopter assistance was called for, and the lifeboat stood by while forty people were airlifted to safety by a coastguard helicopter and the remaining eleven by a Navy helicopter. The lifeboat then managed to pass a towline between the *Eendracht* and a tug, and eventually the training ship was towed to safety.

The following airfields now have helicopters on round-the-clock standby for emergency work with the RNLI:

England
Boulmer (RAF Sea Kings), Chivenor (RAF Sea Kings), Culdrose (RN Sea Kings), Leconfield (RAF Sea Kings), Lee-on-Solent (HM Coastguard AW139s), Portland (HM Coastguard AW139s), Wattisham (RAF Sea Kings).

Scotland
Kinloss (Rescue Co-ordination Centre Sea Kings), Lossiemouth (RAF Sea Kings), Prestwick (RN Sea Kings), Stornoway (HM Coastguard S92s), Sumburgh (HM Coastguard S92s).

Ireland
Dublin (S61Ns), Sligo (SCINs), Shannon (Rescue Co-ordination Centre S6INs).

Wales
Valley (RAF Sea Kings)

The nearest lifeboat, Hayling Island's *Aldershot*, was already on service, rescuing a sailboarder. But the ketch's Mayday was picked up by Frank Dunster, an off-duty lifeboatman; and Frank decided to launch his own single-engined inflatable, *Hayling Rescue*, which he kept in the local marina, as a stopgap until the other lifeboats arrived. He had a hard time getting to the *Donald Searle* in his tiny boat; and when he did at last reach her, he found she was in real trouble, being flung violently this way and that in shallow water close to a sub-merged wreck. He realized that the offshore lifeboat (which he knew was on its way from Bembridge) would have difficulty operating in the shallows, while his own tiny inflatable couldn't hope to rescue the large number of people aboard the ketch. So he radioed for helicopter assistance, then tried to bring his tiny boat alongside. On his second attempt, the *Donald Searle* reared up near-vertical, but one man jumped and was hauled aboard. At his next attempt, the ketch fell off the crest of a wave, coming within inches of crushing the inflatable like an eggshell. On his fourth attempt, a woman jumped, but plummeted into the sea, and if Frank Dunster hadn't hauled her aboard

Two of the traumatised survivors from the *Donald Searle*.

within seconds she would have been crushed between the two boats.

With two sodden and traumatized survivors aboard, and his inflatable threatening any moment to capsize in the huge seas, Frank headed for home. On his way back to Hayling Island, he passed the *Aldershot* heading for the casualty. *Aldershot* had just been hit by a huge wave, 'the height of a double-decker'; she had been flung into the air, both engines had stalled, and her helmsman, Rod James, felt sure she was going to somersault and capsize. 'I was hanging on to the steering wheel,' he said after-wards, 'to stop myself falling out. And I took a deep breath, thinking the boat was going to turn over, with me underneath.' But at the last moment, the engines restarted. The crew got *Aldershot* under control, and they were heading once again for the ketch. They got there at the same time as the helicopter.

Rod James now had to make a tough decision. There were still fifteen people onboard the *Donald Searle*; if she foundered, there would be little chance of saving them all. He therefore decided to try to get as many as he could aboard his inflatable, while the helicopter winched up the rest. Seven times, 'with great courage and skill', he manoeuvred as close as he could to the violently pitching vessel. Five times, a single person jumped and was hauled aboard. When the inflatable was full to over-flowing, one of her crew, Christopher Reed, managed to scramble aboard the ketch to help with the helicopter winching. The overcrowded *Aldershot* then headed back for Hayling Island, while the offshore lifeboat from Bembridge (which had just arrived) stood by.

Because conditions for helicopter winching were clearly going to be hazardous, the Bembridge boat decided to try to continue the rescue herself. She managed to take off one more person from the ketch. But at a price. In the heavy seas the two vessels crunched together; both were damaged, and it was agreed to use the helicopter to lift off the remaining passengers and crew. Within little more than an hour of the Mayday being transmitted, the rescue was complete. A satisfactory end to a near-disaster which, in the words of one of the lifeboatmen, 'should never have happened'.

The qualities needed to carry out this sort of inshore rescue are the traditional courage, determination and good seamanship that have long been the hallmark of offshore lifeboatmen; and the men and women who today crew our inshore inflatables are cast in the same mould as the oarsmen of Greathead's Originals. There is also an additional quality that is sometimes asked of them: kindness.

The crew of the Hayling Island inshore lifeboat *Aldershot*.

In the old days the majority of people rescued by lifeboats were the crews of fishing boats or merchant vessels, adults with some knowledge of the sea. There was often neither time nor need for personal, one-to-one contact. Nowadays the majority of people rescued are pleasure-seekers and holidaymakers, many of them children and many of them with little understanding of the sea. There is therefore a lot to be said for an approach that is not only caring but seen to be caring. A smile and a joke can be as helpful as a strong arm.

When Faye Lasdell drifted out to sea and was left alone on her inflatable crocodile, she wasn't afraid of the men who came to rescue her because they were 'funny and kind'. And she wrote them a charming letter:

Dear Lifeboatmen,

Thank you very much for saving me on 6th August 1995. I am very grateful.

Love, Faye Lasdell age 7.

PS Faye's family are very grateful too. Thank you!

Lifeboat crews might be forgiven if they occasionally get a bit fed up with rescuing people who have got themselves into difficulties. But most see the funny side of it. Witness a coxswain's cheerful shout as he towed back a none too seaworthy dinghy and its lifejacket-less crew: 'Bring 'em back alive!'

'It is not walls tha
but thos

make a city,
who man them'

ike many charities today, the RNLI is much concerned with raising money. No wonder, when it costs over £2.6 million to build a modern (Tamar class) lifeboat, and around £339,000 a day just to keep the Institution ticking over. Fundraising is a sine qua non of survival. Yet no matter how much money comes in, and no matter how splendid the lifeboats are and how state of the art their equipment, when it comes to the crunch everything still depends on the crew.

A hundred years ago most lifeboatmen were fishermen, with a sprinkling of ex-servicemen, merchant seamen, tradesmen, farmers, coast-guards and local gentry. The skills demanded of a crew were seafaring skills, in particular the ability to pull an oar and handle sail. Even as late as the 1950s, a historian of the RNLI could write: 'Every member of Whitby's lifeboat, except the mechanic, is a fisherman by trade ... and the fishing industry and the work of the lifeboat [are] indissolubly bound together'.

Times have changed. To quote a recent article in *The Lifeboat*: 'A lifeboatman in the 1800s was wise in the ways of the sea, knowing his coast as well as his village street. A lifeboatman today could be anything from garage mechanic to teacher to company director, and the skills required are to operate some of the most sophisticated equipment in the maritime world.' This highlights the two major differences between the crews of yesterday and the crews of today. Lifeboatmen and women today can be drawn from any walk of life, and what is asked of them is not so much physical strength as the ability to work as a team and to operate equipment.

This latter requirement has brought about another big difference between yesterday's crews and today's. Modern lifeboatmen and women are much better trained than their predecessors. In the old days, most crew members needed little tuition in seamanship

ABOVE Lerwick's Gold Medal crew in November 1997.

LEFT The Abersoch lifeboat crew in the early 1900s.

because they were already professional seafarers. It is true that the Institution's top-hatted inspectors used to pay regular visits to lifeboat stations all round the coast, but their attention was focused not so much on the crews as on the boats and equipment. It was not until engines began to replace sails that the need to train at least some members of the crew became apparent.

At first, it was only coxswains and mechanics who were trained. But as marine engines and ancillary equipment – VHF, radar, satellite D/F, etc. – became increasingly sophisticated it was realized that the more crew members had specialized skills, the better. Such skills needed to be taught. Today's lifeboats are, like the old oar-pulled Originals, still manned by volunteers. But these volunteers are every bit as professionally competent in their part-time calling as their full-time (and fully paid) counterparts in other countries.

This is due, at least in part, to their training. If you want to become a lifeboatman or woman, this is what will be expected of you: You must be over seventeen (with parental approval) or over eighteen (without it). You must pass a reasonably demanding medical. It would be helpful if you had some knowledge of the coastline close to your lifeboat station, and some ability at small boat handling. And, most important of all, you must fit in with and be acceptable to the rest of the crew.

A lifeboat crew is a team: 'tous pour un, un pour tous'. For as the strength of a chain is the strength of its weakest link, so in a lifeboat one moment of frailty by one member of the crew is likely to put everyone's life at risk. Successful rescues often depend not only on every member of the crew doing their job, but on their doing it in collaboration with their companions. The men and women who crew a modern lifeboat must therefore have absolute trust in one another.

During an initial probationary period, you will be expected to help with routine maintenance of the boat, take part in practice launches and exercises, and, most importantly, attend weekly crew meetings so that you can get to know the rest of the crew and they can get to know you. Next, assuming you are found acceptable, you will start acquiring the skills essential to your new part-time calling. A first step will be to study at home the various training manuals and videos provided by the Institution; these cover basic subjects such as navigation and boat handling. A second step will be to attend classes at one of the Institution's mobile training units. These pay frequent visits to all lifeboat stations. They are staffed by qualified instructors who train crew members (generally in the evenings) in subjects such as first aid, how to operate radar, and co-operation with helicopters. Crew members who attain a sufficiently high standard in the various subjects are given a certificate of proficiency. A third step will be to attend an intensive sea training course. Classroom-based theory sessions in the Lifeboat College in Poole give practical hands-on training in the College's survival pool and full-bridge simulator. There are also intensive training exercises in lifeboats in Poole harbour and beyond. These exercises live up to their name of 'intensive', and include helicopter winching, capsizing and self-righting, and coping with such horrendous situations as chemical asphyxiation. There is also a big, once-a-year exercise when large numbers of lifeboats are called on to cope with a simulated major disaster – say, fire aboard a ferry and the evacuation of badly injured passengers.

In addition to all this, before an all-weather lifeboat goes on service, her crew take part in extensive tests. Before the boat leaves the builders' yard, she undergoes some forty hours of proving trials under the supervision of a member of the RNLI's technical department, and these trials are carried out in the presence of the mechanic, coxswain and two or three crew members from the lifeboat's intended station. Once the boat is officially accepted, she goes to Poole, where her crew join her for a week's intensive training. The crew then sail her to her station under the eyes of a Divisional Inspector and a Divisional Engineer. Finally, the crew spend a further fortnight carrying out as many exercises as possible under as many conditions as possible. A lifeboat nowadays only goes into service once her crew are happy with her and feel at home in her – a far cry from the days of the Originals, when crews were expected to make the best they could of a boat often ill suited to their needs.

The value of all this training should become apparent when you take part in a demanding service. It should help you cope with an emergency. However, no amount of training can ensure that you *will* cope. That is something that will depend on the sort of person you are.

So what sort of person do you need to be to become one of a lifeboat crew?

Between the First and Second World Wars, a competition was held in schools to 'Describe the sort of person a good lifeboatman should be.' The language of the answers may be archaic (and far from politically correct!), but the image conjured up is as valid today as it was in the 1930s. Some answers stressed the need for courage: 'As the Lion is the King of Beasts, so the lifeboatman is the King of Heroes'; 'He is the hero of the seven seas.' Some stressed the need for determination: 'He must be dogged as the British bulldog.' Others emphasized the Christian ethic: 'He must put God first, other people second, self last.' Some of the responses gave primacy to the need for good seamanship: 'He should be a sea dog down to his last hair'; or, less demandingly, 'He needs to know the front end of his boat from the back.' Some stressed the need for kindness: 'He is gentle and tender towards those he has rescued,' and for modesty: 'Lifeboatmen do good deeds and then say no more about them . . . they do not swank.' Other answers paid tribute to lifeboatmen's wives, though for reasons that would cause raised eyebrows today: 'He must choose a wife who will be ready with warm blankets and hot-water bottles'; 'He must have a good wife or someone similar to get off his wet clothes'; 'Their wives must be willing to let them go out late at night.'

If asked to pick a handful of services that reflect these characteristics and demonstrate the sort of people lifeboatmen and women need to be, I would choose William Hillary's rescue of the crew of the *St George* (Douglas, 1830); the efforts of the Brooke and Brighstone Grange lifeboats to save the crew of the *Sirenia* (Isle of Wight, 1888); Robert Patton's attempt to save a lame man from the salvage steamer *Disperser* (Runswick, 1934); James Dougal's rescue of two divers in a hurricane (Eyemouth, 1991); and Richard Pearce's rescue of two girls from the Palace Pier

(Brighton, 1995). Apart from other considerations, these services cover almost the length and breadth of the British Isles, almost the whole span of the Institution's history, and almost the whole range of its lifeboats, from the oar-pulled Originals to the 'rubber ducks' and ocean-going giants of the twenty-first century.

On the night of 20 November 1830, the Royal Mail steamer *St George* was driven on to St Mary's Island at the approaches to Douglas harbour. In those days two vessels, *St George* and *Mona's Isle*, were vying for supremacy in the lucrative passenger run from Liverpool to the Isle of Man. On 20 November both vessels were at sea when wiser masters would have stayed in harbour. Both reached Douglas in the twilight at low tide, and because the water wasn't deep enough for them to enter harbour both anchored in Douglas Bay, and their passengers were ferried ashore. As the light faded the wind backed south. The Master of *Mona's Isle* was a local man. He knew the saying: '*Yn chiuney smoo erbee geay jiass smessey jee*.' He weighed anchor and made for the open sea. But the master of the *St George*, Lieutenant John Tudor, was not from the island; he remained at anchor, telling himself the tide was rising, the weather was clearing, and he would soon be entering harbour. However, a little after midnight the wind suddenly increased, and huge white-crested waves came surging into Douglas Bay, piling up house-high in the shallow water. John Tudor had his full crew of twenty-two onboard. They got up steam, dropped their emergency anchors and tried to ride out the storm. But in the small hours their anchor cables parted, and before their engines could take effect the *St George* was flung on to the rocky foreshore of St Mary's Island, a couple of hundred yards from the harbour entrance. Her hull was ripped open; water poured into her, and she came to rest 'bow-down and broadside to the most rugged part of the isle, lurching violently as the waves smashed into her'. Some of her crew tried to launch one of her ship's boats, but it capsized and the men were flung into the sea; they were lucky to be hauled back on board. Distress rockets soared skyward and were swirled over what was then the little fishing village of Douglas.

One would have thought that Douglas – home of William Hillary and scene of so many disasters in the past – would have had a lifeboat. However, the old one was damaged and the new one not yet commissioned. It was therefore a scratch boat with a scratch crew that went to the aid of the *St George*.

William Hillary was coxswain. He was fifty-nine and no great shakes as a seaman. Yet he was very much the driving force behind the rescue, motivated, we are told, by his 'overwhelming humanity' – his determination that, no matter what the risk or the cost, he would save the lives of those who had been shipwrecked.

It took his crew two hours, battling head into wind and sea, to reach a position upwind of the casualty from which they could drop anchor and prepare to veer down on her. Their first idea was to come alongside and hope the crew could jump into the lifeboat. However, as they got closer they saw that the seaward side of the *St George* was a place of death. Huge waves were one moment sweeping green over the ship, next moment receding to leave reefs of rock glistening in the moonlight. They backed away.

William Hillary takes his rowing boat
True Blue into the dangerous channel
between the paddle-steamer *St George*
and the rocks of St Mary's Isle. In a
rescue that called for great courage, all
the crew of the *St George* were saved.

It seemed to Hillary that their only hope was to come in on the
landward side of the wreck. Their boat had a shallow draught, and
he reckoned it might be swept on the crest of a wave clean over the
submerged rocks. When John Tudor saw what the rescue boat was
attempting he shouted at them not to be foolhardy. But Hillary was
in no mood to back off. He edged into the narrow gap between the
St George and the rocks. They had almost made it when a huge
wave flung them against the hull of the wreck. Their rudder was torn away. Six of
their ten oars were broken or lost. And before they could regain control, another
wave tossed the lifeboat clean out of the water, and Hillary and three of the crew
were washed overboard.

The three crewmen were quickly rescued. But Hillary was injured. Flung against the stern of the lifeboat, six of his ribs were broken and his breastbone crushed. No more than half-conscious, he managed to grab one of the ropes dangling over the side of the *St George*. The crew spotted him, and he was hauled aboard.

In spite of his injuries, and the fact that he was far from being the most experienced seaman onboard, Hillary insisted on taking command. He could see that it wouldn't be long before the *St George* broke up with the loss of all aboard her. Their lifeboat was damaged but still afloat, so their only chance was to use it. He ordered the debris cluttering the side of the wreck to be cut clear, with the idea of allowing the lifeboat to be swept over St Mary's Rock and into the calmer water beyond.

For two hours, doused by green seas and sheets of spray, the crew hacked away at the rigging and mast. At last a passageway was cleared, and thirty-six exhausted men (twenty-two of the crew and fourteen of the rescuers) slid down the ropes and into the lifeboat. Hillary waited until a larger than usual wave loomed over them. He gave the order to cast off. The lifeboat was lifted up by the swell. For a moment it looked as though they were going to be swept clean over St Mary's; but at the last moment the wave subsided, and the lifeboat crunched into the rocks. As she lay broadside on, another wave swept over her. Several men were washed out of the boat, but managed to cling to gunwales or lifelines; until, as Hillary put it afterwards, 'thanks to Merciful Providence', they were swirled into a patch of calm water in the lee of the rock. As they clung to their near-foundering lifeboat, hardly daring to believe they were still alive, they heard voices and the plash of oars. Two boats from Douglas had put out to help them. The rescuers were rescued.

In the small hours of the morning the *St George* broke up. By dawn all that was left of her was a couple of engine-room boilers, and a few fragments of twisted metal and splintered wood. It was several months before Hillary's broken ribs no longer hurt him; the injury to his breastbone was to trouble him for the rest of his life.

It is easy to be critical of several aspects of the rescue of the crew of the *St George*. Hillary showed no particular skill in seamanship; he took risks that many would consider unacceptable. He jeopardized the lives of his crew, and his rescue owed as much to luck as to skill. But overshadowing, and to some extent negating, all this was his courage. That night he lived up to the motto he had chosen for his family crest: 'With courage nothing is impossible.' And in the final analysis courage is perhaps the quality that lifeboatmen and women need more than anything else.

To save the crew of the grain ship *Sirenia* the crews of the Isle of Wight lifeboats needed not only courage but also determination and a refusal to admit defeat. On the morning of Saturday, 9 March 1888, while walking to his father's farm, young Henry Cotton noticed what looked like 'a small white cloud' bobbing up and down over the top of the cliffs on the south coast of the Isle of Wight. It was some moments before he realized that what he was looking at was the billowing sails of a ship that had gone aground at the foot of the cliffs. He ran to his father's cottage, and the Cotton family, nearly all of them lifeboatmen, hurried to the Brighstone Grange lifeboat station.

There was a fair amount of fog that morning and a heavy sea, a not uncommon combination off the Isle of Wight; and the 1500-ton *Sirenia*, laden with wheat from California, had run on to the Atherfield Ledge at low tide. At first, her master, Captain McIntyre, thought she was in no great danger; he expected that as the tide rose the *Sirenia* would float clear. The crews of the Brooke and Brighstone Grange lifeboats knew better. Maroons thundered out above the roar of the waves as the *Worcester Cadet* and the *William Stanley Lewis* prepared to launch. But into what a sea! 'I had never seen such huge waves breaking on the beach,' one of the Brighstone Grange crew later told a reporter. It took Brighstone Grange's *Worcester Cadet* two hours of hard rowing to reach the casualty, 'climbing an endless succession of long grey seas, the crew repeatedly soaked by deluges of icy water as each swell broke over the lifeboat's bow'. Getting alongside was difficult. Getting a line onboard was even more difficult. The first was broken by a mountainous wave; but the second held, and two women and three children (the youngest in a wickerwork basket) were lowered into the lifeboat. All this time the weather had been worsening, and the coxswain was afraid that if too many of the crew crowded into the boat she might be swamped and the children washed overboard. He therefore agreed with Captain McIntyre to land the women and children on the nearby shore, then come back for the crew. It was getting dark by the time the *Worcester Cadet* beached beside the Atherfield Ledge. By now a fair-sized crowd had gathered at both the top and the bottom of the cliffs, among them a working party from Brighstone Grange who had brought with them the lifeboat's carriage; this was now lowered seventy-five feet down the slippery, unstable cliff to enable the *Worcester Cadet* to be relaunched.

The lifeboatmen, by this time, had been at sea for something like six hours, but with the weather worsening they knew they needed to get back to the stranded vessel as soon as they could. There was time for a quick mug of tea, but no time for rest.

Both the relaunch and the return passage to the *Sirenia* were a nightmare, and in the rising wind and steepening sea the *Worcester Cadet* was repeatedly swamped. As they manoeuvred alongside, they were three times flung against the grain ship's steel hull 'with such force that I thought our boat must be broken in pieces. Ten of our oars were lost.' Thirteen of the crew managed to jump or lower themselves into the lifeboat. But in the moment of casting off, just as they had severed the rope holding them to the *Sirenia*, they saw 'a huge wave, higher than any of the others, a mountain of black water with a fringe of white at the top', looming over them. The lifeboat was upended and swept near-vertical towards the shore. When the giant wave had passed, the *Worcester Cadet* broached to, and the next wave broke flush on top of her. She capsized. She self-righted almost instantly, and, miraculously, twenty-two out of the twenty-six aboard her managed to clamber back into the boat. But her first coxswain, Moses Munt, and second coxswain, Thomas Cotton, along with two of the rescued seamen, had disappeared. With only four oars and a damaged, water-logged boat there was no hope of even trying to search for them. The *Worcester Cadet*

was swirled willy-nilly towards the shore, spewed up on the beach and hauled to safety by the men and women at the foot of the cliffs.

The grain ship, *Sirenia*, which was wrecked off the Isle of Wight on 9 March 1888.

Two of her crew had been drowned, several had been injured, all were suffering from hypothermia and exhaustion. But they at once set to work to repair their boat and get together a full crew. For there were more than a dozen men still onboard the *Sirenia*.

Meanwhile the Brooke lifeboat, the *William Stanley Lewis*, was also in difficulty.

So enormous were the waves that morning, sweeping into Brooke Chine, that the coxswain of the lifeboat, John Hayter, reckoned it would be 'suicidal' even to attempt a launch. The lifeboat was therefore loaded on to her carriage and dragged to nearby Grange Chine. But even here, in more sheltered conditions, launching proved impossible. The *William Stanley Lewis* was flung back, broadside on, up the beach, and damaged. Two of her crew were injured. New crewmen came forward. The boat was repaired, taken to Chilton Chine, lowered down the face of the cliffs and successfully launched.

It is six miles from Chilton Chine to the Atherfield Ledge. In the huge seas and strengthening south-west gale, the *William Stanley Lewis* was repeatedly swamped and several times nearly capsized. By the time she got to within hailing distance of the *Sirenia*, the sun had set. Suddenly, out of the darkness, a huge wave rose up above them. The lifeboat rolled to within an ace of capsizing, and three of her crew were washed overboard. Two managed to cling to their lifelines and were hauled back, but the second coxswain, Reuben Cooper, was swept away. His cries for help could be heard from both the lifeboat and the *Sirenia*. Flares were flung overboard, forming pools of flickering blue light, but there was no sign of Reuben. Coxswain Hayter shouted to McIntyre that he would try to take off his crew. Captain McIntyre, however, pleaded with the coxswain to go on looking for his missing crewman; he and his men, he said, would take their chance of rescue later.

In the search that followed, the *William Stanley Lewis* was swept clean over the Atherfield Ledge, a combination of wind, tide and current first driving her through 'a veritable Hell of waters', then preventing her return. Lesser men would have given up and run downwind to safety. But the crew of the Brooke lifeboat dropped anchor; they would, they agreed, wait for daylight, the turn of the tide, and a chance to get back to the stranded vessel. To quote a contemporary report: 'Throughout the remainder of that fierce night the men sat and shuddered and bandaged their blistered hands . . . They were chilled to the bone, drenched to the skin and had been without food or drink for many hours.' But they stood by the *Sirenia* throughout the hours of darkness, and in the half-light of dawn they tried to get back to her.

As they headed into the white water over the Ledge, it seemed to the onlookers, many of whom had spent all night on the cliffs, that they were heading for certain death. There were cries of warning and dismay. Even Captain McIntyre shouted at them to turn back.

For more than an hour the crew of the *William Stanley Lewis* struggled to fight their way westward. But in their weakened condition and with their few undamaged oars, they lacked the physical strength to make headway against current and wind. Yet it was only when they saw that the Brighstone Grange lifeboat was preparing to relaunch that they gave up. By the time they struggled back to their station, after a service of more than fifteen hours in horrendous conditions, several of them were so cold, cramped and exhausted they had to be lifted out of the lifeboat.

By now, the *Sirenia* was in imminent danger of breaking up. Her hull had been ripped open, water had flooded into her hold, and her cargo of wheat, swollen by the damp, had burst through her deck. There was now only one hope left for the thirteen men still aboard her: the *Worcester Cadet*.

During the night, the Brighstone Grange lifeboat had been patched up. Many of her crew had been injured; all were at the end of their tether; yet three of them, the Cotton brothers and sixteen-year-old Frank Salter, volunteered to make yet another attempt at rescue. 'I've been out twice,' Salter is reported to have said, 'so I can go out again. Just give me a cup of tea.' These three were joined by lifeboatmen from Ventnor, Atherfield, Bembridge and Sandown, also by a local smuggler, Fred

Bastiani. They launched in mid-morning, managed to get alongside the shattered *Sirenia*, and in a particularly hazardous rescue took off the rest of her crew and brought them safely ashore.

The service to the *Sirenia* was long and costly. For more than two days lifeboat crews were almost constantly attempting to launch, repairing their boats, or at sea in testing conditions. Three lifeboatmen were killed. Several were injured. And for many years afterwards, Saturday, 9 March, was known on the Isle of Wight as 'Black Saturday'. However, as the Chief Inspector of Lifeboats subsequently wrote in his report, 'The perseverance of the men both in the boats and on shore was worthy of admiration'. The Isle of Wight crews did indeed prove themselves 'dogged as the British bulldog', and it was thanks to their doggedness, their refusal to admit defeat, that almost the whole crew of the *Sirenia* were saved.

Courage and determination are qualities that many people like to think they might perhaps be able to summon up in a crisis. But how many of us can say that we would be willing, in the words of the Bible, to lay down our life for our friends? Robert Patton was.

In the early hours of 8 February 1934, the salvage vessel *Disperser* was sinking. There was a full gale that morning, with squalls of rain and a heavy sea beating down on the Yorkshire coast. When the *Disperser* got into difficulties a tug took her in tow, but about five miles north-east of Staithes Nab the salvage vessel seemed about to founder. The tug came alongside and managed to take off seven out of eight of her crew, but the eighth crewman was disabled and it proved impossible to rescue him. The Runswick lifeboat was alerted, and prepared to launch.

Lifeboatmen at Runswick, the old generation and the new. On the left, the older generation: Bowman Joseph Taylor, Second Coxswain Tom Patton and Coxswain Andrew Tose. On the right (left to right): Bowman Robert Taylor, Coxswain Robert Patton (who gave his life on service in 1934) and Second Coxswain George Taylor (photograph taken in 1931).

Runswick was typical of the many small stations that opened in the mid-nineteenth century, did sterling work for a hundred or so years, but was then closed, partly because of the development of long-range seagoing lifeboats, and partly because the decline in the fishing industry led to a shortage of crewmen. In 1934, however, the station was still operational, and had just been given a new Liverpool class motor boat, *The Always Ready*, together with a tractor to launch her – so the women of Runswick no longer had to wade waist-deep into the water to get their lifeboat afloat. The coxswain, Robert Patton, came from a family of lifeboatmen; his father had been awarded a bronze medal in 1924. Robert joined the lifeboat crew at the age of sixteen, and for thirty years hardly missed a launch, except during the war years when he served in minesweepers.

The Always Ready launched at four twenty-five a.m., and the matter of fact words of *The Lifeboat* tell us what happened:

After about an hour the lifeboat sighted the *Disperser*, and with considerable difficulty in the heavy seas got alongside the sinking salvage vessel. The crew shouted at the man still aboard her to jump. Instead he lowered himself over one side and clung to the rails. Robert Patton seized him and told him to let go; but he clung only tighter. Suddenly the lifeboat was carried [by a wave] away from the steamer. Robert Patton could have loosened his hold, but he knew that if he did so the man would almost certainly fall into the sea. He therefore held on, was dragged overboard, and fell into the sea between the lifeboat and the steamer. But he still held onto the man. Then a heavy sea flung the lifeboat back against, the steamer, and Patton's lifebelt took the full force of the blow. The rest of the crew dragged the man on board; but before they could rescue their coxswain, he had twice more been crushed between lifeboat and steamer. [Shortly after this the *Disperser* sank.] The lifeboat returned to Runswick at 6.15, and the coxswain was taken to hospital. Several of his ribs had been broken; his pelvis had been fractured in three places, and he had other [internal] injuries. When, two days later, he was visited by an officer of the Institution, he was conscious and able to speak. He had known the risk he had run [he said] but the man was a cripple; had he dropped into the sea he would have had little chance of survival.

'I couldn't let the poor lad go,' Robert Patton said. 'He might have drowned'.

A week later, he died.

Four thousand people came to his funeral. The Institution gave his widow a pension. The Carnegie Hero Fund helped to finance his daughter's education. And Runswick's lifeboat was renamed *The Robert Patton – The Always Ready*.

You might say that this little-known coxswain from Runswick was the archetypal lifeboatman of yesterday – a man loved and respected by the people of the fishing community where he spent almost the whole of his life, and who did indeed, in the words of the school competition, 'put God first, other people second, self last'. Lifeboat crews are seldom asked to make the sort of sacrifice that Robert Patton made. But when they launch, the possibility that they might be asked to make this sacrifice must often be at the back of their minds.

James Dougal, acting coxswain of the Eyemouth lifeboat. He displayed fine seamanship while rescuing two sub-aqua divers trapped off St Abbs Head in a hurricane.

In quite a few services, courage, determination and self-sacrifice may not be enough, by themselves, to effect a rescue. What is also needed is good seamanship. This quality was in evidence during the rescue carried out by James Dougal on 6 October 1990. The east coast of Scotland was hit that evening by a sudden hurricane – 'the worst in living memory' – and a group of sub-aqua enthusiasts found themselves trapped on a lee shore. As light was fading, a coastguard spotted four divers in the water, in obvious difficulty, off the rocky headland of St Abb's. Eyemouth's Waveney class lifeboat, with acting coxswain James Dougal at the helm, set out to rescue them.

The first problem was getting out of harbour. Huge waves were sweeping diagonally across the entrance and surging over the sea walls. In the kaleidoscope of rain, spray and spume, visibility was virtually zero, and good judgement was needed first to prevent the lifeboat capsizing in the cross-sea, then to avoid the reefs of half-submerged rocks outside the harbour entrance. Once in the open sea, they were hit by thirty-five-foot waves driven straight at them by a wind reaching 120 miles per hour. It took them half an hour to cover the three miles to St Abb's, and by the time they got there it was dark.

St Abb's Head is not a good place to approach in the dark, especially when an onshore hurricane is driving so much spray and spume over the surface of the sea that radar is ineffective. Amazingly, coastguards had spotted two of the divers clinging to an offshore creel-buoy. These same coastguards could now see the Eyemouth lifeboat, pinpointed by the beam of her searchlight; and using their radio, they began to guide the lifeboat towards the buoy.

To say this was a tricky business would be an understatement. Sixty yards to starboard lay the Cathedral Rock; sixty yards to port lay the Ebb Carr Rocks. Neither could be seen by the naked eye and neither showed up on the radar, as Dougal edged cautiously between them towards the buoy, with only the coastguard's voice to guide him. His crew were on deck, secured by lifelines, clinging to whatever support they could find, and scanning the sea for the divers. At last they spotted them. But in the huge seas and high wind it proved impossible to come alongside for fear of injuring them. Lifelines were thrown, and on the third attempt the divers managed to grab one. They were drawn to the bow of the lifeboat and, with no little difficulty, hauled aboard.

For the moment they were safe, but they were by no means out of danger. Two divers were still missing, and the Eyemouth lifeboat now started to search for them. It wasn't long, however, before James Dougal became concerned for the two men he had rescued. Both were violently seasick, were suffering from shock, exhaustion and hypothermia, and were becoming dangerously weak and disorientated. An RAF helicopter had been alerted, and by seven p.m. was hovering overhead. However, the weather was judged too bad to winch the men up, and at seven forty-five the helicopter returned to base and the lifeboat was recalled.

This was not the end of the story. Returning to Eyemouth, James Dougal found conditions even worse than when he had launched, with huge waves, whipped up by the hurricane-force winds, turning the harbour entrance into a death-trap. He therefore headed for Burnmouth, three or four miles to the south, where the entrance was more sheltered.

However, here too there was a problem. The hurricane had brought down both telegraph lines and power pylons; the town was without electricity and the harbour entrance was unlit. It was a challenge the people of Burnmouth rose to. Under the guidance of local fishermen, cars were positioned along the harbour walls. Their headlights were switched on. And, like an aircraft landing with the help of a flare-path, the lifeboat came in through the narrow entrance to a safe anchorage. By nine p.m. the two divers were under the care of the Scottish Ambulance Service, and within forty-eight hours had made a full recovery. It was learned afterwards that

The crew of
Brighton's Atlantic
21, who rescued
two girls swept
under the Palace
Pier, Brighton by
heavy seas,
8 September 1995.

their companions had also survived; they had been washed ashore near St Abb's, bruised and battered, but not seriously injured.

This was a rescue that demanded fine seamanship – not only in the old-fashioned sense, which implies a knowledge of the sea and an ability at boat handling; but also in its more modern sense which, for lifeboat crews, implies, as well as the traditional skills, the knowledge of how to make the best use of their equipment and the ability to work with others. If James Dougal had not 'known the front end of his boat from the back', the divers in difficulties that evening off St Abb's Head would never have been rescued.

Another characteristic often asked of lifeboat crews is that they should 'be gentle and tender towards those they have saved'. These qualities were much in evidence in a rescue that took place off Brighton on 7 September 1995.

It was a little before midnight. The wind had subsided to a near-gale; but huge waves were still thundering on to Brighton beach and sweeping green into the marina. Brighton's Atlantic 21 rigid inflatable had just returned from service and was lying at the foot of her slipway when a coastguard's cri de coeur came over the radio. 'Immediate! Immediate! Two girls have been swept into the sea under Palace Pier'.

Three lifeboatmen, Richard Pearce, Joe Purchess and Martin Ebdell, were in their drysuits and halfway through a cup of coffee when the call came through to the crew room. In less than a minute and a half they had launched and were heading for the entrance to the marina. They were halfway there, when their boat was slammed backwards by a huge wave. Pearce called for their spotlight, and none of them liked the scene that it lit up. 'It looked', Pearce wrote afterwards, 'like a huge washing machine. There didn't seem to be a way through'.

With backwash from the sea walls and a bludgeoning wind threatening any moment to capsize them, it needed all Pearce's skill to get them out of the marina. Getting back again, perhaps with casualties aboard, was obviously going to be a problem; so they radioed Newhaven and asked for their larger Arun class lifeboat to stand by. Pearce takes up the story:

> Above the noise of our twin outboards and the roar of the sea, I could hear snippets of radio chatter from the coastguards on the beach. They could see the girls hanging onto the pier supports. Encouraged by the fact that they were still there, I gave the inflatable full throttle, running across the back of the larger rollers and down the face of the smaller ones, like a surf-boarder. Arriving east of the pier, we couldn't see the girls. We called the coastguards [and they told us] they were about 20 yards offshore, being intermittently submerged by the huge seas running under the pier . . . I spotted a life-ring which had been thrown from the pier, its line still attached to the pier handrail. Hoping this was an indication of where the girls would be, I picked out a wave running down under the pier, its breaking white top just visible in the dim light of the street lamps, and drove the lifeboat towards the life-ring, timing our speed so that we came under the pier just after the wave had passed.

Beneath the pier huge waves were racing towards the shore, and the supporting pillars and crossbeams were now laid bare, now under twenty feet of water. They spotted the girls almost at once, but were separated from them by a network of girders. They were trying to manoeuvre closer when there was a sudden jolt and a report like a gunshot. An underwater metal spike, left untrimmed after the previous day's maintenance work on the pier, had punctured their sponson tube, deflating almost the whole port side of the lifeboat.

Pearce rammed their damaged inflatable against one of the crossbeams to give it support, and Joe and Martin yelled at the girls to jump. One let go, fell into the sea, and was hauled aboard. But the other, screaming hysterically, still clung to the pier. As Pearce tried to manoeuvre closer to her, the lifeboat was submerged by a large wave. Martin's legs became pinned against one of the crossbeams, his hand was crushed and one of his fingers broken. Then another wave flung the lifeboat almost into the air at an angle of sixty degrees. Martin's legs were freed, and the girl clinging to the pier support was swept away. She grabbed Martin's injured hand, and the two of them were half-washed, half-dragged into the lifeboat.

'Get us out of here!' Joe shouted.

Pearce knew they had no hope of surviving beneath the pier. They couldn't land because of the dumping surf. Their best bet was therefore to find as sheltered a patch of open sea as they could, and hope their crippled inflatable would stay afloat until they were rescued.

They called up the coastguards: 'Got girls. Severe damage to boat. Request urgent assistance'.

Brighton's Atlantic 21 in dry dock, together with two of her crew, the day after the Brighton Pier rescue.

And urgent assistance was needed. For the instant they backed out from under the pier, a wave swept waist-deep the length of the lifeboat, almost swamping them and tumbling girls and crew aft. They headed out to sea, beyond the surf line, to where the waves were not so steep, inflated their self-righting airbag as a precaution against capsizing, and settled down to wait.

Before long they became seriously concerned for the girls. They gathered their names were Vicky and Lisa, and that they had been partying on the beach, doing what thousands of young people have been doing for thousands of years, playing 'catch me if you can' with the waves, when a particularly large wave had swept them out to sea. They had been wearing lightweight clothes, and were now shivering with cold, numb with shock, and suffering from hypothermia. The crew wrapped them up in as much warm clothing as they could, and did their best to comfort them, while struggling to keep their near-foundering lifeboat head into the waves. One girl had lost her contact lenses, and lay huddled at the bottom of the boat staring at the little red capsizing light, which gave her something to focus on, and clutching Pearce's leg, which gave her something to hang on to. The other girl did her best to keep talking to Martin and Joe, but became increasingly incoherent and weak. If ever casualties were in need of tender loving care it was Vicky and Lisa.

By the time a rescue helicopter was homing in on them, both girls were barely conscious and in no condition to be winched up. Another disincentive to winching was the danger that if the helicopter hovered directly overhead, the downdraught from its rotor blades might swamp their damaged inflatable. The helicopter pilot therefore stood off and trained his searchlight on them, to guide in the larger lifeboat now on its way from Newhaven.

The arrival of the Arun class *Keith Anderson* marked the beginning of the end of the Brighton Pier rescue. Transferring casualties and crew to the ocean-going lifeboat and taking the damaged inflatable in tow were far from easy; but almost exactly an hour and a half after the first call for help came over the radio both rescuers and rescued had been landed safely, and the girls and Martin Ebdell were on their way by ambulance to hospital. All, physically, made a quick recovery.

To add postscripts. A replacement Atlantic 21 arrived in Brighton marina on the morning the rescue took place. Within an hour it had been called out on service. Martin Ebdell was discharged from hospital the following morning. That afternoon he was best man at a friend's wedding.

One of the girls was so traumatized by her experience that she had to have counselling. Eventually, she gave up her course at Brighton and went back to her home in Sheffield, about as far from the sea as she could possibly get. The other girl became a staunch RNLI supporter and fundraiser, and a few years later at the Royal Tournament took part in a re-enactment of her rescue.

Most of the five services described above have one thing in common: they were carried out by men who, to outward appearances and in the eyes of their contemporaries, were ordinary, 'everyday' people (the one exception being William Hillary, who was far from ordinary). This underlines a point made by the current RNLI slogan that their crews are 'ordinary people doing extraordinary things'.

Over the last 180-odd years, lifeboatmen and women have gradually built up the reputation of being brave, determined, self-sacrificing, skilled in seamanship and gentle – a somewhat daunting image for lesser mortals to live up to. However, these characteristics are latent in a fair number of people and can be brought to fruition by dedication and training. So it is probably true to say that quite a few of us could, if we were prepared to make the necessary commitment, become members of a lifeboat crew.

But the commitment needs to be total.

The dictionary definition of commitment is 'an obligation that restricts freedom of action', and lifeboat crews soon discover just how time-consuming and restricting their work can be. First, there are the actual rescues. At some stations there may not be more than a dozen rescue services a year; but at others, such as Brighton, Poole and Southend, there may be sixty or seventy – and that does not include false alarms and hoaxes. This means that lifeboat crews can be called out on average more than once a week. They must also attend weekly meetings, go to training lectures and sit exams. But most restrictive of all is their commitment to be on call, all day and every day, 365 days a year, unless they are on holiday or for some reason far distant from their lifeboat station.

Crew members always carry with them a pager (arguably the most sophisticated

OPPOSITE
Some of the crew
of Poole's offshore
lifeboat (above)
in civvies,
(below) in uniform.

of its kind in the world) and, when called, they are expected to be at their lifeboat station within ten minutes. (Many crew members reckon to be on station within five minutes; and many lifeboats, particularly inflatables, reckon to launch within seven or eight minutes of being alerted. For research has proved that the more quickly a lifeboat arrives, the greater the chances of a successful rescue.) This means that lifeboatmen and women must be prepared any moment instantly to drop whatever they are doing, no matter how important or how pleasurable, and make a dash for their station. So if lifeboat crew members have children, their partner or some other responsible person must always be on hand to look after the children if their pager is activated. It is therefore not only crew members who need to be committed to lifeboat work. Commitment is also asked of their partners.

It would not be too fanciful to describe these partners as the unseen props on which the Institution depends. In the old days, lifeboatmen's wives had to live with the knowledge that their husbands might at any time be called on to launch in what were little more than glorified rowing boats, probably in heavy seas and foul weather. They must often have felt as Elizabeth Cook, wife of the explorer James, felt: she, it is said, found it impossible to sleep on nights when there was a storm, 'because she couldn't help thinking of those poor men at sea'. It might be thought that nowadays, with more sophisticated boats and better equipment, lifeboat work would be less hazardous. But storms in the twenty-first century are as frenetic as in

the nineteenth. Lifeboats today tend to go farther, in worse conditions, and to make more rescues than they did a hundred years ago. Lifeboatmen still die on rescue work. It is still not unheard of for an entire crew to be lost: it happened off the Cornish coast near Penlee in 1981. Lifeboatmen and women today face the same risks as their predecessors. This their partners know and have to live with.

There is also another problem for today's partners. A hundred years ago, it was widely accepted that a man's place was at work and a woman's was in the home. Husbands and wives often led quite separate lives, and spent comparatively little time doing things together. Nowadays, in contrast, partners tend to share as many activities as possible – looking after children, cooking, home improving, leisure pursuits, sport, etc. But being a member of a lifeboat crew is not an activity that can easily be shared. It is, on the other hand, an activity that is both demanding and time-consuming. And some crew members' partners might be forgiven if they feel that they are missing out on the sort of togetherness and freedom of action enjoyed by many of their contemporaries. They get plenty of anxiety and plenty of hassle, but little in the way of recognition. Yet the debt that the public owes them is incalculable.

There are also, of course, plus points to being one of a lifeboat crew, and for many people the gains far outweigh the losses. The first and greatest plus point is the knowledge that one is doing something wonderfully worthwhile. And how many of us can, in all honesty, say that of either our careers or our leisure activities?

The other plus point is the camaraderie. Those who play team games will know that a side that contains players of no more than average ability can sometimes achieve great results. This is because they know one another's strengths and weaknesses, and play together as a team. In the same way, the men and women who serve on a lifeboat station can sometimes become so bonded one to another that their combined strength is greater than the sum of their individual strengths. By knowing and helping each other, they bring out the best in each other. Although they would deny and probably be embarrassed by the comparison, they are a bit like the members of an exclusive club, where membership cannot be bought but has to be earned. Those who know what goes on in lifeboat stations are nearly always impressed by their informality, their atmosphere of friendship and mutual respect, and by the fact that people of different ages, backgrounds and abilities are working together for a common cause. And no one would deny that the cause they are working for is a good one. Lifeboat crews have been compared with the members of an elite military unit or a sports super team. There is some truth in both comparisons; but saving lives is preferable to taking them, and more worthwhile than kicking a ball between a couple of posts.

Another comparison sometimes made is that 'lifeboat crews are like a well-knit family'. There is perhaps even more truth in this, because not so long ago lifeboatmen often were of one family. Throughout most of the nineteenth and the first half of the twentieth centuries, when many lifeboats were stationed in relatively small fishing villages and were manned mainly by fishermen, it was not unusual for several members of the same family to serve in the same crew. Nor was it unusual for

OPPOSITE

A hundred years ago a woman's role in the RNLI was restricted to supporting her menfolk, fundraising and helping to launch (left: the women launchers of Dungeness). Today women participate in all the Institution's activities, working for example as tractor drivers, administrators and members of lifeboat crews.

Lifeboats often used to be manned by members of the same family. (Opposite top) Harry Nicholas of Sennen Cove. (Above) The Oilers and Tarts of Dungeness. (Opposite bottom) The Davies family of Cromer, who were between them awarded nineteen bronze, five silver and three gold medals.

father, son and grandson to serve consecutively in the same boat. The work of these families, many of whom gave their lives on service, deserves to be recorded.

In the 1920s, over half the crew of the Sennen Cove (Cornwall) lifeboat were members of the Nicholas family; and between them, over a span of fifty years, the Nicholases were awarded two silver and six bronze medals. In the 1930s, every member of the Ballycotton (County Cork) lifeboat was a member of either the Sliney or the Walsh family; and between them the Slineys and the Walshes won one gold, three silver and eight bronze medals. In the 1940s, nine out of fourteen of the regular members of the Cromer (Norfolk) lifeboat were members of the Davies family; and between them the Davieses were awarded an amazing three gold, five silver and nineteen bronze medals.

Many other families have a long tradition of service to their local lifeboats: to mention only a few, the Armstrongs of Newbiggin, the Cables of Aldeburgh, the Evanses of Moelfre, the Kirkpatricks of Longhope, the Stephensons of Boulmer, the Tarts of Dungeness, and in our own day the Clarks of Lerwick.

At a time when bad news often gets more prominence than good, it is heartening to know there are still men and women who are ready to cross the road and give a helping hand to those in trouble: 'ordinary people doing extraordinary things'.

The RNLI

in the 21st Century

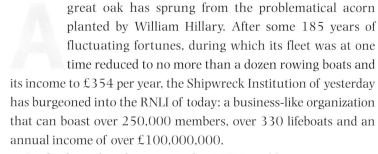

great oak has sprung from the problematical acorn planted by William Hillary. After some 185 years of fluctuating fortunes, during which its fleet was at one time reduced to no more than a dozen rowing boats and its income to £354 per year, the Shipwreck Institution of yesterday has burgeoned into the RNLI of today: a business-like organization that can boast over 250,000 members, over 330 lifeboats and an annual income of over £100,000,000.

On the face of it, this present-day RNLI would seem to have little in common with its pie-in-the-sky predecessor. However, a closer look reveals that the Institution has remained surprisingly faithful to the vision of its founder. It is still a charity. Most of its crews are still unpaid volunteers.

The Teesmouth lifeboat *City of Sheffield*, accompanied by helicopter, on service to the *Stora Korsnas link I*, on fire with a potentially explosive cargo.

Most countries with a coastline now have some sort of lifeboat service. Usually this is provided by the state. In Britain and Ireland it is provided by a charity. Some people feel that so important a job should not be dependent on the benevolence of the public, but should be brought under state control. However, there are strong arguments against this. Abroad, the RNLI is now widely regarded as the most effective and dependable lifeboat service in the world. Why change a successful format, especially when the majority of RNLI personnel are happy with the status quo? Another reason for eschewing state control is that once a service comes under the aegis of the government, it is almost certain to lose control of its finances and become involved in politics. This can be a recipe for disaster. A final point against switching to a state-run service is the effect that this would be likely to have on the crews.

Lifeboat crews always have been and always will be the prop and stay of the Institution. There have been times when lifeboats were not all they should have been, and management not all it should have been. But the courage and commitment of the crews has been constant. They have proved again and again that being a lifeboatman or woman is not a job but a vocation. Would it remain a vocation if the Institution came under state control, and its crew members became salaried employees?

Under the present system crews who put their lives at risk do so not because it is something they are ordered or paid to do, but because it is something they volunteered to do. Under state control all sorts of ethical and legal problems would be bound to surface. For example, could it ever be morally right to order a person, other than a member of the armed forces, to risk his or her life? And what would happen if a person was ordered to take part in a launch and refused? A lifeboat service run by a charity may sound an anachronism. But if we look at what the present-day RNLI does and how it does it, there would seem to be a strong case for keeping things as they are.

The RNLI today exists for one purpose only: to save lives at sea.

William Hillary's original appeal was for an organization 'having for its objects FIRST: The preservation of human life from shipwreck, which should always be considered as the first great and permanent object of the Institution'. In the old days, most rescue services did indeed go to the aid of ships that had been wrecked, more often than not commercial or fishing vessels driven ashore in winter. However, some forty years ago the nature of the Institution's work began to change. The table below shows how today the majority of rescue services are to holidaymakers or pleasure-seekers who have got into difficulties in summer. Viewed another way, these figures show that on every day of the year there are now on average twenty-three lifeboat launches, with twenty-two people, several of whom would otherwise have died, being brought to safety, and three people are saved from certain death – statistics which give some idea of the scale of present-day lifeboat work but little idea of what is actually involved.

Lifeboat Launches in 2007

To the aid of	Number of launches	
Aircraft	28 (39% offshore, 61% inshore)	Total launches
Commercial/MOD	256 (52% offshore, 48% inshore)	**8,141**
Fishing vessels	677 (71% offshore, 29% inshore)	
Manual pleasure craft	711 (14% offshore, 86% inshore)	
Miscellaneous	379 (19% offshore, 81% inshore)	People rescued
		7,834
Persons ashore	1,033 (22% offshore, 78% inshore)	
Persons in the sea	1,204 (20% offshore, 80% inshore)	
Power pleasure craft	1,863 (26% offshore, 74% inshore)	Lives saved
		306
Sail pleasure craft	1,717 (40% offshore, 60% inshore)	
Unidentified/Distress	285 (46% offshore, 54% inshore)	

A lifeboat rescue today is a complex operation. In the nineteenth century, the first people to know that a ship was in trouble were usually coastguards, who had either spotted distress flares or seen the vessel itself being driven ashore. These coastguards would then rush to the nearest lifeboat station; the honorary secretary would have to be found, permission would have to be sought for a launch, maroons would have to be fired to assemble the crew, and finally the lifeboat would have to be dragged, often for several miles, to its launch site. Sometimes all this could take literally days. Almost always it took several hours. In the twentieth century things were speeded up by the introduction of telephones and radios. However, communication between the would-be rescuers remained a problem right up to the start of the present century, when a call out and communication system specially tailored to meet RNLI requirements came into operation. Today, this system not only pages crew members, but gives them information about the casualty. It provides voice communication between the lifeboat, the lifeboat station and key personnel such as coxswains and mechanics; it is self-monitoring, fail-safe and secure; it includes a printer in the crew room that displays the latest information about the casualty, and enables this information to be disseminated by means of voice prompts and codes. It is helping the Institution to provide a quicker and better-informed service.

When crew members get a call on their pager, they are expected to be at their lifeboat station within ten minutes. People who live and work some distance from a station are therefore virtually precluded from joining a crew. This is inevitable, for nowadays speed of launching, especially for inshore inflatables, is often a prerequisite for success – the majority of stations reckon to launch within six or seven minutes of receiving a call.

As soon as the lifeboatmen and women who have been alerted on their pagers arrive on station, they kit up in preparation to launch. Generally speaking, it is those who arrive first who form the crew. There are obvious exceptions to this. It is no good launching an offshore boat without a mechanic or an inshore boat without a helmsman; and if the rescue operation looks like being a particularly difficult one, the coxswain may wait for the arrival of his more experienced crew members. Those who get to the station and are not included in the crew help with the launch.

There are three basic ways of launching a lifeboat: from a mooring afloat or floating boathouse, down a slipway, or from a carriage or trolley manoeuvred across the shore.

Launching a boat that is afloat is comparatively simple. All the crew have to do is board the boat, cast off and head out to sea. This is the RNLI's preferred method of launching. It can, however, only be used where there is either a safe, sheltered, deep water anchorage, or a floating boathouse.

Slipway launching looks spectacular but needs to be meticulously controlled. The crew board the lifeboat while it is still in its boathouse. The chains holding the boat in position are released, and the boat slides out of its boathouse, down its slipway and into deep water. To recover the lifeboat, it has to be manoeuvred so that its keel rests on the bottom of the slipway; a cable is then attached to it and it is winched up,

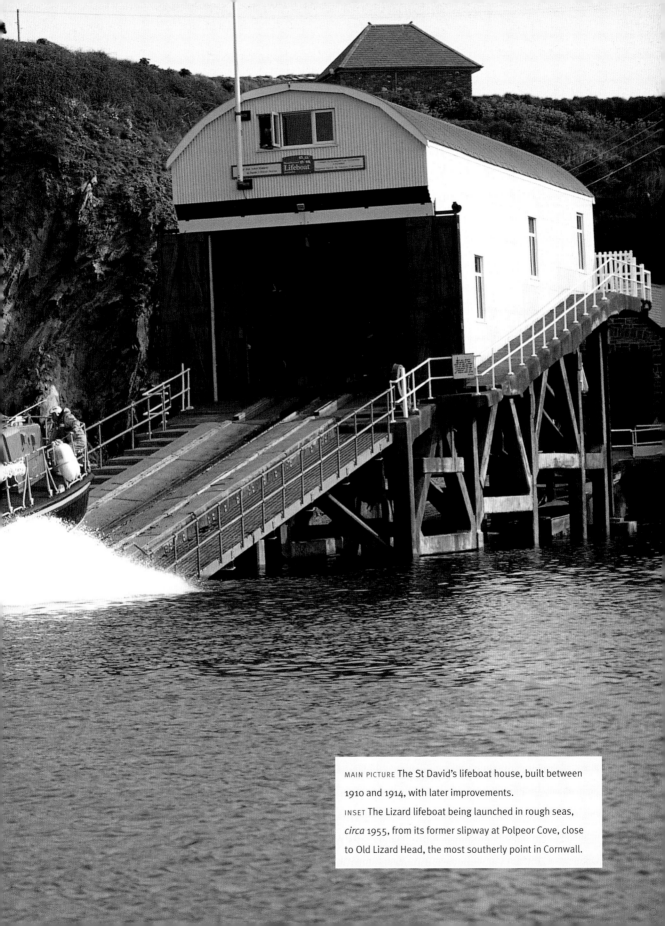

MAIN PICTURE The St David's lifeboat house, built between 1910 and 1914, with later improvements.

INSET The Lizard lifeboat being launched in rough seas, *circa* 1955, from its former slipway at Polpeor Cove, close to Old Lizard Head, the most southerly point in Cornwall.

stern-first, into the boathouse. In bad weather both launching and recovery, especially the latter, can be hazardous.

Beach launching is necessary when there are no floating or slipway facilities; for example, in anchorages that dry out at low tide, or on beaches too flat, shifting or exposed to build a slipway. In these cases, the lifeboat is loaded on to a specialized carriage or trolley, and pushed into the sea bow-first by a waterproofed caterpillar-tracked vehicle.

When a lifeboat returns from service, it has to be inspected for damage, washed down, refuelled and resecured; its equipment has to be checked and, if need be, replaced. All this is done as quickly as possible so the coastguards can be told that the lifeboat is once again ready if needed. This work not only helps to train crew members, it provides the opportunity for them to get to know one another and to form a team.

This process of forming a team is helped by the fact that in recent years lifeboat stations have become more user-friendly. In the old days, lifeboat houses used to consist of a single building, sometimes of an ecclesiastical appearance, with Gothic windows, buttresses and a steeply pitched roof. Such buildings were generally big enough to house a lifeboat but not much else; there were often no toilets, no hot water, and no cooking or changing facilities. The crew therefore spent as little time in them as possible. This was no problem in the nineteenth century, when most lifeboat stations were sited in small fishing villages or in the harbour areas of commercial ports, and when the majority of crew members were fishermen. There was no need

RIGHT Today, lifeboat stations are more likely to be fine modern buildings sited in a holiday resort, such as this one in Morecambe.

Tractors

Most lifeboats launched from a beach have to be loaded on to a trolley or carriage, then dragged, often some distance, over sand, shingle or mud.

When lifeboats were comparatively small and light, human pulling power was usually enough to haul the boats to their launch sites. But as lifeboats (and the carriages used to transport them) became heavier, horses were called into service.

For years horses played a major role in the work of the RNLI; without them, many launches could never have taken place. However, they were gradually superseded on the road by cars and in the field by tractors; their numbers declined, and by the end of the First World War they were not always at hand when needed.

In 1920 the RNLI began trials at Hunstanton (Norfolk) to see if agricultural tractors could be adapted for beach launching. A three-ton Clayton and Shuttleworth tractor, with a forty horsepower petrol-driven engine, and fourteen-inch caterpillar tracks, attempted to tow the Hunstanton lifeboat and carriage (combined weight seven and a half tons) over soft sand at a reasonable speed. It succeeded. Orders were placed for twenty Clayton and Shuttleworths, and the first, duly modified, went into service in 1922. However, it was soon found that these tractors lacked the power to cope with particularly difficult conditions – steep shingle or cloying

In the early 1920s, tractors began to replace horses as a means of beach-launching.(Top) A tractor designed by the Four Wheel Drive Lorry Company towing the Hoylake lifeboat *Hannah Fawcett Bennett* back to the boathouse in 1929, and (bottom) some more recent examples of RNLI tractors.

mud. Tests were therefore made with a larger tractor designed by the Four Wheel Drive Lorry Company; four were ordered, the first going into service in 1928.

Over the next fifty years a succession of commercial tractors were adapted to RNLI needs: in 1952 the ninety-five horsepower Fowlers; in 1962 the 100 horsepower Leylands; in 1977 the Case 1150 Bs with their enclosed watertight cab. All had one big disadvantage. Commercial vehicles are usually in production for only a relatively short time; once they go out of production, spare parts and maintenance become

a problem. The Institution therefore asked its technical staff to design a purpose-built tractor, and after four years of research and trials the Talus MB-H came into service: a giant of seventeen and a half tons with a 210 horsepower engine, built by Bigland of Knighton and specially designed to operate in soft sand and shallow water.

Bigland-built tractors proved reliable and efficient. In recent years they have been modified and updated to meet RNLI requirements, and two types are now in service.

Talus MB-H semi-submersible vehicle for launching offshore lifeboats

Weight:	19 tonnes (with track pads)
Length:	5.486 m
Width:	2.44 m
Height:	2.91 m
Power:	220 hp diesel
Gears:	hydrostatic: hi-low ratio; hydraulically driven, forward and reverse
Max. speed:	10 mph
Ground performance:	maximum draw bar and winch wire pull on flat surface, 15 tonnes
Water performance:	capable of working in 5 feet (1.52 m) of water, achieving the above performance with allowances for saturated surface conditions

The MB-H tractor has a totally enclosed cab for the driver, is fully waterproof and capable of operating at greater depths than previous tractors. Headlights are fitted in glazed waterproof boxes, which also include side and tail lights, turn indicators and flashing blue lights. Two floodlights are mounted on the cab roof.

Talus MB-H tractors operate from Aldeburgh, Anstruther, Bridlington, Clogher Head, Dungeness, Filey, Hastings, Hoylake, Ilfracombe, Kilmore Quay, Llandudno, Margate, Newcastle (Co. Down), New Quay, Seahouses, Peel, Pwllheli, Ramsey, Rhyl, Scarborough, Skegness, St Ives, and Wells.

Talus MB764 semi-submersible vehicle for launching inshore lifeboats

Weight:	6.9 tonnes with 90% water ballast tyres
Length:	3.88 m
Width:	2.575 m
Height:	2.95 m with hull extension; 2.3 m without extension
Power:	80 hp at 1900 rpm
Gears:	8 forward, 2 reverse
Max speed:	12 mph
Ground performance:	maximum draw bar pull in first gear with full engine power on dry surface, 5.8 tonnes.
Water performance:	capable of working in 5 feet (1.52 m) of water achieving the above performance with allowances for saturated surface conditions

For the MB764 a boat-like hull is built round the engine, gearbox and axle of a commercial skid unit. This construction allows the wheels to function outside the hull, which is designed to remain buoyant up to normal working depth. Extensive toughened glass panels protect the driver and give wide vision.

Talus MB764s operate from Abersoch, Aberystwyth, Appledore, Atlantic College, Beaumaris, Clifden, Hayling Island, Kilrush, Kinghorn, Arran (Lamlash), Largs, Red Bay, St Bees, St Catherine, Silloth, Skerries, Tignabruaich, Trearddur Bay, and Youghal.

in those days for the crew to have a place where they could change and socialize, because they probably lived within walking distance of the station and already knew one another. It became a different story in the latter part of the twentieth century, when stations in small fishing villages tended to be superseded by stations in popular holiday resorts, and lifeboat crews were drawn from all walks of life and from a far larger community – people whose work for the RNLI was often their only point of contact with one another.

Different circumstances called for a different type of lifeboat house, and a modern station now not only houses and provides launching facilities for its boat, it also provides a workplace-cum-home-from-home for its crew, a place where lifeboatmen and women can do their training and form a team. In its 'Design Philosophy' the Institution laid down guidelines for its new stations: 'High quality construction with low maintenance is considered essential to the good management of charitable funds … new buildings should be designed to require only minimum maintenance for 30 years … all new marine structures (i.e. slipways) should be designed to have a life of 50 years … public access is to be encouraged to certain areas of lifeboat stations.'

Appendices give the requirements not only for a boat room, but for a whole complex of associated rooms. These include a crew room/training room ('ideally with views over the launching area and an internal view from crew room to boat room … capable of accommodating a minimum of 18 people for training and meetings'); a galley ('a small domestic kitchen, to include stainless steel sink, space for fridge and microwave'); a changing/washing/drying/toilet area ('to include cabinets with dehumidifiers, space for a minimum of 12 sets of crew kit, WCs to allow uni-sex use, lockers for crew clothing and a shower room'); a workshop/mechanic's store ('to include workbench, deepbowl sink with hot and cold water, and space for storage of oil, grease, spare parts, etc.'); a souvenir sales outlet ('only to be included where local conditions are judged to justify the cost … the entrance and approach to be fully accessible to wheelchairs'); and, finally, storage facilities ('to include oil/antifreeze store, petroleum store, diesel fuel store, and a delivery store … with steel doors of sufficient width to accept a "Europallet"').

Even more important than the stations are the boats themselves. There is no such thing as the perfect all-purpose lifeboat. However, improvements in design and materials have led to the evolution of two different types of boat, which are now well able to cope with the work expected of them. In June 2001 the RNLI had a fleet of 130 all-weather boats (plus 43 in one relief fleet), all good sea boats, self-righting, and able to operate in all weather conditions as far away from land as they are needed. It also had 182 inshore boats (plus 68 in one relief fleet); these are small, fast-response and rigid inflatables, able to operate in moderate conditions close to land. Which boats are sent to which stations obviously depends on local conditions, the type of casualties they are most likely to have to deal with, and the type of launching facilities available.

There are now (in 2008) five types of all-weather offshore lifeboats in service with the RNLI, three of inshore lifeboats, two of inshore rescue craft and one of hovercraft.

Maps showing the locations of RNLI stations (as at July 2008).

RNLI RESCUE MAP

Lifeboat stations and lifeguard areas around the
United Kingdom and Republic of Ireland

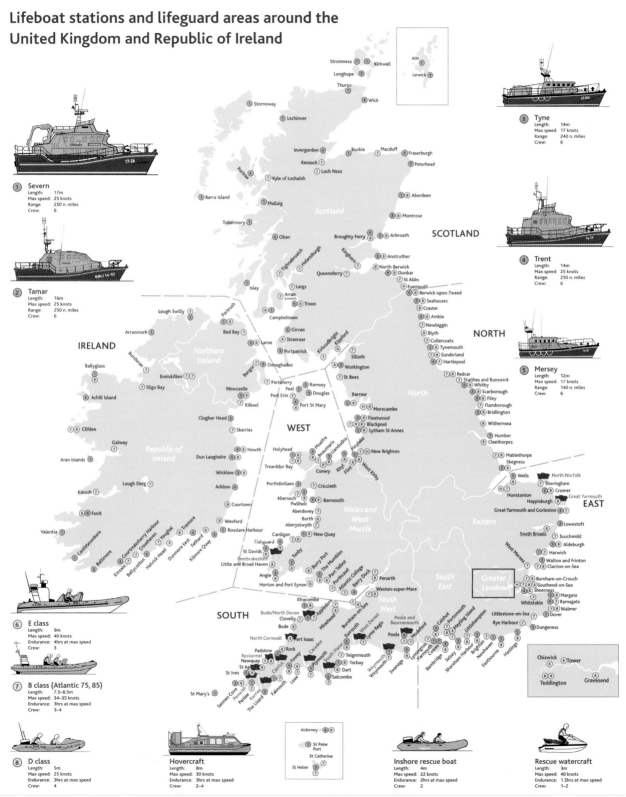

Severn
Length: 17m
Max speed: 25 knots
Range: 250 n. miles
Crew: 6

Tamar
Length: 16m
Max speed: 25 knots
Range: 250 n. miles
Crew: 6

E class
Length: 9m
Max speed: 40 knots
Endurance: 4hrs at max speed
Crew: 3

B class (Atlantic 75, 85)
Length: 7.5–8.5m
Max speed: 34–35 knots
Endurance: 3hrs at max speed
Crew: 3–4

D class
Length: 5m
Max speed: 25 knots
Endurance: 3hrs at max speed
Crew: 4

Tyne
Length: 14m
Max speed: 17 knots
Range: 240 n. miles
Crew: 6

Trent
Length: 14m
Max speed: 25 knots
Range: 250 n. miles
Crew: 6

Mersey
Length: 12m
Max speed: 17 knots
Range: 140 n. miles
Crew: 6

Hovercraft
Length: 8m
Max speed: 30 knots
Endurance: 3hrs at max speed
Crew: 2–4

Inshore rescue boat
Length: 4m
Max speed: 22 knots
Endurance: 2hrs at max speed
Crew: 2

Rescue watercraft
Length: 3m
Max speed: 40 knots
Endurance: 1.5hrs at max speed
Crew: 1–2

SCOTLAND

IRELAND

Northern Ireland

Republic of Ireland

WEST

NORTH

North

Wales and West Mercia

Eastern

EAST

South East

Greater London

South West

SOUTH

South West

Chiswick · Tower
Teddington · Gravesend

Alderney
St Peter Port
St Catherine
St Helier

Regional boundary   Divisional boundary   1 – 5 All-weather lifeboats   6 – 8 Inshore lifeboats   Lifeguard areas   July 2008

SAP code: plain   INF021
SAP code: laminated INF022
SAP code: plain A4   INF023

The Royal National Lifeboat Institution, West Quay Road, Poole, Dorset, BH15 1HZ   Telephone: 0845 122 6999   rnli.org.uk   A charity registered in England, Scotland and the Republic of Ireland

Offshore boats

Tamar class specifications

Length	16 m (45 feet 11 inches)
Beam	5 m (14 feet 10 inches)
Draught	1.35 m (4 feet 3 inches)
Displacement	30 tonnes
Construction	fibre-reinforced composite (FRC)
Engines	two Caterpillar 1000 hp diesels
Fuel capacity	4300 litres
Range	250 nautical miles
Speed	25 knots
Crew	6
Method of launching	slipway or afloat

The first Tamars joined the fleet in 2006 and are replacing Aruns and Tynes as the institution's principal all-weather offshore lifeboats. They carry a wealth of sophisticated equipment, including SIMS, a computerised Systems and Information Management System that enables the crew to operate onboard controls remotely without leaving their position.

Offshore boats

Severn class specifications

Length	17 m (55 feet 9 inches)
Beam	5.9 m (19 feet 3 inches)
Draught	1.38 m (4 feet 6 inches)
Displacement	41 tonnes
Construction	fibre-reinforced composite
Engines	two Caterpillar 3412 hp diesels
Fuel capacity	5500 litres (1200 gallons)
Range	250 nautical miles
Speed	25 knots
Crew	6
Method of launching	from afloat mooring

The Severn class was introduced in 1991, and is still in production. A total of forty-six have been built, the last in 2004.

Trent class specifications

Length	14.26 m (46 feet 9 inches)
Beam	4.9 m (16 feet 1 inch)
Draught	1.1 m (3 feet 2 inches)
Displacement	27.5 tonnes
Construction	fibre-reinforced composite
Engines	two MAN diesels
Fuel capacity	4000 litres (900 gallons)
Range	250 nautical miles
Speed	25 knots
Crew	6
Method of launching	from afloat mooring

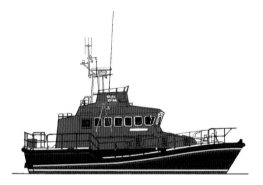

Trents are a slightly older and slightly smaller version of the Severn. Their electronic equipment includes radar, laser chart plotter, echo sounders, speed log, anemometer, GPS (for satellite navigation), MF radio transmitter and receiver, VHF radio telephone, MF/VHF direction finder, an intercom system and closed-circuit television. A total of thirty-eight have been built, the last in 2004.

Mersey class specifications

Length	11.77 m (38 feet 7 inches)
Beam	4 m (13 feet)
Draught	0.98 m (3 feet 2 inches)
Displacement	14 tonnes
Construction	aluminium or fibre-reinforced composite
Engines	two Caterpillar 280 hp turbocharged diesels
Fuel capacity	1100 litres (245 gallons)
Range	145 nautical miles
Speed	17 knots
Crew	6
Method of launching	slipway or moored afloat

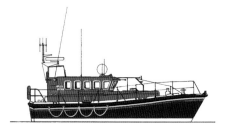

Merseys, introduced in 1986, are lightweight ocean-going boats designed for beach launching. During the launch their propellers are protected by tunnels and substantial bilge keels. A total of thirty-eight have been built, the last in 1993.

Tyne class specifications

Length	14.3 m (47 feet)
Beam	4.6 m (15 feet)
Draught	1.3 m (4 feet 2 inches)
Displacement	24.4 tonnes
Construction	steel (aluminium wheelhouse)
Engines	two 425 hp General Motors diesels
Fuel capacity	2800 litres (612 gallons)
Range	240 nautical miles
Speed	18 knots
Crew	6
Method of launching	by slipway from boathouse

Tynes were developed, from a design by the National Maritime Institution, specifically for slipway launching from old-style boathouses, hence their strong steel keels, shallow draught and protected propellers. A total of forty were built, the last in 1990.

Inshore boats

Forty years ago there were no inshore lifeboats in the RNLI's fleet. Today they outnumber the all-weather boats.

D class specifications

Length	4.95 m (16 feet 2 inches)
Beam	2 m (6 feet 6 inches)
Displacement	745 lb (approx.)
Engines	single 40 hp outboard
Construction	nylon coated with hypalon
Crew	2 or 3
Endurance	3 hours
Speed	125 knots
Method of launching	manually or from trolley

The D class were the original inshore lifeboats; reasonably fast, light and with a very shallow draught, they can respond quickly to emergency calls, and work close inshore in confined and shallow waters. First introduced in 1963, they are still in production and to date nearly 600 have been built.

Atlantic 21 class specifications

Length	6.9 m (22 feet 9 inches)
Beam	2.4 m (8 feet)
Displacement	2750 lb (approx.)
Engines	two 50 hp outboards
Construction	glass-reinforced plastic hull, nylon tubes
Crew	3
Endurance	3 hours
Speed	30 knots
Method of launching	usually by tractor-towed trolley

Faster and more seaworthy than the D class, the Atlantic 21 twin-outboard, rigid inflatables formed the core of the inshore fleet in the 1970s, '80s and early '90s. The last of the hundred-odd boats was built in 1994, and they are now being replaced by Atlantic 75s and 85s.

Atlantic 75 class specifications

Length	7.3 m (24 feet)
Beam	2.64 m (8 feet 8 inches)
Displacement	3200 lb (approx.)
Engines	two 70 hp outboards
Construction	glass-reinforced plastic hull, nylon tubes
Crew	3
Endurance	3 hours
Speed	32/34 knots
Method of launching	usually by tractor-towed trolley

An improved version of the Atlantic 21, the Atlantic 75 is one of the fastest lifeboats in service. Introduced in 1993, over 100 have been built to date. The Atlantic 75's redesigned hull gives its crew a softer ride than the Atlantic 21, while, as in the old Atlantic 21, a manually operated gas buoyancy bag enables the boat to self-right.

Atlantic 85 class specifications

Length	8.5 m (27 feet 10 inches)
Beam	2.8 m (9 feet 2 inches)
Displacement	2.4 tonnes
Engines	two x 115 hp
Construction	fibre-reinforced composite
Crew	3 or 4
Endurance	3 hours at maximum speed
Speed	35 knots
Method of launching	trolley, floating boathouse or davit

An improved version of the Atlantic 75, the 85 is currently being brought into the fleet. New features include a faster top speed, radar, VHF direction-finding, space for a fourth crew member and more room to carry survivors. And perhaps most importantly, the 85s can operate in daylight in up to force 7 winds and at night in up to force 6. They can also be beached in an emergency without damaging their engines or steering gear.

Hovercraft

Length	8 m (26 feet 3 inches)
Draught	virtually nil
Weight	2.4 tonnes
Construction	marine grade aluminium with
	moulded fibre-reinforced composites
Speed	30 knots
Endurance	3 hours at maximum speed
Crew	2–4
Launch	bespoke transporter

The RNLI had often considered the possibility of adding hovercraft to their fleet, and in the 1990s tests were carried out at Poole, Hunstanton, Morecambe, Flint and Southend: locations chosen because their extensive areas of shallow water and mudflats present obvious difficulties to the operation of conventional inshore lifeboats.

The advantage of a hovercraft in such conditions is that it has virtually no draught. Lift is provided by the build-up of air-pressure under the hull; thrust is provided by two large fans in the stern that work the aeroplane propellers, and steering is provided by aerofoil-shaped 'rudders' mounted behind the propellers.

The trials were – with reservations – successful. Crews found their hovercraft easy to fly, though some special training was needed. Launching was no problem, provided there was access for the transporter. On the plus side, it was found that the hovercraft could carry more sophisticated equipment (such as infra-red imaging) than the conventional inshore lifeboat. But on the minus side, they couldn't operate in bad weather.

Because of this limitation, they are unlikely to be widely used. They can, however, provide an invaluable specialist service in areas of shallow water.

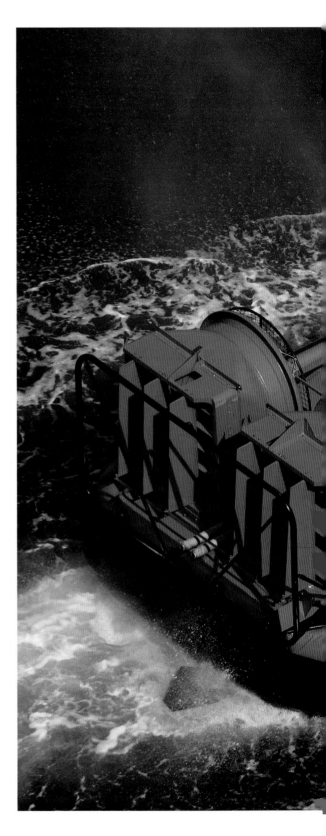

A rescue operation nowadays depends not only on such obvious factors as the commitment of the crew and the speed of their paging, the efficiency of the lifeboat station and its launching facilities, and the quality of the boats. These are like the tip of an iceberg. Much more goes on beneath the surface.

As a lifeboat crew achieves success by working as a team, so a lifeboat station achieves success through the teamwork of its many 'players in the wings': men and women whose contribution to a rescue may appear peripheral, but in fact is often vital. This photograph shows the personnel of a typical present-day lifeboat station: Wells in Norfolk. They number over a hundred. And they all do their bit. The coastguards, for example, are the people who first alert the RNLI to an emergency, and who co-ordinate the efforts at rescue. The honorary medical adviser and the crew of

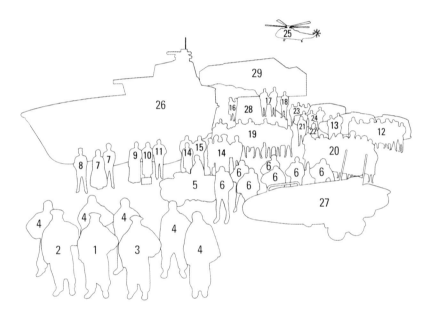

The lifeboat crew of the Wells-next-Sea lifeboat station and onshore support team

1 Coxswain/mechanic – Mersey class lifeboat. The coxswain is responsible for all decisions once the lifeboat is at sea and for the safety of the boat and its crew. At this station the coxswain is also the full-time mechanic and has to make sure that both lifeboats are in good working order at all times, replace any damaged equipment and run the engines at least once a week to make sure the lifeboats are ready for launching in an emergency.

2 Second coxswain – Mersey class lifeboat

3 Assistant Mechanic – Mersey class lifeboat

4 Crew – Mersey class lifeboat

5 ATV (all terrain vehicle) driver

6 Inshore lifeboat crew

7 Station honorary secretary and his wife. The station honorary secretary is responsible for the general administration of the station and deciding whether the lifeboat should be launched.

8 Deputy launching authority

9 Chaplain

10 Honorary medical adviser

11 Honoray treasurer

12 Coastguard rescue teams. The many Coastguard Co-ordination Centres are responsible for co-ordinating the response to incidents at sea. They receive radio messages and 999 (112 in the Republic of Ireland) telephone calls. If they decide a lifeboat is needed, they will page the honorary secretary of the nearest lifeboat station.

13 EAA NHS Trust with Emergency Response vehicle

14 The Rt. Hon the Earl of Leicester, patron and president of station branch, with Lady Leicester and committee members

15 Chairman of station branch

16 Tractor drivers

17 Head launchers

18 Maroon firer

19 Crew and launchers

20 The lifeboat guild members

21 Beach warden

22 RNLI SEA Check Co-ordinator

23 Beach voluntary lifeguards

24 Norfolk Constabulary

25 Sea King helicopter, RAF Wattisham, 22 Squadron SAR

26 Mersey class lifeboat

27 D class inflatable lifeboat

28 Talus MBH launching tractor

29 Lifeboat house

the NHS emergency response vehicle care for casualties when they are brought ashore. Without the support of their lifeboat branch members, many stations would be less happy and efficient places. The honorary secretary is responsible for the over-all administration of the station. In addition, he has the responsibility of authorizing every launch that takes place from it. In some cases, this is no problem. But in others – say, when the weather is particularly horrendous, or when the mission has virtu-ally no hope of success – the honorary secretary has to decide whether he is justified in putting the lives of his crew at risk. This, to say the least, is a job that calls for sound judgement.

Other people whose work behind the scenes is of vital importance are those responsible for the Institution's finances. Historically, the RNLI has been at its most effective when its finances have been on a sound footing. It has been less effective – in the 1840s, 1890s and 1970s – when there were insufficient funds to maintain and at the same time modernize the fleet. At the start of the twenty-first century the Institution's outgoings are daunting. It costs nearly £340,000 a day just to keep things running efficiently. The cost of building and equipping a new (Tamar class) lifeboat is £2,600,000. Every time an inshore lifeboat is launched the cost is over £2,000, rising to nearly £6,000 for all-weather offshore boats. In 2007 there were 8,144 launched. It is not therefore surprising that in the financial year 2007 total expenditure was over £123,000,000.

How, you may wonder, does the Institution generate the income to meet these huge expenses? Not a penny comes from the government. Only a tiny proportion (less than one per cent) comes from corporate financing. An even smaller propor-tion comes from the RNLI lottery. Virtually all the RNLI's income is provided by the generosity of the public. The diagram below shows how, in 2007, this money was donated.

It can be seen that legacies are now the Institution's main source of income. This wasn't always so. In its first thirty years the Shipwreck Institution received less than £5000 from bequests in its supporters' wills. In many years there were no bequests at all. It was not until 1856, when Captain Hamilton Fitzgerald left the Institution an amazing £10,000, that bequests began to make a sizeable contribution to income. In the second half of the nine-teenth century and throughout most of the twentieth, as the work of the RNLI came to be increasingly appreciated by the public, more and more people remembered the Institution in their wills. In 1880 bequests totalled £25,000, in 1920 £48,000, in 1950 £399,000, and by 1980 nearly £6,000,000.

Sources of income totalling £158M

❭ Legacies	60
❭ Raised voluntary income	30
❭ Net investment income	5
❭ Net merchandising and other trading	3
❭ Other income	2

However, in the mid 1990s this support showed signs of declining; in 1996 the amount received from legacies was less than in 1992. The Institution realized it

Fundraising is now the institution's second-largest source of income, after legacies. This 1939 picture shows the old-fashioned collection boxes.

could not rely on the public automatically to increase its support each year. What was needed was a campaign to promote public awareness of what lifeboatmen and women were currently doing, and how utterly dependent they were on public donations. As part of this campaign the Institution published a booklet entitled *Preserving All You Value: How a gift to the RNLI in your will can help save lives in the years to come.* This outlines the enormous cost nowadays of running the lifeboat service, and stresses how much it helps the Institution to have some idea of what its future income from legacies is likely to be. In a separate questionnaire members were asked if they were thinking of making a bequest in their will. The response was 'overwhelming'. A typical reply came from Dorothy Eldridge: 'I am glad to support the RNLI because I have such great admiration for the volunteers who man our lifeboats. It is therefore a natural step (for me) to pledge a legacy gift'.

Most legacies come in the form of money. However, over the years the Institution has had some not so simple bequests, including a pig farm, a caravan park, a night club, a house in Tenerife occupied by Dutch squatters, and a loquacious parrot. All are grist to the mill. And it seems likely that as long as lifeboat crews retain the affection and admiration of the public, legacies will continue to swell the Institution's income.

The second-largest source of income is from fundraising. Ever since Charles Macara and his wife organized their first street collection in Manchester in 1891, fundraising has been part of the fabric of the RNLI. Not only has it provided money, it has helped to keep the Institution in the public eye, ensuring that the work of lifeboat crews is brought to the attention of people not only in coastal areas, but in inland towns and villages all over the country.

In the old days, most fundraising was done by ladies, often guild members, who sold flags and rattled collecting boxes. Throughout the first half of the twentieth century this was effective. The ladies made house-to-house calls, carrying little paper and silk flags stuck into pincushions specially made to fit RNLI collecting boxes; the paper flags were sold for a minimum of 1d, the silk ones for silver. Fashions change. Today people, and especially young people, like to raise money in a totally different way, by taking part in sponsored and often personally challenging fun events. A glance at a few such events that have taken place in the last couple of decades provides evidence both of the continuing support of the public, and of the spirit of adventure of the fundraisers.

In 1990 a donation arrived with the following letter:

Dear Sirs,

Two of my locals at the Horse Shoe Inn bet me £50 each that I wouldn't dare wear 'Drag' on Christmas eve ... I took them up on their bet. The enclosed photo shows the three of us, together with a very game barmaid – I'm the one with the dark hair! A very successful evening, resulting in a cheque to Fleetwood [Lifeboat] Station for £245.

Yours faithfully

Phil Hindley, Licensee.

In 1891 shire horses had pulled lifeboats through the streets of Manchester for the first ever street collection. A hundred years later Webster's shire horses pulled a traditional brewer's dray on a tour of twenty-seven lifeboat stations in the north of England. They raised over £1500.

On 22 May 1992, Portrush held its annual raft race. There were tug o' war, climbing the greasy pole, fireworks, a parachute drop and mock rescues by a lifeboat. The climax was a race by 104 rafts competing for the prize of the 'Most Ingeniously Devised Method of Propulsion'. Over 25,000 people attended; over £22,000 was raised.

In 1993, The Lifeboat tells us, 'After raiding their toy cupboards and wardrobes, Amy Bromilow, aged eight, and her sister Rebecca, aged ten, held a jumble sale outside their home in Stoneclough, raising £80 63p for [the] Farnworth and Kearsley [lifeboat] branch.'

The twenty-first anniversary of the Cromer Ladies' Guild occurred in 1994. A special cake was baked for the occasion by founder members, and was cut at a party for 150 members and their guests; £850 was raised. This is typical of the fundraising work that goes on behind the scenes literally every day of the year. Since it was founded in

OPPOSITE

Putting the fun into fundraising. People rattling collecting boxes have now been joined by a new type of fundraiser: young people taking part in sponsored and often personally challenging events.

1973, the Cromer Ladies' Guild has raised over £92,000 for the Institution.

In 1966 the children's television programme Blue Peter asked for 60,000 paperbacks to be sent to the BBC; it was hoped to sell these in aid of the RNLI. In fact, 250,000 books were donated, and the money raised from selling them paid for four inshore lifeboats: Blue Peter I, II, III and IV, stationed at Littlehampton, Beaumaris, North Berwick and St Agnes. As a result of subsequent appeals, two more Blue Peter boats (stationed at Cleethorpes and Portaferry) were added to the fleet. Then in 1993 the programme launched yet another appeal on behalf of the RNLI for 'Pieces of Eight'. It asked for 'treasure' – any unwanted bric-a-brac that could be auctioned – to be sent to a warehouse in Ringwood. Over one and a half million parcels came in (all delivered free by the Royal Mail), their contents ranging from a diamond pendant to a rusty spoon. When sold, these 'Pieces of Eight' realized well over £1,000,000, enough to pay for the replacement of the existing six Blue Peter inshore lifeboats and to pay for a Trent class lifeboat stationed at Fishguard – 'a gift from a community of the air to a community of the sea'.

In 1996 Barrie Simpson-Wills celebrated his sixty-fifth birthday by making an Alpine paragliding flight. Taking off from close to the top of the 7500 foot Plan d'Aiguille, Barrie found that increasing wind made it impossible for him to reach his

intended landing field. However, he managed to put down on a country road between two moving cars – one of the drivers winding down his window with the greeting 'Bonjour, monsieur!' Following a film show of his flight, cheques totalling £1300 were sent to the RNLI and a Marie Curie hospice.

In 1997 hundreds of sponsored Storm Force (the RNLI's youth club) members played 'Monopoly Live' round the streets of London, dashing almost non-stop from the Old Kent Road to Mayfair. Several youngsters managed to reach all twenty-six locations on the Monopoly board (not including Jail!), and the game raised over £8300.

The choir of the Cromer Smugglers don't like being called a pop group, but they are certainly popular. In 1998 they went on tour under the guidance of lifeboat mechanic Paul Wegg, 'giving a unique rendering of sea shanties and folk music'. In Holland, they were signed up by an agent wanting to sell their CDs on the continent. They are now extensively booked for national and international gigs, and have raised enough money to pay for Tynemouth's D class lifeboat.

In 1999 the wives and girlfriends of the Llandudno lifeboat crew took on the local police in a charity football match. Rumour has it that for one reason or another more than half the policemen got red cards. The women had the satisfaction not only of winning 6–4, but of raising £2200.

On New Year's Day 2000, Martyn King and Alison Shaw went walkabout. Having sold many of their possessions and given up the comfort of their home, they set out on a two year, 7000 mile walk round the coast of the British Isles, with the intention of visiting every lifeboat station en route. With supporters like these putting the fun into fundraising, the RNLI would seem assured of both income and publicity.

Its next most lucrative source of revenue is from investments. At the moment, this income amounts to a healthy £13,000,000 per year; but stock markets are volatile, and no matter how astute the Institution's investment consultants may be, this sort of return cannot be guaranteed year after year.

Another major source of income is from membership. The Institution now has over 250,000 members. There are several categories – Governors, Offshore (Shoreline) and Storm Force, to mention only a few – and between them they contribute over £9,000,000 to annual income. However, the contribution these members make is far greater than the figures indicate. Many belong to one of the 2000-odd branches or guilds that support the Institution. And to quote the journal: 'These ordinary men and women from all walks of life are, alongside our lifeboat crews, the bedrock of the RNLI . . . For when an individual joins a branch or guild committee they are doing something more than offering support; they are giving something of their own lives in Service'.

RNLI (Sales) Ltd now makes a sizeable contribution – nearly £2,000,000 last year – to annual income. This is a commercial company, owned by the RNLI, which covenants its profits back to the Institution. This somewhat complicated arrangement enables the charity to raise funds by trading without having to pay taxes such as VAT. The sales organization is not merely linked to the Institution, it is bonded to it: its board of directors consists entirely of RNLI staff and committee members, and its sole objective is to raise money for the Institution by selling its gifts and souvenirs. This is big business, with an annual turnover of some £8,000,000 – almost £2,000,000 of which is returned to the RNLI as profit, and with some 650 different items – ranging from a 50p pencil to a £295 model of the *Victory* – being held in stock. One key to handling such diverse merchandise, and orders that sometimes pour in at a rate of 2,000 a day, is good warehousing and distribution. Orders from RNLI shops and the souvenir orders for Branches and Guilds are now fulfilled from the Lifeboat Support Centre in Poole, while orders from the Gift Catalogues are handled by an external fulfilment provider.[i] But perhaps the real key is the small but dedicated team, who know that all their hard work helps not to line some director's pockets, but to save lives at sea.

The last major source of income is corporate sponsorship. On the face of it, corporate sponsors provide less than one per cent of the Institution's income. But there is more to it than that. Many sponsors have entered into a partnership with the RNLI, whereby both parties gain. For example, Volvo can say that their cars, like lifeboats, are designed to save lives. The Royal Bank of Scotland can say that each time a customer uses one of their credit cards, a percentage goes to the Institution. Duckhams can say that if their oil is good enough to be used in lifeboats, it is good enough to be used anywhere. Several sponsors have donated lifeboats to the RNLI – in the case of the Fred Olsen Line, no fewer than three. Many not so well-known sponsors also make valuable contributions. For example, Drayton Manor Theme Park has a 'Lifeboat Ride'; for every person who uses it 1p is donated to RNLI funds.

Expenditure totalling £124M

❭ Rescue — 46%
❭ Operational maintenance — 36%
❭ Cost of generating voluntary income — 15%
❭ Prevention — 3%

At the start of the twenty-first century, the Institution's incomings seem to be in a healthy enough state.

But what of its outgoings? The diagram above shows how annual income for 2007 was spent.

These figures can be taken as an indication of how the RNLI sees its future.

The RNLI

moving forward

ears ago, the Royal Navy used to be known as the 'Silent Service', the inference being that it was so pre-eminent in its field it had no need to boast of its achievements. In the same way it used to be thought that the RNLI had no need to sell itself to the public because the exploits of its lifeboat crews spoke for themselves. However, to be successful in the twenty-first century everything needs to be promoted, and in recent years the Institution has been making a conscious effort to enhance its image and make people, particularly young people, aware of what it does. As part of this packaging it has produced a leaflet, *2000 and Beyond*, which sets out its aims for the future.

[Our] vision is to be recognized universally as the most effective,

innovative and dependable lifeboat service.

In all we do or say, we will:

(a) Recognize the courage, commitment and humanity of our crews

(b) Maintain our volunteer ethos

(c) Harness staff professionalism and expertise in support of our volunteers

(d) Strive for high standards

(e) Preserve our independence and the trust of the public

(f) Encourage open and effective communication.

Some of this may be stating the obvious. Yet objectives can be more easily achieved if they are set out for all to see.

The modern face of the RNLI: a Griffon
450TD Hovercraft.

Equipment carried by offshore and inshore lifeboats.

It would seem from '*2000 and Beyond*' that the Institution's priorities for the future will be its crews, its lifeboats and its relationship with the public. Lifeboat crews always have been and always will be the bedrock of the Institution. In the old days, crew members needed to be brave and able to pull an oar, but not a great deal else was expected of them. Today, as well as being brave, they are expected to be proficient in subjects such as first aid, and the operation and maintenance of marine engines and electronic equipment; they also need knowledge of many other skills such as pilotage, and procedures for towing and helicopter transfer. In a word, they need to be trained. In the 1990s an RNLI team led by George Cooper campaigned for the building of an international college: 'a centre of excellence', where lifeboat crews from all over the world could be given the new type of training they needed. Land adjacent to the RNLI's headquarters in Poole was purchased, building was started in the spring of 2003 and a year later the RNLI's Lifeboat College was officially opened by HM the Queen.

It was to prove a centre of excellence in more ways than one. It was soon awarded full membership of the International Association of Conference Centres, and its design by Dean and Dyball was voted best Medium-sized Project for 2004, and in its first four years nearly 5,000 volunteers from all over the world attended its training courses.

Indoors, the College has classrooms for theory sessions, and – more importantly – a survival pool and a sophisticated simulator. Outside, lifeboats are available for exercises in Poole Harbour and beyond. All lifeboat crews (most of whom now come from non-maritime occupations) attend these courses, and volunteers who turn up expecting a gentle swim and some not too demanding computer games are in for a rude awakening. The survival pool has a state-of-the-art simulator able to create four-metre waves, gale-force winds, thunder and lightning, and engine vibrations so realistic that some trainees are seasick. Simulator-instructors can programme any kind of exercise, from saving a single person who has fallen overboard to coping with a supertanker on fire and sinking in a high-density shipping area. Sophisticated software enables them to alter the light, the state of the sea and the needs of the casualty. And everything is recorded. So when trainees are debriefed they can watch a replay of their exercise and the instructor can talk through with them what they did right or wrong, and how their performance might be improved. Many lifeboat crews who have subsequently saved lives described these courses as invaluable. 'We could never have done what we did,' one wrote, 'if we hadn't been so well trained.'

The College has also been successful in other ways. Its sixty bedrooms can provide accommodation not only for trainees, but for those visiting the RNLI's headquarters and ancillary centres. The College also has first-class conference facilities and a welcoming and highly professional staff. When not fully occupied by RNLI members, there are many organizations with a similar ethos to the RNLI who are happy to use – and to pay to use – the College's facilities.

But perhaps most importantly of all, the College has become a place where crews from all over the country can meet not only one another, but also staff, shore-workers and fundraisers. To quote the College's Principal, Sue Hennessy, 'The College is more than somewhere you go for a training course: it is a place where all members of the RNLI family are welcomed.'

The basic objective of this training is, of course, to ensure that crews are equipped to do all that is humanly possible to save lives at sea. There is, however, another objective: 'to provide quality evidence in case of litigation'.[ii]

In brief, the College has ensured that in a safe and controlled environment our lifeboat crews and our lifeguards are given the best training in the world.

Will they also be given the best lifeboats in the world? Ever since the days of Lukin and Wouldhave there has been controversy over what is the best type of lifeboat. Today the controversy is made more complicated by the fact that rescue boats are becoming increasingly specialized, and a well-balanced fleet now consists of several different kinds of boat.

In the mid 1990s an RNLI team was asked to formulate both a short-term and a long-term strategy for the fleet of the future. For the short term, the team suggested two targets: (a) to be able to reach any point up to fifty miles off the coast within two

RNLI lifeboat crews and lifeguards work together to provide a ring of safety around our islands: Lifeboats, Lifeguards, Life first.

and a half hours of launching; and (b) to reach ninety-five per cent of casualties within thirty minutes of launching. These targets have now been achieved: (a) by introducing an increasing number of Tamars and re-engined Severns fitted with SIMS to operate offshore, and (b) by introducing an increasing number of Atlantic 75s and 85s and rescue boats and rescue watercraft to operate inshore. As a result, the RNLI is now close to having what it considers 'the perfect fleet'.

For the long term, the team made radical proposals. They saw their brief as being not merely to improve the existing fleet, but to visualize what would be the perfect fleet, assuming the RNLI was given a clean slate. From a detailed analysis of services carried out in the last decade, they concluded that by the year 2020 the Institution ought ideally to have four types of lifeboat. The tables below outline the specifications proposed.

Proposed lifeboat specifications for 2020

Type I. A large, all-weather, self-righting lifeboat, launched from afloat

Weight:	40 tonnes plus
Endurance:	10 hours
Speed:	25 knots
Crew:	4/7 (age limit 55)
Carrying capacity:	100 plus
Towing capacity:	up to 50 tonnes

Carrying a daughter boat (i.e. a small, 20-knot, manhandlable, 2-crew inflatable easily launched from its parent lifeboat)

Type II. A smaller, faster, all-weather, self-righting lifeboat, launched from afloat, carriage or slipway, transportable by road

Weight:	20 tonnes
Endurance:	5 hours
Speed:	35 knots
Crew:	3/4 (age limit 55)
Carrying capacity:	50 plus
Towing capacity:	up to 50 tonnes

Type III. A fast, medium-sized inshore lifeboat, with righting capacity, housed, and transportable by road

Weight:	Not yet determined
Endurance:	2½ hours
Speed:	35 knots
Crew:	3 (age limit 45)
Carrying capacity:	10 plus
Towing capacity:	up to 15 tonnes

Type IV. A smaller, slower, inshore lifeboat, with righting capacity, housed, and transportable by road

Weight:	Not yet determined
Endurance:	2½ hours
Speed:	25 knots
Crew:	2 or 3 (age limit 45)
Carrying capacity:	10 plus
Towing capacity:	up to 15 tonnes

The table below shows roughly where, by 2020, they might be stationed.

Proposed boats in service by 2020

Area	Type I (large offshore)	Type II (fast offshore)	Type III (medium inshore)	Type IV (small inshore)	Total
Scotland	21	7	11	6	45
Ireland	15	12	10	17	54
North of England	4	15	13	18	50
South of England	12	11	18	19	60
West of England	2	12	18	26	58
East of England	7	10	18	16	51
Total	61	67	88	102	318

It is interesting to see that Type II is already at the experimental stage and will definitely be powered by water jets. Type III has already been fulfilled by the B class Atlantic 85s. And Type IV has been fulfilled by a redesigned and upgraded version of the D class inflatable.

Until recently, the RNLI concerned itself largely with coping with accidents after they had happened. However, in the mid 1990s the ever increasing demand for lifeboat services led to the feeling that prevention was needed as well as cure; and the Institution initiated a campaign to make seagoers (and particularly holiday-makers, beach users, extreme sports enthusiasts and pleasure boat owners) aware of the fact that inshore waters, as well as bringing relaxation and pleasure, can also bring danger and death. Together with organizations such as the coastguards and the Royal Yachting Association, the Institution launched a Sea Safety Campaign.

A first step was to establish friendly relations with the other organizations concerned with sea safety. Once this had been done, everyone pooled their expertise and their records. This made possible the creation of a national database for sea-related emergencies; and when the information held there was analysed, it became possible accurately to identify such things as the most frequent causes of accidents, and the most effective types of response. This liaison work is now ensuring that the policies of the future are being shaped by the lessons of the present.

A second step was to produce a series of videos and booklets designed to make people aware of the potential hazards of shore-based and sea-based activities. The videos cover such subjects as *First Aid Afloat* and *Marine Diesel Engines: All you need to know about them*. Some of the booklets cover general subjects such as *Beach Safety Guidelines*; others are more specialized, such as *Guidelines to Reduce Machinery Failure in Pleasure Craft*.

Every year thousands of people get into difficulties on our beaches and inshore waters. On average the RNLI and the RLSS (Royal Life Saving Society) between them rescue over 2500 people annually – people who, if they had not been rescued, would almost certainly have drowned. The diagram below gives a breakdown of the type of casualty to which lifeboats are called out nowadays.

A great many of these launches would not have had to be made had people observed a few basic precautions, as set out in the *Safety on the Sea* booklets.

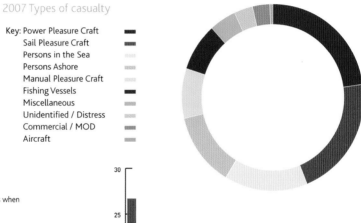

2007 Types of casualty

Key: Power Pleasure Craft
Sail Pleasure Craft
Persons in the Sea
Persons Ashore
Manual Pleasure Craft
Fishing Vessels
Miscellaneous
Unidentified / Distress
Commercial / MOD
Aircraft

CASUALTY ACTIVITY

Casualties were participating in a wide variety of activities when the incidents occurred

Activity	Total 2007	% of total
Bodyboarding	500	26.7
Swimming	363	19.4
Surfing	360	19.2
Walking / running	216	11.5
Inflatables	145	7.7
Passive recreation	82	4.4
Climbing	46	2.5
Powered craft	37	2.0
Kayaking / canoeing	35	1.8
Kitesurfing	32	1.7
Windsurfing	20	1.1
Skimboarding	11	0.6
Playing football	9	0.5
Sailing	6	0.3
Fishing	5	0.3
Cycling	2	0.1
Horseriding	2	0.1
Paddling	2	0.1
Snorkelling	1	0
Total	1,874	100.0

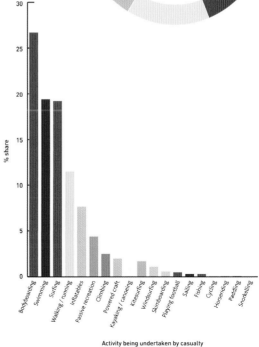

Activity being undertaken by casualty

More than 5,000,000 of these booklets have been distributed free. Each contains six-teen pages of advice, tips, telephone numbers and cartoons that would enhance any newspaper or magazine. A typical example is 'Safety Guidelines for Recreational Boat Users'. Information is given on subjects that include buying a suitable boat, acquiring the basic skills you need before you put to sea, what to do before you set out, the equipment and safety apparatus you ought to have aboard, and how to attract attention in an emergency.

Another recently launched safety initiative is Sea Check. An analysis of lifeboat services has revealed, not surprisingly, that the largest number of emergencies stem from the failure of a boat's engines or equipment. These failures are sometimes due to ignorance and inexperience – it is not unheard of for navigation side lights to be installed pointing upwards! And they are sometimes due to poor maintenance; for whereas fishing and commercial vessels that are in use all the time tend to be main-tained and serviced as a matter of routine, pleasure craft that are used only occa-sionally are not always so well looked after. It was therefore decided to offer an advisory service to all leisure boat owners, with trained and experienced inspectors first carrying out a thorough check on their safety equipment, then offering free advice as to what was needed to make the vessel concerned – be it a luxury yacht or an eight-foot sailing dinghy – as safe as possible.

A pilot scheme was set up. Questionnaires were sent to a cross-section of boat owners, and the response was astonishing. Over seventy per cent replied – the aver-age response to this type of questionnaire is under five per cent. Within a year, Sea Check's 400 voluntary, unpaid inspectors had reported on 2300 boats, and as a result of their reports over half the owners concerned updated their safety equip-ment. It is hoped that the number of volunteer inspectors will soon be increased to 2000, and that they will report and advise on some 20,000 pleasure craft each year. The Sea Check teams will never know how many lives are being saved by their efforts. But it may be significant that in the early 1990s the number of lifeboat launches made every year was sharply rising; by the late 1990s it had levelled off.

Other recently introduced safety initiatives include an Offshore Membership cate-gory for sea users – this now has over 30,000 supporters – and the upgrading of the RNLI's travelling roadshow, which consists of two forty-foot trailers that have walk-through interactive displays. It is hoped these will attract some 200,000 people a year. In addition, a campaign has been launched to make young people aware of the need to reduce sea-related accidents and to get them interested in the work of the RNLI.

Since the youngsters of today will be the lifeboat crews of tomorrow, it was a bit disquieting for the RNLI to discover in the 1990s that it was not altogether on the same wavelength as a lot of young people. There appeared to be a widespread feeling of goodwill towards the Institution, but for many young people it had a dated image – old men in oilskins heaving at oars and ladies in hats rattling collecting boxes. Many youngsters had little idea of what the RNLI was currently doing. *2000 and Beyond* outlines how the Institution hopes to remedy this: by 'expanding the chil-dren's sea safety campaign', by 'addressing family audiences more effectively' and by 'creating a regional youth education programme'.

Acting on the old adage that prevention is better than cure, the RNLI has launched a Sea Saftey Campaign. The cartoons (right) are from an April 2000 leaflet, *Safety Guidelines for Recreational Boat Users*.

HOW TO GET ADVICE BEFORE BUYING YOUR BOAT

- Decide on the type of boat that you can handle and is most suitable for your purpose
- Make sure it is in good condition
- It is worth considering an independent survey
- Find out what equipment you will need
- Advice can be obtained from the **British Marine Industries Federation (BMIF)** who operate a free information service.

Call Boatline on 01784 472222

GET SOME TRAINING

- Before putting to sea, for your family's sake, you **MUST** acquire basic skills in Seamanship, Navigation, Rules of the Road, use of safety equipment and boat/engine maintenance
- Your skills, and those of your crew, are your greatest asset, particularly if things go wrong.
- Join a suitable sailing or boating club.
- For information on where training is available in your locality.

Call the RYA on 023 8062 7400

BE SAFE AFLOAT

- Lifejackets and safety harnesses are essential and should be provided for everyone on board. They could ensure your survival, but only if worn
- Ensure sets of warm and protective clothing are available including sunglasses
- Everyone must know what to do in a man overboard situation – It could be **YOU!**
- Advice on carrying additional safety equipment can be obtained from any of the organisations shown on page 15. The lives of your family must be worth a phone call

HOW TO ATTRACT ATTENTION IN AN EMERGENCY

- A VHF radio, which can be portable, will enable you to summon help by calling the **Coastguard** on channel 16. This may also alert other vessels in your vicinity who may be able to provide assistance
- If you use a radio you need to obtain an operators certificate and an annual licence. For more information call the **RYA on 023 8062 7400**
- Carry a portable foghorn and use the whistle fitted to your lifejacket to attract attention if necessary

A leaflet, *Get Splashed*, has been brought out for the under-nines. Already half a million copies have been distributed free, and more are on the way. It contains sensible advice put across as fun – drawings, letters, cartoons, puzzles, games, competitions, etc., and has been widely praised and enjoyed. Those under sixteen can join the RNLI youth club, Storm Force (membership is £5 per year). Members receive a quarterly magazine, and have the chance to join a shore-based youth crew and meet other like-minded young people who enjoy a challenge. Finally, the Institution has appointed a number of regional education officers, whose job is to liaise with schools and youth clubs, and ensure that young people are kept aware of what the RNLI is doing in the twenty-first century.

In addition to all this, the Institution now offers a comprehensive education programme, covering sea and beach safety and the work of the RNLI. This includes free print-based resources for schools and youth groups, and the opportunity to visit a lifeboat station and a beach covered by RNLI lifeguards. The Institution has a website – Shorething! – for students, parents and teachers. It is hoped that making young people aware of our work and our volunteer ethos may point the way to their becoming active and responsible citizens.

Two faces of the RNLI. ABOVE A young fundraiser. OPPOSITE The Lerwick lifeboat *Soldian*, which carried out many difficult and hazardous rescue-services around the Shetland Islands.

During the first decade of this century there has been considerable expansion of the services offered by the RNLI. Today its vision is not only to save lives at sea, but also to save lives on inland waterways and beaches.[iii]

It is good to know that the Institution is moving with the times and planning for the future. Yet all its plans and all its expenditure will be of little use if it should ever lose its greatest asset: the commitment of its crews. That is the heartbeat it relies on. Everything else may need to change: that needs to stay constant.

So many lifeboat launches today are comparatively low-key affairs – picking up a family cut off by the tide, towing back a pleasure craft with a failed engine – that perhaps we need to be reminded that some services are still unbelievably hazardous. Storms in the twenty-first century are as frenetic as they were in the nineteenth; ships are still driven ashore and pounded to destruction by huge seas and hurricane-force winds. It is true that lifeboats are now bigger and better than they were in Hillary's day; but it is also true that they go on service in conditions in which not even Hillary would have put to sea. There are occasions when the traditional virtues of courage and good seamanship are as necessary today as they were in the age of oars and sail.

One such occasion was a rescue that took place in the summer of 2004. The Nash Sandbanks, off the south coast of Wales, have claimed the lives of many fishermen. It seemed that more lives were likely to be lost on the morning of 24 August when a local fishing vessel, the *Gower Pride*, suffered engine failure, and found herself being swept by a force 8 gale on to the sands.[iv]

Between 1980 and 2000 the *Soldian* and her successors launched 331 times and saved 290 lives. In the small hours of 21 September 1982, the yacht *Hermes of Lune* sent out a Mayday from close to the Skerries, the most easterly of the Shetland Islands. It was a wild night: a hurricane from the south-west, huge seas and torrential rain. Lerwick's lifeboat was the Arun class *Soldian*, and her coxswain Hewitt Clark, a matter-of-fact, retiring, family man, soon to be the recipient of more honours than any other serving lifeboatman. When, after a difficult passage, *Soldian* reached the Skerries, the wind was force twelve: 'so strong it had blown the sea flat, and turned its surface into a solid sheet of spume'. Without the lifeboat's powerful searchlights the casualty would have been impossible to find; but eventually Clark spotted her, embayed in a remote sound and in danger of being driven ashore. He managed to manoeuvre alongside, and took off two of her crew. Her third crewman, the skipper, asked to be left on his yacht in the hope of saving her, while the lifeboat stood by.

By using his engines, sometimes almost at full power, Clark managed to stay close at hand throughout the night. By dawn, the wind had moderated to a mere 70 miles per hour, and *Soldian* was able to launch her inflatable dinghy. Its crewmen, Andrew Leask and Ian Newlands, succeeded in running a line from the yacht to the shore. In shallow, rock-strewn waters this was no easy task. The dinghy was operating at the very limit of its capabilities, and Ian had to spend most of the time lying flat, face-down on its bow to prevent it flipping over. As the weather slowly improved, it became clear that the *Hermes of Lune* was no longer in danger. So Clark put one of her crew back on board, and returned to Lerwick. The lifeboat berthed at nine thirty-five a.m., having been at sea for eight and a half hours, most of the time in appalling conditions. For this service Hewitt Clark was awarded a bronze medal, and Andrew Leask and Ian Newlands the Thanks of the Institution inscribed on Vellum.

On 13 January 1989 the fishing vessel *Boy Andrew* ran aground on the rocks of Trebister Ness, three miles south of Lerwick. She transmitted a Mayday, and *Soldian* went to her aid, reaching her a little after five a.m. Although conditions were difficult – high winds and heavy seas – the situation didn't seem at first to be life-threatening. As the *Boy Andrew* was aground in shallow water, the lifeboat wasn't able to get alongside; however, she used her inflatable dinghy to rescue all the crew except the skipper who, once again, chose to remain on board in the hope of saving his ship. An attempt by the lifeboat to tow *Boy Andrew* off the rocks was unsuccessful, due largely to a falling tide. *Soldian* then took the rescued fishermen back to Lerwick. But in mid-morning the weather worsened. Returning to the wreck, the lifeboat found another fishing vessel, *Altair*, attempting to pull *Boy Andrew* off the rocks, while a helicopter from Sumburgh was hovering overhead. There were now four people aboard the *Boy Andrew*: her skipper, two of the crew of the *Altair* who had been transferred to the casualty by helicopter to help secure the towline, and the helicopter winchman.

As *Boy Andrew* was hauled off the rocks, Clark stood by. And it was as well he did; because everything went wrong at once. At eight minutes past one, *Boy Andrew* was hauled stern-first off the Ness; she immediately started to sink. At ten minutes past one, Clark drove the lifeboat alongside the foundering vessel – no easy job in the heavy seas and shallow water. The fishermen leapt safely into the lifeboat; but the winchman slipped, and fell into the sea between the two vessels. With great presence of mind, Clark used full power to swing the lifeboat away before the winchman was crushed; he then manoeuvred so that the man was swirled clear of the sinking vessel by the lifeboat's wash. At twelve minutes past one, the winchman was picked up by the helicopter, and Clark reported that *Boy Andrew* had sunk, but all aboard her had been saved. For this service he was awarded a second bronze medal, and two of his crew the Institution's Thanks on Vellum.

A few years later, on 17 January 1993, another night of high winds and heavy seas, another fishing boat was in trouble. Sixteen miles off the south tip of Bressay, the m.f.v. *Ardency* was out of control and close to foundering; she was shipping water, and her pumps were not functioning. *Soldian* got to her a little after midnight to find a helicopter overhead, trying to lower emergency pumps to her. With the wind gusting to over 100 miles per hour, and *Ardency* corkscrewing gunwale-under, every attempt was failing. Clark managed to pass a heaving-line to the fishing vessel; then he took her in tow, and began to haul her slowly into the shelter of the nearest land. When *Ardency* became more stable, the pumps were lowered to her, and as soon as they began to operate effectively, the danger of foundering receded.

Clark, however, decided to keep the fishing vessel in tow and haul her back to Lerwick. The official report says laconically that the service was 'difficult', that 'the tow-line broke and it took three-quarters-of-an-hour before it could be re-established,' and that 'the wind was Force 14' and 'the seas very high'. Matter of fact words that

(Left) The *Michael and Jane Vernon* alongside *Green Lily* in a Force 14 hurricane. (Right) Survivors from the *Pionersk*. All her crew were saved after a service of which Lerwick's honorary lifeboat secretary wrote, 'I have never seen a coxswain and crew so physically and mentally shattered.'

give little indication of how testing conditions were: not a glimmer of light, near-continuous sleet-cum-rain, thirty-foot waves that threatened any moment to capsize them, and soaking spray and a cutting wind blowing at eighty miles per hour which penetrated even the best protective clothing. Dawn was breaking as *Soldian* at last towed the labouring fishing boat into the safety of Lerwick harbour, after a service that called for fine seamanship and earned Hewitt Clark his third bronze medal.

On 31 October 1994, a 10,000-ton Russian factory ship, the *Pionersk*, went aground on the same spot as the *Boy Andrew* – Trebister Ness. These were familiar waters for the Lerwick lifeboatmen, and within fifteen minutes of casting off, *Soldian* was approaching the casualty. She was lying impacted into the rocks, her bow facing seaward, and yawing violently as the seas swept over her; bunker oil and refrigerant gas were spewing out of her shattered hull. Clark decided to take off the crew via a ladder dangling over her stern; but after just four men had clambered down to the lifeboat, the ladder was dislodged by heavy seas. Clark then

The *Pionersk*, aground and breaking up off Trebister Ness.

had no option but to try to ease the lifeboat into the narrow seaway between the *Pionersk*'s stern and the shore, and come alongside the factory ship's port quarter where a pilot ladder had been lowered. It was a nightmare scenario: pitch dark except for the beam of *Soldian*'s searchlight, high winds, huge seas, rocks close at hand, and men retching in the stench of the escaping oil and gas. The crew of the factory ship could come down the ladder only one at a time; and Clark could hold the lifeboat alongside only for two or three seconds before the seas either rolled the two boats apart or threatened to crash them together; in those two or three seconds the Russian seamen had to jump one at a time into the lifeboat.

To have come safely alongside half a dozen times would have been a fine feat of seamanship. Incredibly, in the small hours of that October morning, Clark came alongside the *Pionersk* no fewer than seventy times. If he had got any one of his approaches wrong, that would almost certainly have been the end of the *Soldian* and her crew. But he didn't, and he managed to take off sixty-four of the Russian seamen. Then the overladen *Soldian* returned to Lerwick. One might have thought her crew had done all that could be expected of them. But as soon as they had landed the traumatized crew, they returned to the wreck and stood by while a helicopter airlifted the rest of the Russian seamen to safety. When at last Clark and his men returned to Lerwick, after an appallingly difficult and demanding service, the honorary secretary reported, 'I have never seen a Coxswain and crew so physically and mentally shattered. They really did give their all.' Clark was awarded a silver medal, and five of his crew the Thanks of the Institution on Vellum, 'in recognition of their courage, determination

Lerwick's Severn-class lifeboat *Michael and Jane Vernon*. In 1997 she rescued the crew of the refrigerated cargo ship *Green Lily* in a service that called for 'enormous courage, leadership, determination and seamanship'.

and teamwork whilst on the lifeboat deck... being constantly sprayed by diesel oil'.

Another and equally difficult rescue took place on 19 November 1997. The refrigerated cargo ship *Green Lily* chose a bad moment to develop engine trouble. She was south-east of Bressay, in conditions described by the Met. Office as 'horrendous'. For the past week gale-force winds had been piling up the sea, and by the early hours of that November morning the waves were forty-five feet from trough to crest, the wind was seventy miles per hour gusting 100, and *Green Lily* was being swept towards a shore where there would be no hope of survival. She sent out a Mayday and three tugs and a helicopter went to her aid.

It was not until midday that Lerwick's new Severn class lifeboat, the *Michael and Jane Vernon*, was alerted, for it was thought that the tugs would be able to tow *Green Lily* to safety. However, conditions proved too difficult for both tugs and helicopter. In the huge seas every hawser parted, and with *Green Lily* wallowing and corkscrewing out of control the helicopter couldn't get a line to her. When Clark and his crew arrived, a third towline had just broken, and the cargo ship was less than a mile and a half from land. She tried to drop anchor. The starboard anchor was payed out successfully, but the port failed; and the luckless *Green Lily* swung bow into wind and started to roll so violently that the waves broke clean over her. The Institution's official 'account of the service' tells us what happened next:

> The [cargo] ship was now in 35 metres of water and only 900 yards off shore. Clark decided he would have to make some sort of approach on the casualty if anyone was to be saved. Any approach would have to be made on the port side, to take advantage of what lee there was, but this would restrict the amount of searoom between the drifting ship and the rocks. He urged the master to get his crew ready for evacuation ... The crew positioned themselves to assist survivors as they abandoned ship [as] the lifeboat approached to within 20–30 feet of the ship's side. The two vessels were moving violently in the huge seas, and the lifeboat [one moment] rose high above the cargo ship's deck, before dropping [next moment] below her waterline in the next trough.

Perhaps only those who have been at sea in a storm can appreciate the difficulty of the rescue that followed. We may say we love the sea, but it is nonetheless an alien and at times unforgiving environment. On land, a miscalculation can often be rectified. Not so at sea. If Hewitt Clark, that afternoon, had given the wheel one more or one less turn, or given the engines a shade more or less power, the odds are that the *Michael and Jane Vernon* would have capsized, been flung fatally against the hull of the cargo ship, or have remained so far from her that no one could have been saved. But he made no miscalculation. 'Operating at the very limit of his boat's capabilities ... he made numerous attempts to put the lifeboat into a position where the survivors could be evacuated, often having to abort runs alongside due to the violent motion of the vessels.' (His crew told him afterwards that *Green Lily*'s rudders and propellers were at times being lifted clean out of the water.) 'Whenever the decks were [approximately] level, the lifeboat crew would grab a survivor and pull him over the ship's gunwale and on to the lifeboat's deck. Each time a man was saved, Coxswain Clark swung away and prepared for another run.'

The freighter *Green Lily*, buffeted by strong waves and winds.

But the time came when there was not enough searoom for another run; for the ships had been driven to within 200 yards of the shore, where huge seas were breaking white over the rocks. Five of *Green Lily*'s crew had been saved; but another ten were still onboard, and it seemed there was little chance of saving them. Then at the last minute one of the tugs, the *Maersk Champion*, managed to grapple the cargo ship's anchor chain and haul her head into wind. Head into wind *Green Lily* rode, for a few minutes, more easily; and in those few minutes the helicopter was able to drop its winchman, Bill Deacon, aboard her, and airlift the rest of her crew to safety. But at a terrible price. Just as the last man was being swung into the air, a huge wave broke flush on the deck of

Green Lily and swept Bill Deacon over the side. A moment later the anchor cable parted, and the cargo ship was driven on to the rocks. Almost at once she began to break up.

Clark was now faced with a nightmare decision. His heart pleaded with him to search for his fellow-rescuer. His head told him that Bill Deacon was surely already dead; for not only had he been washed overboard, but *Green Lily* had been seen to roll back on top of him. He also had to consider the fact that some of the men they had rescued were suffering from the sort of seasickness and hypothermia that can be life-threatening. Clark headed back for Lerwick, as fast as conditions would allow. But the moment the survivors had been put ashore safely, the *Michael and Jane Vernon* returned to the wreck.

It would have been a miracle if they had found Bill Deacon's body. And the miracle didn't happen. At considerable risk, Clark took the lifeboat as close inshore as he dared. But *Green Lily* was breaking up. Debris from her shattered hull and cargo from her shattered hold were being flung about in the huge seas. Oil was being spewed out of her tanks. And it was getting dark. The *Michael and Jane Vernon* searched for as long as it was possible to search. Only when a wave broke flush on top of the lifeboat, coating it from stem to stern in a film of oil, did they admit they were on a mission impossible. In spite of all they had achieved, it was a silent crew who dropped anchor that evening in Lerwick, after a service that earned Hewitt Clark a gold medal, and all five of his crew bronze medals. The Institution's Thanks on Vellum was awarded to the helicopter crew.

The service carried out that November afternoon encapsulates the story of the RNLI. What made this rescue possible was the commitment and teamwork of the Lerwick crew. The lifeboatmen would be embarrassed by any suggestion that they were supermen; they would much prefer to be thought of as 'ordinary people doing extraordinary things'. And perhaps a matter-of-fact account of the service they carried out is a more fitting tribute both to them and to the Institution than a fulsome valediction.

There are times when lifeboat crews have to face heartbreak – the empty overturned raft, the child's body floating face-down in the sea. But there are also times when they have the satisfaction of having done something wonderfully worthwhile. As a Gorleston crewman put it: 'You come off the lifeboat physically wrecked and bruised; but after a successful rescue you're on Cloud Nine for days. It is a hell of a feeling.' And it would seem that this is appreciated by a large percentage of the public. Not long ago the coxswain of the Lowestoft lifeboat got an unexpected letter:

Dear Mr Catchpole,

Just a few lines of very dear thanks.

Mr George Bird, who you and your crew saved, was and still is my grandad thanks to the bravery and courage of you men.

My grandad is 73 and I love him very much, if he had died a big part of me would have died as well.

So once again I just can't thank you enough.

Love, Debbie.

Let Debbie's words speak for us all.

Endnotes

[i] The Lifeboat Support Centre.

In the summer of 2004 a huge new warehouse was opened in Poole: its purpose, 'to store and distribute everything needed to run every station, lifeboat-unit and fundraising office in the UK and the Republic of Ireland'. This requirement was subsequently extended to include the holding of sales stock.

The warehouse now holds over 750,000 different items, ranging from 3-tonne lifeboat engines to loo rolls. And it is the proud boast of Manager Ruth Gentry and her dedicated team that their warehouse is open 24 hours a day, 365 days a year, and that every item held in it will be located and ready to be despatched within half-an-hour of it being asked for. This necessitates, among other things, holding a huge stock – currently valued at over £7,000,000. But as Ruth says: 'We are talking about lives. And I can't say to anyone, "sorry, you can't launch your lifeboat today, because I haven't got a spare pump for the engine".'

The creation of this new warehouse, with its 30-foot storage racks and mezzanine floor areas, has necessitated a new computer system for ordering and locating stock, a new team structure, and new responsibilities for the workforce. Staff suddenly found themselves expected to operate computer software, drive trucks and learn how to abseil (in case a truck breaks down on one of the upper storage levels).

Some found these changes stressful; but they have led to increased efficiency. The crew of a lifeboat today know that they will get a response of unparalleled speed and efficiency to their every request.

To quote Vince Jones, a Lifeboat Mechanic at Moelfre: 'Often we need items urgently, whether it is a pack of pager batteries or an inshore lifeboat engine. It is quicker now and easier to get the items from Poole, and that is very positive.'

[ii] Not so long ago, RNLI property and crews were sacrosanct: nobody stole the Institution's equipment or defamed its personnel. This is not so today. Security at headquarters, depots and lifeboat stations has had to be tightened, following an increase in theft. A lifeboat crew recently went to help a yachtsman who had transmitted a Mayday. The crew risked their lives to save him. He then tried to sue them because they hadn't been able also to save his yacht! It is not enough nowadays for men and women to go to the help of others, they must be seen to have the right qualifications to do so – an indication perhaps of the culture of litigation we now have to face.

[iii] Extending its lifeboat services inland has been on the Institution's wish list for many years, and Lough Erne in Northern Ireland was chosen as a test site. Lough Erne covers more than fifty square miles and is used in summer by over 600 visitors a week, many of them canoeists, dinghy-sailors or extreme sports enthusiasts. Each year there used to be accidents and fatalities. The spadework for setting up a rescue service was done by a local charity, the Lough Erne Rescue, and the Institution liaised with local volunteers to carry out tests with an Atlantic 21 stationed at the Yacht Club. The volunteers went through the usual demanding training, and on 23 May 2001 the RNLI's first inland waterways station was officially opened. It was quickly to prove its worth, being called out sixteen times in its first summer.

It wasn't long before other inland stations were opened, and today the RNLI operates rescue services on five inland waterways, including the tidal reaches of the Thames.

Over 100,000 people use the Thames every day, and there are on average more than 100 life-threatening incidents every year. Lifeboats first came to the river at the request of the government, following the *Marchioness/Bowbell* disaster, and they are now stationed at Tower Bridge, Chiswick, Gravesend and Teddington. It was found that the most efficient service was provided by a mix of D-class, B-class Atlantics and (uniquely) E-class lifeboats. Many of these boats aim to launch within ninety seconds of being alerted. This means that their crews – some paid, some unpaid – operate on a rota system, and some of them are always on station and ready to respond instantly. In the last six years lifeboats on the Thames have been launched 4,528 times, rescued 1,737 people and have saved 309 lives.

Improvements to the training of its crews and in the quality and coverage offered by its lifeboats have kept the RNLI abreast, if not ahead, of the times. But it would be fair to say that these improvements have not been fundamental. They have not altered the Institution's basic *raison d'être*: to save lives at sea.

However, during the last few years something has been happening that *has* changed the RNLI fundamentally. It has become increasingly concerned not only with saving lives at sea, but with preventing accidents – and hence of course saving lives – on our beaches.

In the twenty-first century many more people die as a result of accidents on and around our beaches than in shipwrecks. For our coastline is now used by an ever-increasing number of holidaymakers, swimmers, surfers, small craft and inflatable users, and extreme sports enthusiasts, many of whom have little knowledge of the sea. The RNLI is now offering these people advice and protection.

Early in 2001 the Institution began negotiations with the Maritime and Coastguard Agency, the Royal Life Saving Society and the Surf Life Saving Association of Great Britain to work out a coordinated approach to beach safety; and later that year the Institution undertook to provide lifeguards and whatever equipment was needed on several more popular West Country beaches.

In the last few years this service has been steadily expanded, and today highly trained RNLI lifeguards can be found on over 100 beaches, most of them in Southern England or South Wales. Their brief is first to prevent accidents from happening – patrolling, monitoring, advising and operating a flag-warning system – and second to respond to accidents if they do happen; for this they are equipped with small, fast, easy-to-launch rescue watercraft and inshore rescue boats. Over 10,000 people a year now receive some sort of help from these RNLI lifeguards, and it has been calculated that you are 500 times less likely to drown at a beach patrolled by lifeguards than at a beach where there is no lifeguard. All this has added a new dimension to the RNLI's commitment to saving lives at sea.

[iv] Within ten minutes of receiving the *Gower Pride*'s SOS, Porthcawl's Atlantic 75, the *Giles*, was heading for the sandbanks. In command was Helmsman Aileen Jones. 'It was very windy,' she writes, 'with big waves breaking right over the pier.' As they neared the casualty, Aileen could see (a) they needed to act quickly or the *Gower Pride* would break up, probably with the loss of all her crew; (b) their best bet was to try to tow the fishing vessel clear of the sands, and (c) the tow would have to be made through the shallow and dangerous water south of the sandbanks. Because conditions were so bad – close to the limits at which an Atlantic 75 could operate – Aileen called up the Mumbles all-weather lifeboat (the *Ethel Anne Measures*) and asked her to come and stand by. She then attempted to take the fishing vessel in tow.

The rescue that followed was no epic of the sea. But it was difficult. It was dangerous. And it called for an extremely high standard of seamanship. It succeeded only because the crew of the *Giles* worked together, and used the capabilities of their lifeboat to maximum effect.

As they headed into the confused water south of the Sandbanks, the *Giles* came close to capsizing. 'It was not a nice place to be,' writes Aileen. 'Quite dangerous. But you are so busy getting on with it, you don't really think about that.' They managed eventually to get close enough to the *Gower Pride* to throw her a tow-line. This was secured to the bow of the fishing vessel, and the tow got under way. They had just fought clear of the sands, when the tow-line parted, and the *Gower Pride* was swept back into danger. Aileen tried again. This time she managed to get alongside the fishing vessel, and one of her crew, Simon Emms, made the perilous leap from boat to boat, taking with him a new tow-line, a VHF radio, and a first aid kit. The tow was then started again: 'Slowly and painfully, with the lifeboat at times being lifted clean out of the water.'

To cut a long story short, Aileen and her crew managed to tow the fishing vessel clear of the sands to where the Mumbles seagoing lifeboat was waiting. Transferring the tow-line wasn't easy, with Simon having to crawl the length of the fishing vessel's slippery and wave-swept deck, 'with nothing much to hang on to'. But eventually the transfer was made, and within the hour rescuers and rescued were relaxing in the safety of Porthcawl harbour.

For her courage, seamanship and leadership Aileen was awarded the RNLI's bronze medal – the only woman and the first female crew member to have received the accolade in the last hundred years. But perhaps the final word on what happened that day should be left to the skipper of the *Gower Pride*. 'They were very brave,' he said. 'If it were not for Aileen and her crew, I wouldn't be here today.'

Rescues carried out by the Lerwick lifeboat *Soldian* are another reminder that some lifeboat services are still unbelievably hazardous. Many of these services took place in appalling weather, with the crew at risk from the moment they left the harbour. Five of their rescue operations led to the award of medals.

Key events in the history of the RNLI

1824   William Hillary's *Appeal to the Nation* leads to the founding of the Shipwreck Institution.

1838   Grace Darling helps her father rescue nine people from the wreck of the *Forfarshire*; she becomes 'Britain's first national heroine'.

1849   The Institution close to bankruptcy; its fleet reduced to 'less than a dozen really efficient boats'.

1850   Appointment of Richard Lewis as secretary.

1854   Lifeboat Inspector John Ward invents the cork lifejacket. Name of Institution changed to Royal National Lifeboat Institution.

1886   Probably the worst disaster in the Institution's history: three lifeboats lost, twenty-seven lifeboatmen drowned, going to the aid of the *Mexico* aground in the Ribble estuary.

1890   The first steam lifeboat, the *Duke of Northumberland*, goes into service.

1891	The birth of fundraising; Charles and Marion Macara organize the first street collection in Manchester.
1899	The Lynmouth lifeboat is hauled eleven miles over Exmoor, up and down gradients of one in four, to beach launch at Porlock.
1904	Introduction of kapok lifejackets: 'so bulky that lifeboatmen say they would rather drown than wear one'!
1909	Introduction of petrol-driven lifeboats.

1914–18	Many lifeboatmen join the services; the average age of a crew rises to over fifty. Nonetheless, lifeboats are launched 1808 times and save 5332 lives.
1920	First trials with agricultural caterpillar tractors; tractors begin to replace horses to assist with beach launching.
1921	Founding of first Ladies' Lifeboat Guild.
1924	First International Lifeboat Conference held in London.
1929	Radiotelephone sets installed in lifeboats, providing speech transmission between ship and shore.
1934	Last ever horse-drawn lifeboat launch (from Wells, Norfolk). Introduction of diesel engines.
1939–46	Again, many lifeboatmen join the services, and the average age of a crew rises to over fifty. Nonetheless, lifeboats are launched 3760 times and save 6376 lives (excluding the many thousands evacuated from Dunkirk).
1956	Introduction of VHF radio.
1957	First use of helicopters to co-operate with lifeboats.
1963	Introduction of radar. Introduction of the first inshore lifeboat, the inflatable D class.
1969	Elizabeth Hostvedt becomes the first female lifeboat crew member.
1970	Introduction of the Beaufort lifejacket.
1972	Introduction of the fast, rigid, inshore inflatable, the Atlantic 21.
1985	A junior membership scheme, Storm Force, is introduced to attract young people.
1996	Launch of Sea Safety Campaign.
2001	First inland lifeboat station opens in Lough Erne. RNLI lifeguards assume responsibility for patrolling selected West Country beaches.
2002	First RNLI hovercraft enters service.
2003	The Lifeboat College opened by HM the Queen.

The Beaufort Scale

BEAUFORT NUMBER	KNOTS	KILOMETRES PER HOUR	CONDITIONS
0	<1	<1	Dead calm: sea like a mirror
1	1–3	1–6	Light air: small ripples on sea
2	4–6	7–12	Light breeze: wind felt on face, small wavelets on sea
3	7–10	13–19	Gentle breeze: wave crests begin to break
4	11–16	20–30	Moderate breeze: frequent white horses at sea
5	17–21	31–9	Fresh breeze: small waves inshore, moderate waves offshore
6	22–7	40–50	Strong breeze: foaming wave crests and some spray at sea
7	28–33	51–62	Near gale: foam from wave crests blown into streaks
8	34–40	63–74	Gale: wave crests break into spindrift
9	41–7	75–87	Strong gale: high waves with rolling crests and dense spray
10	48–55	88–102	Storm: sea appears white, with high overhanging waves and streaks of dense foam
11	56–63	103–17	Violent storm: sea covered in streaks of foam, waves high enough to hide vessels, crests blown into froth; visibility restricted
12	>64	>118	Hurricane: sea completely white with driven spray; air filled with foam; visibility seriously impaired

LEFT The Exmouth Lifeboat, 1998.

RIGHT Sir Francis Beaufort (1774-1857), originator of the Beaufort Scale of Wind Speed.

Annual receipts

1824	£9706	1878	£34,493	1925	£235,818	1972	£3,123,277
1825	£9826	1879	£30,125	1926	£211,964	1973	£3,860,065
1826	£3392	1880	£38,507	1927	£228,975	1974	£4,944,781
1827	£1269	1881	£36,419	1928	£299,263	1975	£5,271,312
1828	£1234	1882	£43,117	1929	£311,054	1976	£6,259,929
1829	£1324	1883	£40,250	1930	£319,434	1977	£6,738,831
1830	£2425	1884	£44,810	1931	£264,040	1978	£8,111,246
1831	£835	1885	£47,035	1932	£268,588	1979	£10,067,404
1832	£984	1886	£43,044	1933	£294,916	1980	£11,886,652
1833	£1615	1887	£56,970	1934	£309,584	1981	£13,952,421
1834	£2227	1888	£50,813	1935	£321,861	1982	£15,697,896
1835	£806	1889	£42,700	1936	£293,915	1983	£16,636,000
1836	£788	1890	£42,523	1937	£308,015	1984	£22,548,000
1837	£899	1891	£65,295	1938	£349,882	1985	£25,518,000
1838	£554	1892	£58,527	1939	£284,153	1986	£31,250,000
1839	£743	1893	£56,550	1940	£356,321	1987	£38,324,000
1840	£1582	1894	£73,526	1941	£386,836	1988	£40,651,000
1841	£729	1895	£81,159	1942	£495,775	1989	£44,444,000
1842–9	not recorded	1896	£117,036	1943	£528,726	1990	£52,433,000
1850	£354	1897	£81,569	1944	£563,507	1991	£51,725,000
1851	£758	1898	£108,625	1945	£609,294	1992	£61,215,000
1852	£2468	1899	£105,176	1946	£588,541	1993	£61,871,000
1853	£703	1900	£101,184	1947	£619,944	1994	£64,666,000
1854	£1885	1901	£107,293	1948	£689,125	1995	£64,462,000
1855	£1744	1902	£105,454	1949	£577,638	1996	£70,608,000
1856	£4983	1903	£112,704	1950	£741,863	1997	£85,645,000
1857	£5327	1904	£118,507	1951	£655,861	1998	£93,746,000
1858	£6112	1905	£114,007	1952	£739,708	1999	£107,300,000
1859	£10,633	1906	£121,073	1953	£775,040	2000	£99,700,000
1860	£14,027	1907	£103,793	1954	£864,235	2001	£127,900,000
1861	£15,092	1908	£115,303	1955	£837,675	2002	£115,700,000
1862	£14,825	1909	£126,215	1956	£1,001,209	2003	£110,400,000
1863	£21,101	1910	£97,322	1957	£997,848	2004	£125,300,000
1864	£31,917	1911	£113,352	1958	£1,118,684	2005	£128,600,000
1865	£28,932	1912	£110,908	1959	£973,322	2006	£149,500,000
1866	£41,718	1913	£122,966	1960	£1,023,629	2007	£167,400,000
1867	£39,305	1914	£111,813	1961	£1,234,909		
1868	£31,668	1915	£139,606	1962	£1,355,792		
1869	£14,409	1916	£146,948	1963	£1,530,541		
1870	£25,711	1917	£150,844	1964	£1,695,282		
1871	£28,140	1918	£181,003	1965	£1,598,334		
1872	£27,331	1919	£151,025	1966	£1,721,485		
1873	£31,740	1920	£185,903	1967	£1,521,124		
1874	£33,500	1921	£174,501	1968	£1,819,887		
1875	£39,835	1922	£91,399	1969	£2,173,508		
1876	£33,801	1923	£180,014	1970	£2,419,259		
1877	£42,442	1924	£241,780	1971	£2,501,380		

Members of the International Lifeboat Federation

The first International Lifeboat Conference was held in London in 1924. Eight countries sent representatives: Denmark, France, Japan, Holland, Norway, Spain, Sweden and the United States. This led to the founding, later that year, of the International Lifeboat Federation (ILF), an organization the aim of which is to encourage co-operation between the lifeboat services of the world. Bound, in the words of its founders, by 'the Brotherhood of the Sea', its members exchange information, so that the technical advances of one nation can be enjoyed by all. For example, in 1971 a technical paper read to the ILF by Peter Silvia of the US Coastguards sounded the death-knell for wooden lifeboats and inaugurated the world-wide use of aluminium and fibreglass-reinforced plastic. Members sometimes respond to an international crisis. In 1970 the RNLI sent twenty inshore boats to East Pakistan to help with flood relief. Similar help on a smaller scale was recently sent to Mozambique.

The Federation now has forty-three member countries. In Europe: Belgium, Bulgaria, Denmark and Faroes, Estonia, Finland and Åland, France, Germany, Greece, Iceland, Italy, Netherlands, Norway, Poland, Portugal, Republic of Ireland, Russia, Spain, Sweden, Switzerland, and the United Kingdom. In Asia: China, Hong Kong, India, Japan, Russia, Turkey. In North and Central America: Bahamas, Bermuda, British Virgin Islands, Canada, Guatemala, Netherlands Antilles, Turks and Caicos Islands, and the USA. In South America: Argentina, Chile, Peru, and Uruguay. In Africa: Morocco, Namibia, and South Africa. In Australasia: Australia and New Zealand.

The Federation's permanent secretariat is the RNLI, West Quay Road, Poole, Dorset BH15 1HZ, UK.

Lives saved by RNLI lifeboats: cumulative annual total

YEAR	NUMBER OF PERSONS RESCUED	CUMULATIVE TOTAL	YEAR	NUMBER OF PERSONS RESCUED	CUMULATIVE TOTAL	YEAR	NUMBER OF PERSONS RESCUED	CUMULATIVE TOTAL
1824	124	124	1855	406	9628	1886	761	32,671
1825	218	342	1856	473	10,101	1887	572	33,243
1826	175	517	1857	374	10,475	1888	800	34,043
1827	163	680	1858	427	10,902	1889	627	34,670
1828	301	981	1859	499	11,401	1890	773	35,443
1829	463	1444	1860	455	11,856	1891	736	36,179
1830	372	1816	1861	424	12,280	1892	1056	37,235
1831	287	2103	1862	574	12,854	1893	598	37,833
1832	310	2413	1863	714	13,568	1894	790	38,623
1833	449	2862	1864	698	14,266	1895	709	39,332
1834	214	3076	1865	714	14,980	1896	461	39,793
1835	364	3440	1866	921	15,901	1897	662	40,455
1836	225	3665	1867	1086	16,987	1898	756	41,211
1837	272	3937	1868	862	17,849	1899	609	41,820
1838	456	4393	1869	1231	19,080	1900	865	42,685
1839	279	4672	1870	784	19,864	1901	490	43,175
1840	353	5025	1871	882	20,746	1902	455	43,630
1841	128	5153	1872	739	21,485	1903	709	44,339
1842	276	5429	1873	668	22,153	1904	528	44,867
1843	236	5665	1874	713	22,866	1905	550	45,417
1844	193	5858	1875	921	23,787	1906	772	46,189
1845	235	6093	1876	600	24,387	1907	1156	47,345
1846	134	6227	1877	1048	25,435	1908	638	47,983
1847	157	6384	1878	616	26,051	1909	644	48,627
1848	123	6507	1879	855	26,906	1910	767	49,394
1849	209	6716	1880	697	27,603	1911	687	50,081
1850	470	7186	1881	1121	28,724	1912	759	50,840
1851	230	7416	1882	884	29,608	1913	574	51,414
1852	773	8189	1883	955	30,563	1914	1112	52,526
1853	678	8867	1884	792	31,355	1915	832	53,358
1854	355	9222	1885	555	31,910	1916	1301	54,659

YEAR	NUMBER OF PERSONS RESCUED	CUMULATIVE TOTAL	YEAR	NUMBER OF PERSONS RESCUED	CUMULATIVE TOTAL	YEAR	NUMBER OF PERSONS RESCUED	CUMULATIVE TOTAL
1917	1348	56,007	1948	638	76,328	1979	1056	105,253
1918	852	56,859	1949	396	76,724	1980	1249	106,502
1919	511	57,370	1950	472	77,196	1981	1115	107,617
1920	584	57,954	1951	406	77,602	1982	1330	108,947
1921	410	58,364	1952	449	78,051	1983	1450	110,397
1922	436	58,800	1953	446	78,497	1984	1371	111,768
1923	721	59,521	1954	561	79,058	1985	1764	113,532
1924	454	59,975	1955	912	79,970	1986	1444	114,976
1925	380	60,355	1956	608	80,578	1987	1510	116,486
1926	459	60,814	1957	719	81,297	1988	1399	117,885
1927	354	61,168	1958	568	81,865	1989	1552	119,437
1928	591	61,759	1959	609	82,474	1990	1634	121,071
1929	363	62,122	1960	470	82,944	1991	1344	122,415
1930	365	62,487	1961	507	83,451	1992	1414	123,829
1931	271	62,758	1962	555	84,006	1993	1332	125,161
1932	395	63,153	1963	588	84,594	1994	1656	126,817
1933	406	63,559	1964	908	85,502	1995	1683	128,500
1934	354	63,913	1965	1100	86,602	1996	1325	129,825
1935	498	64,411	1966	1128	87,730	1997	1485	131,310
1936	491	64,902	1967	1394	89,124	1998	1418	132,728
1937	524	65,426	1968	1233	90,357	1999	1044	133,772
1938	673	66,099	1969	1376	91,733	2000	899	134,671
1939	1407	67,506	1970	1463	93,196	2001	801	135,472
1940	2345	69,851	1971	1721	94,917	2002	790	136,262
1941	1445	71,296	1972	1622	96,539	2003	355	136,617
1942	830	72,126	1973	1837	98,376	2004	441	137,058
1943	640	72,766	1974	1417	99,793	2005	311	137,369
1944	931	73,697	1975	1101	100,894	2006	245	137,614
1945	687	74,384	1976	1166	102,060	2007	306	137,920
1946	790	75,174	1977	1164	103,224			
1947	516	75,690	1978	973	104,197			

The Lifeboat Enthusiasts' Society

The Lifeboat Enthusiasts' Society was founded in 1964. Its objective was, and still is, to facilitate the work of those who have a particular interest in the historical and/or technical aspects of the Institution. Not only does the Society provide a useful focal point for these enthusiasts, perhaps more importantly the work of its members has resulted in a valuable repertory of archive material. Originally there were eight members. Today there are 700.

At first, it was the Institution's history that attracted most enthusiasts. One of the founder members, Grahame Farr, became the Enthusiasts' first official archivist; his researches enabled him to compile and publish detailed records of many lifeboats, lifeboat stations and lifeboat services. His successor, Jeff Morris, the current archivist, has continued the painstaking research work and has written, in particular, many valuable station histories.

Other enthusiasts have more specialized interests. Some collect lifeboat photographs, lifeboat stamps or lifeboat postcards. Others make model lifeboats, either static or radio-controlled; several of these models are works of art, involving more than 2000 hours of painstaking construction. A small number of enthusiasts own ex-lifeboats, which they have either restored to their original glory or converted to yachts or pleasure cruisers. A small group meets regularly at the Historic Naval Base at Chatham to restore and maintain the lifeboats now kept permanently on display there.

Many members are involved, in one way or another, with the work of their local lifeboat station or branch; and in some areas enthusiasts' research groups are recording and studying every aspect of local RNLI operations.

More information about the Society can be obtained from PR Department, RNLI, Poole (Tel. 01202 663000; e-mail info@rnli.org.uk)

Select Bibliography

A full bibliography of all that has been written about lifeboats and the RNLI would occupy several hundred pages. I have listed below only those works that I used and found particularly valuable.

Primary sources

RNLI LIBRARY AND ARCHIVES:

Minutes of committees and subcommittees, 1824–2000

Annual reports, 1824–2000

The Lifeboat journal, 1852–2000

Grahame Farr Archives

Publications of the Lifeboat Enthusiasts' Society, in particular the station histories, many written by Jeff Morris

Records of lifeboat services

Secondary sources

Cox, Barry, *Lifeboat Gallantry* (Spink & Son, 1998)

Dixon, Geoffrey, *Thesis on the Charitable Status of the RNLI* (privately printed, 1990)

Fry, Eric, *Lifeboat Design and Development* (David and Charles, 1975)

Hillary, Sir William, *An Appeal to the British Nation on the Humanity and Policy of Forming a National Institution for the Preservation of Lives and Property from Shipwreck* (G. and W. B. Whittaker, 1823)

Horgan, Denis J., *Water Safety and Rescue* (privately printed, 1997)

Howarth, Patrick, *The Lifeboat Story* (Routledge & Kegan Paul, 1957)

Kelly, Robert, *For Those in Peril* (Shearwater Press, 1979)

Kipling, Ray and Susannah, *Strong to Save* (Patrick Stephens, 1995)

——, *Never Turn Back* (Sutton Publishing Ltd, 2006)

Leach, Nicholas, *For Those in Peril* (Silver Link Publishing, 1999)

Lewis, Richard, *A History of the Life-boat and its Work* (Macmillan, 1874)

Macara, Sir Charles, *Recollections* (Cassell, 1921)

Mitford, Jessica, *Grace had an English Heart* (Viking Press, 1988)

Morris, Jeff, *Lists of British Lifeboats (Parts I, II and III)* (Lifeboat Enthusiasts' Society, various dates)

Vince, Charles, *Storm on the Waters* (Hodder & Stoughton, 1946)

Wake-Walker, Edward, and Thompson, Tim, *Gold Medal Rescues* (David and Charles, 1992)

——, *The Lifeboats Story* (Sutton Publishing Ltd, 2007)

Warner, Oliver, *A History of the RNLI, 1824–1974* (Cassell, 1974)

Index

Figures in **bold**
refer to illustrations.

ALB lifejackets, 147
Aberdeen, 19, 83, 85
Abersoch, 199
  lifeboat crew, **168-9**
Aberystwyth, 153, 199
Admiral Berkeley, 36, **36-7**
Admiralty, 16, 22, 26, 27,
  46, 53
Admiralty Coventry two-
  stroke engines, 127
Adventure, 17
Agnes Cross, 79, **79**, 80
Airbags, 137, 138
Albatross helicopter, 164
Albert, Prince Consort, 53
Aldeburgh, 189, 199, 208
Aldershot, 166-7
  crew, **167**
Alice, 39
all-weather offshore fleet,
  200, 201, 204-11, 229
Allendale Animal Sanctuary,
  162
Allen, Fred, 161
Altair, 236
Always Ready, The, 178-9
Amble, rescues by lifeboats
  based at, 153, 156
Angle, 77
Anglesey, 56, 71
animals, **44**, 44-5, **45**, 162
  see also horses
Anstruther, 199
Appledore, 159, 199
  rescues by lifeboats based
  at, 159
Arbroath, 19, 39
  accident to lifeboat based
  at, 131, 132
Ardency, 240-1
Arklow, 41
Armstrong, Margaret, 94,
  97
Armstrong family (of
  Newbiggin), 189
Arran, 199
Arun class lifeboats, 182,
  184

Asp Rock, 159
Atherfield, 178
Atherfield Ledge, 175, 177
Atlantic, 77, 120,148
Atlantic 21 inflatable
  lifeboats, 150, 152, 158,
  159, 161, 162, 181,
  183, 184, 214, 249
Atlantic 75 inflatable
  lifeboats, 152, 214, 233
Atlantic 85 lifeboats, 216
Atlantic College, 95, 199
Augustus Frederick, Prince,
  22-3
Aurora, 19
Ayr, 19

BBC, 231
Barton, 56
  rescue by lifeboat based at,
  65
Baldonnel airfield, 165
Ballycotton, 36, 123, 126
  rescue by lifeboat based at,
  122-3, 123-6
  lifeboat crew, **124-5**, 189
Ballycotton Bay, 123, 124
Bamburgh, 15, 16
  Castle, 15
Bangladesh/East Pakistan,
  154, **155**, 253
Baring, Thomas, 53
Barmouth, 41
Barnett, Tames Rennie, **81**,
  81-2, 128, 137
Barnett class lifeboats, 77,
  130, 131, 137, 148
barometers, 56, **56**
Barra, 118
  rescues by lifeboats based
  at, 129, 131, 138
  illustration of lifeboat, **139**
Bastiani, Fred, 178
Battle of Britain (1940), 114
Bawdsey Haven, 19
beach launching, **48-9**, **76-
  7**, 92, 94, 196, 198-9
Beachy Head, 128
Beaufort, Sir Francis, **251**
Beaufort lifejackets, 146,
  146, 147, 241

Beaufort Scale, 251
Beaumaris, 199, 221
Beeching, James, 57, 58
  See also Beeching class
  lifeboats
Beeching class lifeboats, 51,
  51, 57-8
Beira, 155
Bell, Sergeant, 39
Bembridge, 166, 178
  rescue by lifeboat based at,
  167
Bencroy, 71
bequests, 56, 222-3
Big Harcar, 31
Bigland, 199
Bilkis, 154
Bird, George, 245
Bird's Eye, 227
Birmingham, 92
Bishopsgate: London
  Tavern, 28, **29**
Blackburn Rovers, 113-4
Blackmore, William, 61
Blackwall, 74
Bliss, David, 157-8
Blogg, Henry, **40**, **41**, 42,
  69, 138, 140
Blue Peter (television
  programme), 225
  presenters, **156**
Blue Peter I, 225
Blue Peter II, 225
Blue Peter III, **156-7**, 225
  crew, **156**
Blue Peter IV, 157-8, 225
Blyth, 82
Board of Trade, 55
Bolt Head, 106
Bolton, 92
Bombard, Professor, 148
Boulmer, 94, 165, 189
  rescue by lifeboat based at,
  116
Bowen, Lieutenant, 39
Boy Andrew, 240
Brahmaputra delta, 154
Bramble, William, 43
Brazen, 36
Bressay, 240, 243
Bridlington, 42-3, 105, 199

Bridson, Norris, 22
Brighstone Grange, 171,
  174
  rescue by lifeboat based at,
  171, 175-6, 177-8
Brighton, 58
  beach launching of lifeboat
  at, **48-9**
  lifeboat crew, **181**, **183**
  rescues by lifeboats based
  at, 172, 181-4
Britannia, 74
British Hovercraft
  Corporation, 137
Bromilow, Amy, 224
Bromilow, Rebecca, 224
Brooke, rescue by lifeboat
  based at, 171, 175, 176-7
Brooke Chine, 176
Broughty Ferry, illustration
  of lifeboat, **133**
  loss of lifeboat based at,
  131, 133
Bruce, David, 132
Bryant, Colin, 114
Buchan, Jackson, 136
Buckie, 136
Burbridge, Lieutenant, 25
Burnmouth, 180
Burton, Captain H. E., 82
Buzi River, 155

CE4 petrol engine, 127
Cable and Wireless, 227
Cable family (of Aldeburgh),
  189
Caister, 56, 63, 78
Caledonian Canal, 128
Campbell, James, 116
Campbeltown, 41
Canavan, Ian, 155
Canning, George, 28
Canterbury, Archbishop of,
  28
Capriclio, 36
Carlington Bay, 14
Carnegie Hero Fund, 179
Carnsore, rescues by lifeboat
  based at, 58, 59-60
Caroline Richardson II, 63
Carr, Robert, 105

Carr reef, 108
Carrig Rocks, 59
Carver, Commander, 78-9, 80
Case 1150 B tractors, 199
Castletown, 21, 22
Casualty Search Dogs, 44
Catchpole, Mr, 241
Cathedral Rock, 180
Chapman, Thomas, 53
Charles Biggs, 86, **88**
Chatham, 256
Chebogue, **118-9**, 120-1
Chichester harbour, 162, 163
children, 232, 234 *see also* Storm Force
Chilton Chine, 177
Chivenor, 165
Christchurch, 19
City of Glasgow, 73, 75, **75**
City of Glasgow II, 77
City of Sheffield, **190-1**
Clarissa Langdon, 116
Clark, Hewitt, 69, 239, 240, 241, 242, 243-4, 244-5
Clark family (of Lerwick), 189
Clarkson, Thomas, 86
Clayton and Shuttleworth tractors, 198
Clifden, 199
Clogher Head, 199
Clyde, Firth of, 158
Clyde lifeboats, 148
coastguards, 104, 105, 193, 221
Coll, 129
communication system, 104, 193
'Compact' lifejacket, 147
Congreve rockets, 38
Content, 26
Cook, Elizabeth, 186
Cook, James, 186
Cooper, Reuben, 177
cork lifejackets, 146, **146**, 248
Cornwall, 60, 187 *see also* names of places in Cornwall
corporate sponsorship, 227
Cotton, Henry, 174
Cotton, Thomas, 175
Cotton family (of Brighstone Grange), 174, 177-8
Countisbury Hill, 93
County Cork, 36, 123 *see also* names of places in

County Cork
County Wexford, 59, 105
Coverack, 128, 129
Cowes, 77, 150, **151**
  Inshore Lifeboat Centre, 150, **151**, 152
Cox, Barry, 39, 63
coxswain, position of, 128, **220-1**
Crail, 108, 109
  rescues by lifeboat based at, 107, 108-9
Cresswell, 94, 97
Crews, 95, 169-89, 191-2, 230-1, 238-9
Crewsaver lifejackets, 146-7, **147**
Cromer, 56, 69, 140, 210
  Davies family of, **188**, 189
  rescue by lifeboat based at, **40-1**
Cromer Ladies' Guild, 224
Cromer Smugglers, 226
Cubitt, William, 65
Cullercoats, 95
Culdrose, 165
Cunningham, Andrew, 108, 109

D class inflatable lifeboats, 143, **149**, 149-50, 153, 154, 155, 161, 212, 226, 249
Dacca, 154
Danbury Place, 23
Darling, Grace, 15, **30-1**, 32-3, 34, **34**, 46, 242
  commemorative locket, **35**
Darling, William, **30-1**, 32, **34**, 34-5
Daunt Rock, 124, 125
  lightship, **122-3**, 123-6
Davies, Captain George, 53
Davies, Gwillym, 117
Davies family (of Cromer), **188**, 189
De Jonge Thomas, 44
Deacon, Bill, 244, 245
Dee estuary, 63
Demerara, 50, 51, 58
Despatch, 44-5
diesel engines, 126, 127-31, 243
Disperser, 171, 178-9
dogs, 44-5
Donald Searle, 163, **163**, 166-7
  survivors, **166**
Doom Bar, 77

Dougal, James, 171-2, 179, **179**, 180, 181
Douglas, 11, 12 19, 21, 22, 24, 25, 41, 47, 171, 172, 210
Douglas Bay, 11, 24, 25, 172
Dove, 26
Dover, 77, 112, 164
  rescue by lifeboat based at, 113-4
Drayton Manor Theme Park, 227
Duchess of Kent, **135**, 135-6, **136**, 141
Duckhams, 223
Duke of Northumberland, **70-1**, 71, 72, 72-3, 74-5, 242
Dun Laoghaire, 204
  lifeboat station, **196-7**
Dunbar, 204
  lifeboat, **55**
Dundalk, 14
Dundee, 85, 92
Dunehn, 82
Dungeness, 94, 112, 128, **186**, 199
  families involved in lifeboat service, 189, **189**
Dunkirk, 99 110, **110-11**, 111, 112, 249
Dunster, Frank, 166
Dumigan, 106

E. C. J. R., 132-3
East Africa, 155 *see also* Mozambique
East Anglia, 56, 63, 64 *see also* names of places in East Anglia
East Pakistan/Bangladesh, 153, **155**, 253
  lifeboat, **112-3**
Ebb Carr rocks, 180
Ebdell, Martin, 181, 182, 183, 184
education officers, regional, 238
Edward VII, medals bearing head of, 68-9, 69
Edward Prince of Wales, **118-9**, 120-1
Edwin Kay, 108-9
Eendracht, 164-5
Eldridge, Dorothy, 223
Elephant, 63
Eliza, 26
Eliza Fernley, 85-6, **86**, **87**

Elizabeth Castle, 38
Essex, *161 see also* names of places in Essex
'Essex legion', 23
Evans family (of Moelfre), 189
Exmoor, 93, 96, 249
Exmouth, 19
  lifeboat, **250**
Expedite, 64-5
Eyemouth, 172
  rescues by lifeboat based at, 179-81

FIBI (Fast Inshore Boat), 233, 234
FRBI (Fast Response Boat), 234
FSB2 (Fast Slipway Boat), 210, 234
Fairles, Nicholas, 18
Fame, 26
Fanny, 38
Farne Islands, 15, 31, 34 *see also* Longstone
Farnworth and Kearsley lifeboat branch, 224
Farr, Grahame, 256
Fast Inshore Boat (FIBI), 233, 234
Fast Response Boat (FRBI), 234
Fast Slipway Boat (FSB2), 210, 234
Fay and Bowen engine, 82
Fernebo, 42
Ferry Engine Company, 127
Festing, Lieutenant, 36, 37
Ffytche, Frances Elizabeth Disney, 23
Fidra, 116-7
Fife, 108, 109 *see also* names of places in Fife
Filey, 199, 208
Finner, 165
First World War (1914-18), 45, 65, 99-109, 121, 249
Fishguard, 225
Fitzgerald, Captain Hamilton, 56, 222
Fitzroy, Admiral, 56, **56**
Fladden fishing grounds, 135
Flat Rock Cove, 157
Fleetwood, 210, 224
  rescue by lifeboat based at, 65-6
Flint, 161
Flushing, 58

Folkestone, 82
Forest Hall, 97
Forfarshire, 15, 31-2, 33, 34, **35**, 248
Formby, 15, 63
Forth estuary/Firth of Forth, 108, 162
Four Wheel Drive Lorry Company, 199
Fowler tractors, 199
Fox, 43
France, 148 *see also* Dunkirk
Fraserburgh, 39, 131, 136, 210
   illustrations of lifeboat, **135**, **136**
   lifeboat disasters, 131, 132, 135-6, 140, 141
Fred Olsen Line, 223
Fry, Eric, 18, 63-4
Fuller, Captain, 148
fundraising, 89, 92, 94-5, 97, 169, 224-26, 243
   illustrations of activities, **90-91**, **92**, **93**, **97**, **219**, **221**, **234**
Fusilier, 49-50, 51, 58

Gammon, William, 120, 121
Ganges delta, 154
Gardner diesel engines, 127, 128
Garland, Barry, 158
George III, King, 22
George IV, King, 28
   medals bearing head of, 68, **68**
George V, King: medals bearing head of, 69
George VI, King, 69
George Patterson, 108
Get Splashed leaflet, 238
Girdler Bank, 49
Global Marine, 227
Godfrey, Thomas, 36, 37
Gold Medal Rescues (Wake-Walker), 117
Goodwins, 128
Gorleston, 63, 77, 79, 80, 83, 245
   rescue attempt by lifeboat based at, 78, 79
Gould, Commander, 127, 128
government, 55, 137, 140, 191
Governors, 226
Grandy, Lieutenant, 36, 37
Grange Chine, 176

Graves, Lieutenant, 25
Great Cumbrae Island, 158
Great Exhibition (1851), 51, 57
Great Yarmouth *see* Yarmouth (Norfolk)
Greathead, Henry, 17-8, **18**, 18-9, 40
Green, J. and F., 74, 75
Green Lily, 243-5, **244**
Griffon 450TD hovercraft, **228-9**
Grimsby, 77, 83
Guernsey, 19 *see also* name of places on Guernsey
Guyana, 59-60

Hall, Commander Basil, 102, 104
Hall, Thomas, 22
Hamburg, 89
Hannah Fawcett Bennett, **198**
Happisburgh, 63
Harcar Rocks, 31, 32
Harold, **70-1**, 71-3, 75
Hartland, 159
Harvey family (of Newfoundland), 44
Harwich, 74, 75, 77, 83
Haslar, 36
Hastings, 199
Hayling Island, 163, 199
   lifeboat crew, **167**
   rescue by lifeboat based at, 166-7
Hayling Rescue, 166
Hayter, John, 176, 177
Hebrides, 129, 138 *see also* names of places in Hebrides
Helen Blake, 105
helicopters, 163, **164**, 164-5, **165**, 166, 167, 180, 183-4, **190-91**, **220-1**, 240, 243, 244, 249
Helmer, Martin, 143, 144
Helmut Schroder of Dunlossit, 138
Henry Vernon, **102**, 102-3, 104
Herd Sands, 51
Hermes of Lune, 235-6
Hibbert, George, 27, 28
Higgans, William, 61
Hill, Arthur, 158-9
Hillary, Richard, 115, **115**
Hillary, Sir William, 9, 19, 22-7, 28, 39, 40, 46-7, 73-4, 115, 171, 172,

173, 174, 184, 191, 192
   Appeal to the Nation, 26-7, **27**, 242
   medals bearing head of, 69, **69**
   portrait, **23**
Hinderwell, Mr, 19
Hindley, Phil, 224
Historic Naval Base, Chatham, 256
History of the Life-boat and Its Work (Lewis), 46
Hoare, Rear-Admiral Desmond, 150
Holland, 226
Holme Sands, 64
Holy Island, 19, 41
Holyhead, 41, 71, 72, 73, 75, 77, 206
   rescues by lifeboat based at, 72-3, 75
Holyhead Bay, 71
honorary medical adviser, 217-8
honorary secretary, 104, 218
Hopelyn, 78-80, 81
horses, 42, 44, **44**, **45**, **76-7**, 93, 198, 224
Hostvedt, Elizabeth, 95, 249
Hovercraft, 218
Hoy, 134
Hoylake, 19, 199
   lifeboat based at, **198**
Humber, 83
Humble, Captain, 31
Hunstanton, 198
Hythe, 112

IBI (Inshore Boat), 234
ILBs (inshore lifeboats) *see* inflatable/inshore lifeboats
ILF *see* International Lifeboat Federation
Icarus, 111
Ilfracombe, 199
income, 43, 52, 56, 92, 107, 140, 191, 225, 233, 249 *see also* fundraising
Independence, 14
Independent Forester Liberty, 158-9
inflatable/inshore lifeboats, 148-53, 200, 201, 212-5, 225, 233, 249 *see also* Atlantic 21 inflatable lifeboats; Atlantic 75 inflatable lifeboats; D class

inflatable lifeboats
inland waters, pilot scheme for, 238
Inshore Lifeboat Centre, Cowes, 150, **151**, 152
Inshore Lifeboat Workshop, **151**
inshore lifeboats *see* inflatable/inshore lifeboats
International Lifeboat Conference, 249, 253
International Lifeboat Federation, 152, 231, 253
Inverness, 128
investments, 226
Ireland, 14, 41, 165 *see also* names of places in Ireland
Irish Sea, 11, 71, 128
Islay, rescue by lifeboat based at, 138
Isle of Inchkeith, 162
Isle of Man, 24, 41, 46, 127
   loss of herring fleet, 11-2
   see also names of places on Isle of Man
Isle of Wight, 77, 171, 174, 175, 178 *see also* names of places on Isle of Wight
Isles of Scilly, 41
Isolda, 124, 125

J. McConnel Hussey, 82
James, Rod, 166
James Stevens, **76-7**
James Stevens No. 3, 77
James Stevens No. 4, 77-8
Jane Holland, **112-3**
Jarman, Isaac, 50
Jessie Hortense, **8-9**
John and Charles Kennedy, 132
John Fielden, 100, **100**
Johnston, Captain Bernard, 14, 15
Johnston, Maggie, 134
Johnston, Robert, 134
Judd, Lesley, **156**
Julia Park Barry of Glasgow, 116-7, **116**

kapok lifejackets, 146, **146**, 243
Keith Anderson, 184
Kelly, Captain, 14
Kelly, Robert, 22
Kentwell, 78, 79, 107-8, **108**
Kilmore Quay, 199

Kilrush, 199

King, Martyn, 226

Kinghorn, 199

Kingsbarns, 109

Kinloss, 165

Kipling, Ray and Susannah, 138

Kirkpatrick, Dan, 134

Kirkpatrick, Margaret, 134

Kirkpatrick family (of Longhope), 189

Knighton, 199

Knights of St John, 23

La Panne, 112

Ladies' Committees, 94-5, 97

Ladies' Lifeboat Guild, 95, 249

  Cromer Ladies' Guild, 224

Land's End, 128

Langlands, Thomas, 100, **101**

Largs, 159, 199

  rescue by lifeboat based at, 158-9

Lasdell, Faye, 167

Last Enemy, The (Hillary), 115

launching beach, **48-9**, **76-7**, 92, 94, 196, 198-9

  from floating situation, 193

  slipway, 193

  with tractors, 198-9

Laura Janet, **84**, 85, 86

Leadbetter, David, 66

Leask, Andrew, 239-40

Leconfield, 165

Lee-on-Solent, 165

legacies, 56, 222-3

Leopold, Prince, 28

Lerwick, 69, 189, 240-4

  illustrations of lifeboats, **239**, **240-1**, **242-3**

lifeboat crew, **169**

  rescues by lifeboats based at, 238-45

Lewes, **160**

Lewis, Richard, 46, 51, 53, 58, 137, 242

Leyland tractors, 199

Life-Boat, The (journal), **53**, 53-4, 59-60, 74, 95, 130, 141, 158, 169, 178-9, 224

lifeboat crews *see* crews

Lifeboat Days, 89, **90-91**, **92**, 92, **93**, **97**, 97, 107

Lifeboat Design and Development (Fry), 18

Lifeboat Enthusiasts' Society, 256

Lifeboat Gallantry (Cox), 39

lifeboat stations, 196, **196**, **197**, 200

personnel, 221-22

lifeboatmen *see* crews

lifeboats

  Arun class, 182, 184

  Atlantic 21 inflatable, 150, 152, 158, 159, 161, 162, 181, **183**, 184, 214, 249

  Atlantic 75 inflatable, 152, 214, 233

  Barnett class, 77, **130**, 131, 137, 148

  Beeching class, 51, **51**, 57-8

  cost, 169

  current fleet, 200-215

  D class inflatable, 143, **149**, 149-50, 153, 154, 155, 161, 212, 226, 249

  diesel engines in, 126, 127-31, 249

  early designs, 16-19

  equipment carried by, **230**

  FIBI, 233, 234

  FRBI, 234

  SB2, 210, 234

  in First World War, 105, 106, 107, 109

  future planning, 231-4

  Greathead's design, 17-19, 40

  inflatable/inshore, 148-53, 200, 201, 212-15, 225, 233, 249 *see also* Atlantic 21 inflatable; Atlantic 75 inflatable; D class inflatable

  Lukin's design, 15, 16, **16**, 18, 40

  Mersey class, 208

  Norfolk and Suffolk, 58, 63-5, 78, **79**

  Northumberland competition/award for design of, 53, 57, 58, 62, 74

  number of launches, 145, 192

  oar-pulled, 39-42

  offshore all-weather, 200, 201, 202-11, 229

  Originals, 18, **18**, 19, 57, 171

  Peake, 58-61

  petrol-driven, 67, 78-83, 109, 126, 127, 249

  privately run, 54, 56

  propellers, 77, 128

  Richardson tubular, 58, 61, 62-4

  sailing, 51, 56-67

  in Second World War, 109, 111-3

  self-righting issue, 131-40

  Severn-class, 169, 202, 233, **242-3**, 243

  single lever control, 128

  steam, 67, 71-8, 248

  Trent class, 204, 225, 233

  trials, 171

  Tyne class, 210

  unimmergibles, 15,16, **16**, 40, 41

  Watson, 58, 65-7, 83, 127, 128, 131, 137

  Wouldhave's design, 17, **17**, 137

  see also names of lifeboats

lifejackets, **146**, 146-7, **147**, 242, 243

Limpopo, River, 155

Linaker, Hiram, 63

litigation, 231

Littlehampton, 128, 225

Liverpool, 15, 23, 161, 172

Liverpool class lifeboats, **54**, 178

Lizard, The, 41, 210 lifeboat, 194

Llandudno, 160, 161, 199, 208, 226

Llanunnas, 117

Lloyd, Samuel, 36

Lloyd's, 129, 131

Lloyds, 18, 27, 43

Loetitia, 64-5

London, **97**, 226, 249, 253

London Tavern, Bishopsgate, 28, **29**

Lone Dania, 138

Long Island (USA), 164

Long Life I, 159

Longhope, 189, 210

  lifeboat disaster, 131, 133-4

Longstone, 34, 35

  lighthouse, 32, 34

Lord Southborough, 110-1

Lossiemouth, 165

Louisa, 65

Louisa Anne Hawker, 159

Lowestoft, 19, 112, 210

  illustration of lifeboat, **108**

  lifeboat station, **196**

rescues by lifeboats based at, 64-5, 79-80, 107-8

Lukin, Lionel 16, **16**, 18, 19 *see also* Unimmergibles

Lynmouth, overland haul of lifeboat based at, 93, **96**, 96-7, 249

Lytham, 89

  illustration of lifeboat, **88**

  rescue by lifeboat based at, 86, 88

Macara, Charles, 85, **85**, 88-9, 97, 224, 249

Macara, Marion, 89, 94, 97, 249

McIntyre, Captain, 175, 177

McLean, John, 117

Macmillan, Harold, 145

MacNeil, John, 138

Maersk Champion, 244

Mahony, Robert, 123, 126

  rescue by lifeboat based at, 130-1

Malta, 23

Manby, Captain George William, 39 *see also* Manby line-throwing mortars

Manby line-throwing mortars, 38-9, **39**

Manchester, 89, **92**, 95, 97, 224, 249

Manx herring fleet, loss of, 11-2

Margate, 111, 114, 199, 208

  rescue by lifeboat based at, 110-1

maroons, **24**

Marryat, Captain, 28

Mary Stanford, **122-3**, 123-6

  crew, **124-5**

Mary Stoddart, 14-5, 17

Matthew Simpson, 127

Mattison, Bella, 95

Maude Pickup, 65-6

medals, 33, 36, 37, 38, **38**, 67, 68-9, **68-9**, 107, 153, 189

membership, 226

Mercantile Marine Fund, 55

Merchant of Fraserburgh, 25

Mersey class lifeboats, 208

Mersey estuary, 63

Meteorological Office, 56

Mexico, 85-6, 88, 89, 242

  survivors, **88**

Michael and Jane Vernon,
  242-5
Miles, Brian, 134, 136, 138
Milford Haven, 120
Millie Walton, 156
Minches, the, 129
Minerva shipyard, Cowes,
  150
Ministry of Shipping, 111,
Moelfre, 189
Mona, 133, **133**
Mona's Isle, 172
Montrose, 19, 210
Morecambe Bay, 65
Morecambe lifeboat station,
  197
Morgan, 63
Morris, Jeff, 256
Mount's Bay, 60
Mozambique, 153, **154**,
  154, 155, 253
Mull, 129,131
Mumbles, 95
  rescue by lifeboat based at,
  118-9, 120-1
Mundesley, 56
Munt, Moses, 175

NHS emergency response
  vehicle, 222
Napoleonic Wars, 13, 39, 51
National Maritime
  Institution, 210
Navy *see* Royal Navy
Nelson, Joseph, 34
New Brighton, 75
  rescue by lifeboat based at,
  63
New Quay, 105, 199
Newbiggin, 94, 189
Newbury, 41
Newcastle (Co, Down), 199
Newfoundland, 44, 45
Newfoundland clogs, 44-5
Newhaven, 19, 182, 184
Newlands, Ian, 240
Nicholas, Harry, **188**
Nicholas family (of Sennen
  Cove), 189
Nicolle, Philip, 38
Nieuport, 110, 112
Noakes, John, **156**
Nora Royds, **84**
Norfolk, 65 *see also* names of
  places in Norfolk
Norfolk and Suffolk class
  lifeboats, 58, 63-5, 78, 79
  diagram, 64
Norfolk Association, 56

lifeboat, 156-7
North Britain, 60-1, **60-1**
North Carr lightship, 133
North Scroby Sands, 78, 79,
  80
North Sea, 63, 99, 115
North Shields, 19
North Stack, 71
North Sunderland, 116
Northumberland, 15, 54
  see also names of places in
  Northumberland
Northumberland, **49**, 50
Northumberland,
  Algernon, Fourth Duke of,
  51, 53, 54
  competition/award, 53, 57,
  58, 62, 74
Northumberland coble, 16,
  18
Nova Scotia, 45

Oakley, Richard, 148
oar-pulled lifeboats, 39-42
Oban radio, 130
Ocean Vanguard, 156
Offshore, 226, 236
offshore (all-weather) fleet,
  200, 201, 202-11, 233
Oiler family (of Dungeness),
  189
Opel, 135
Original, 18, **18**, 57
Originals, 18, 19, 57, 171
Orkneys, 41, 83, 128, 133,
  134 *see also* names of
  places in the Orkneys
Osborne's yards,
  Littlehampton, 128
overland hauling, 92-3, **96**,
  96-7
overseas rescue operations,
  154-5
Owen, William, 73

P & O, 227
  lifeboat disaster, 77-8
Palace Pier (Brighton Pier)
  rescue, 172, 181-4
Palling, 56
Palmer, George, 41
Parkins, Captain Curtis E.,
  164
Parliament, 18
Parson-Ford Porteagle
  engines, 127
partners, 186-7
Patton, Robert, 171, 178,
  178, 179

Patton, Tom, **178**
Pavitt, John, 159
Peake, Captain, 36, 37
Peake, James, 58 *see also*
  Peake lifeboats
Peake lifeboats, 58-61
  diagram, 59
Pearce, Richard, 172, 181,
  182, 183
Peel, 199, 208
Peel, Sir Robert, 28
Pellew-Plenty brothers, 41
Pembrokeshire, 120 *see also*
  names of places in
  Pembrokeshire
Penlee, 187
Pentland Firth, 83, 133-4
Penzance, 19, 60
  rescue by lifeboat based at,
  58, 60-1, **60-1**
Perkins P4 diesel engines,
  127
Perrot, Sir Edward, 53
Peterhead, 135
  rescues by lifeboat based at,
  116, 116-7
Peterhead Bay, 116
petrol-driven motor lifeboats,
  67, 78-83, 109, 126,
  127, 249
pigeons, 45, 45
Pile, Patrick, 143, 144
Pilling Sands, 65, 66
Pionersk, **240-1**, 241-2,
  242
  survivors, **241**
Plan d'Aiguille, 225
pleasure craft, safety of, 236
Plymouth, 19
Pomona, 107
Poole, 112, **142-3**, 170,
  171, 184, 210, 231
  lifeboat crew, **185**
Porlock, 96-7, 249
Porlock Bay, 93
Porlock Hill, 93, 96
Port Erin, 127
Port Eynon, 106
Port St Mary, 204
Port Talbot bar, 120, 121
Portaferry, 225
Porthtowan beach, 156,
  157, 158
Portland, 165
Portpatrick, 127
Portrush, 224
Portsmouth, 36
Prestwick, 165
Prince Consort, 53

propellers, 77, 128
Prudential, 110
Psychedelic Surfer, 150
Purchess, Joe, 181, 182,
  183
Purves, Peter, **156**
Pwllheli, 199

Quakers, 22
Quale, Robert, 22
Queen, 73, 75
Queensferry, 162
Queenstown, 124

R, A, Colby Cubbin No, 3,
  138, **139**
RAF, 164
RLSS (Royal Life Saving
  Society), 235
RNLI (Royal National
  Lifeboat Institution)
  founded, 9, 20-9
  in age of oars, 31-47
  in age of sail, 49-67
  and steam boats, 71-8
  and petrol-driven motor
  sailers, 78-85
  improved public perception
  of, 85
  during World Wars, 99-
  121, 123-7
  after Second World War,
  127-41, 143-67
  present day, 9, 191-227
  future, 229-38
  key events in history of,
  248-9
  lives saved, 254-5 *see also*
  crews; fundraising:
  income; lifeboats; medals:
  women
RNLI (Sales) Ltd, 226-7
Racehorse, **20-1**, 21-2,
  26
Radcliffe, Roger, 158
radiotelephones, 104, 249
Ramsey, 11, 199
Ramsgate, 16, 19, 41, 49,
  50, 164
  rescues by lifeboat based at,
  49-50, 110
Recompense, 65
Reculver, 114
Red Bay, 199
Red Cross, 154
Redcar, 19
Reed, Christopher, 166
Reid, Lieutenant, 24, 25
Relief Fleet, 210, 214

Residential Training College, 230-1, 249
Rhyl, 63, 161, 199
Ribble estuary, 85, 86, 88, 248
Richard Lewis, 60-1, **60-1**
Richardson, Henry, 62 *see also* Richardson tubular lifeboats
Richardson tubular lifeboats, 58, 61, 62-4
diagram, **62**
Ringwood, 221
Ritchie, Andrew, 132
roadshow, travelling, 232
Robert Lindsay, 132
Robert Patton, The – The Always Ready, 179
Roberts, Mary, 99
Robertson, Captain David, 53
Rockwood, Michael, 18
Rohilla, **98-9**, 99-104, **103**
Rose, 39
Round Britain Power Boat Race (1969), 150
Rowney, Commander Harold, 83
Royal Bank of Scotland, 227
Royal Charter, 56, **57**
Royal Dockyard, Woolwich, 58
Royal Life Saving Society (RLSS), 235
Royal Mail, 225
Royal National Lifeboat Institution *see* RNLI
Royal Naval Air Service, 45
Royal Navy, 45, 112, 164, 229
Royal Yachting Association, 235
'rubber ducks' *see* inflatable/inshore lifeboats
Runswick, 92, 178, 179
lifeboatmen, **178**
rescue by lifeboat based at, 171, 178-9
Runswick, 116-7 Russell, Lord John, 46
Rye, 19

S. G. E., 127
Sable Island, 45
safety *see* Sea Safety Campaign
Safety on the Sea booklets, 235-6, **237**
sailing lifeboats, 51, 56-67

St Abb's, 179, 180, 181
St Agnes, 225
rescue by lifeboat based at, 156-8
St Andrews, 19, 41
rescue by lifeboat based at, 109
St Ann's Head, 121
St Anne's-on-Sea, 85, 89
illustrations of lifeboats, **84**
lifeboat disaster, 86
St Bees, 199
St Catherine, 199
St Croix, Francis De, 38
St Croix, Jean De, 38
St Croix, Philip De, 38
St Davids, 210
rescue by lifeboat based at, 117, 120
lifeboat station, **194-5**
St George, 171, **172-3**, 172-4
St Helier, 38
St Ives, 199
St Mary's (Isles of Scilly), 41, 202
St Mary's Island, 24, 172
St Mary's Rock, 174
St Peter Port, 19
St Pierre et Miquelon, 44
Salcombe, 106
illustration of lifeboat, **106**
lifeboat disaster, 106
sales, 226-7
Salford, 92, 97
Salisbury, **93**
Salter, Frank, 177-8
Saltwick, 116-7
Saltwick Nab, 99, 101
Samtampa, 121
Samuel Lewis, **54**
Sandown, 178
Salles, G. W. de: medals designed by, **69**
Saunders, S. E., 150
Scarborough, 10, 83, 85, 101, 131, 199
lifeboat disaster, 132-3
Schermuly, Alfred, 148
Scotland, 39, 41, 116, 128, 129, 133, 135, 165, 179
see also names of places in Scotland
Scott, Andrew, **152**, 153
Scottish Ambulance Service, 180
Sea Check, 236
Sea Lords, 26, 27

Sea Safety Campaign, 235-8, 249
Seaham, 131
lifeboat disaster, 133
Seahouses, 199, 208
Second World War (1939-45), 109, 110-21, 164, 249
self-righting issue, 131-40
Self Writer (magazine), **162**
Sennen Cove, 189
Severn class lifeboats, 169, 204, 233, **242-3**, 243
Shannon, 165
Sharp, Dr John, Bishop of Northumberland, 15, 16
Shaw, Alison, 226
Sheffield, 92
Sheffield Daily Telegraph, 89
Shetland Islands, 239 *see also* names of places in Shetland Islands Shingles, the, 49, 50
Shipping, Ministry of, 111
Shipwreck Institution, 9, 15, 20-29, 32, 33, 36-40, 41, 43, 46, 47, 51-5, 68, 73, 218, 248
Shipwrecked Fishermen and Mariner's Benevolent Society, 54-5
Silloth, 199
Silvia, Peter, 247
Simpson-Wills, Barrie, 225-6
single lever control, 128
Sir Arthur Rose, 130-1
Sir William Hillary, 113-4
Sirenia, 171, 174-8
illustration, **176-7**
Skegness, 199
lifeboat, **54**
Skerries, the, 199, 239
Skerryvore lighthouse, 138
Skirranes, the, 21
Shiley, Patrick, 124, 125-6
Sliney, William, 124
Sliney family (of Ballycotton), 189
slipway launching, 193
Small, Mr, 83
Smith, Robert, **104**
Société des Hospitaliers Bretons, 148
Soldian, 239-42
illustrations of, **239**, **240-1**
Solva, 117
Somali, 115-6
Sound Fisher, 71-2

South Goodwins lightship, 164
South Ronaldsay, 134
South Shields, 17, 51
South Stack, 71
Southampton, 92
Southend, 184
Southport lifeboat, **86**
disaster, 85-6
Southwold, 56, 143, 144
rescue by lifeboat based at, 143-4
Spirit of Fife, 162
sponsorship, corporate, 227
Stacks, the, 71, 72, 73
Staithes Nab, 178
steam lifeboats, 67, 71-8, 248
Stephenson family (of Boulmer), 189
Stevens, John, 51-2
Stewart, Robert, **152**, 153
Stockport, 92
Stogdon, David, 148, 154
Stoneclough, 224
Storm Force, 226, 238, 249
Storm over the Waters (Vince), 112
Stornoway, 165
Strachan, John 158, 159
street collections, 89, 92, 94-5, 97, 224 *see also* Lifeboat Days
Stromness, 41, 83, 204
Strong to Save (Kipling), 138
Stronsay, 83
Success, 108-9
Suckling, Captain, 21
Suffolk, 107 *see also* names of places in Suffolk
Sunsburgh, 165, 240
Sralen, 65
Swansea, 41, 120
Swansea Bay, 120
Swya-y-Mor, 117, 120

TGB, 134, **134**
Talus
MB764 tractors, 199
MB-H tractors, 199
Tamar class lifeboats, 202
Tapti, 129-31
Tart family (of Dungeness), 94, 189, **189**
Tay estuary/Firth of Tay, 108, 183
Taylor, George, **178**
Taylor, Joseph, **178**
Taylor, Robert, **178**

Taylor's Bank, 63
Teesmouth, 101
  lifeboat, **190-1**
Tenedos, 124
Tennyson, Alfred, Lord, 106
Thames, River, 16
  estuary, 49, 83, 128
Thirsk, 227
Thomas, Coxswain, 63
Thompson, Tim, 42
Thurso, 41, 83
Tiger Inn, Bridlington, 43
Tignabruaich, 199
Tiree, 129, 138
Titanic, 99
Tobermory, 131
Tongue lightship, 49
Torrible, James, 36, 37
Tose, Andrew, **178**
Totland Bay, 77
tractors, **198**, 198-9, 249,
  216-7
training, 169-71, 230-1
Trearddur Bay, 199
Trebister Ness, 240, 241
Trent class lifeboats, 206,
  225, 233
Trinity House, 16, 18
Trio, 35
True Blue, **172-3**
Tudor, Lieutenant John,
  172, 173
Two Sisters, 26
2000 and Beyond leaflet,
  228, 229, 236
Tyne, River, 17
Tyne class lifeboats, 210
Tynemouth, 82, 83, 101,
  226
  illustrations of lifeboats,
    10-1, **102**
  rescues by lifeboat based at,
    82, 102-3

Uckfield, **160**
unimmergibles, 16, **16**, 40,
  41,
Upgang, 101
Usher, John, 43

Valley, 165
Ventnor, 178
Victor Kingisepp, 135, 136
Victoria, Queen, 53
  medals bearing head of, 68,
    68
videos, 235
Vigilant, 24-5
Vince, Charles, 112

Viscountess Wakefield, 112
Volvo, 227

Wake-Walker, Edward, 117
Walberswick, 143, 144
Wales, 41, 161, 165 *see also*
  names of places in Wales
Walker, Lieutenant, 36, 37
Walker, Richard, 114
Walmer, 112, 148, 164
Walsh family (of
  Ballycotton), 189
Walton Hall Park, Liverpool
  161-2
Ward, Captain J. R., 53
Ward, John, 248
Ward, Captain Ross, 146
Washington, Captain (later
  Rear-Admiral) John, 53
Watson, George Lennox, 65,
  74, 81, **81**, 137 *see also*
  Watson class lifeboats
Watson class lifeboats, 58,
  65-7, 83, 127, 128, **129**,
  131, 137
  diagram, **66**
Watt, Ian, 130, 131
Wattisham, 165
Waveney class lifeboats, 179
Wegg, Paul, 226
Wellington, Duke of, 46
Wells, 104, 199, 221, 249
  lifeboat crew, **220-1**
West Kirby, 161, 162
West Mersea, 161
West Whitby, 19
Wexford, 41
Whitby, 99, 100, 101, 102,
  105, 133, 169
  illustration of lifeboat,
    100
  rescue by lifeboat based at,
    100
White, J. Samuel, and
  Company, 77
Whitehaven, 19
Wick, 135
Wick radio, 134
Wicksteed, Tony, 148, 149
Wilberforce, William, 28
William and Emma, 106,
  106
William Arthur Millward, **55**
William Riley, 101
William Stanley Lewis, 175,
  176-7
William Taylor of Oldham,
  128-9, **129**
Willie and Arthur, 63

Wilson, Thomas, 27-8, **28**,
  46
Winterton, 56
Wiseman, David, 117
Witch, 16
Woltemade, Wolraad, 44
women, 89, 92-7
  illustrations showing role
    of, **94-5**, **186**
  see also partners
Worcester Cadet, 175-6,
  177-8
Wordsworth, William, 32
Worthing, 105
Wouldhave, William, 17, **17**,
  18, 19, 137
Wyndham-Quinn, Hon. V.
  M., 148-9
Wyon, Alan G.: medals
  designed by, **69**
Wynn, Leonard Charles:
  medals designed by, **68**
Wyon, William: medals
  designed by, 68, **68**

Yare, River, 78
Yarmouth (Isle of Wight),
  127
Yarmouth (Norfolk), 56, 58,
  80
York Hotel, Douglas, 24, 75
Yorkshire Post, 89, 102-3
Youghal, 199
young people, 236, 238 *see
  also* Storm Force

Zambezi, River, 155
Zillah, 66